Aikido

O-Sensei's Sublime Synthesis

volume 2

An Anthology of Articles from the *Journal of Asian Martial Arts*
Compiled by Michael A. DeMarco, M.A.

Disclaimer

Please note that the authors and publisher of this book are not responsible in any manner whatsoever for any injury that may result from practicing the techniques and/or following the instructions given within. Since the physical activities described herein may be too strenuous in nature for some readers to engage in safely, it is essential that a physician be consulted prior to training.

All Rights Reserved

No part of this publication, including illustrations, may be reproduced or utilized in any form or by any means, electronic or mechanical, including photocopying, recording, or by any information storage and retrieval system (beyond that copying permitted by sections 107 and 108 of the US Copyright Law and except by reviewers for the public press), without written permission from Via Media Publishing Company.

Warning: Any unauthorized act in relation to a copyright work may result in both a civil claim for damages and criminal prosecution.

Copyright © 2016
by Via Media Publishing Company
941 Calle Mejia #822 • Santa Fe, NM 87501 USA • E-mail: md@goviamedia.com

All articles in this anthology were originally published in the *Journal of Asian Martial Arts*.
Listed according to the table of contents for this anthology:

Drengson, A. (1992)	Volume 1, Number 2	pages 58–69
Paz-y-Miño, G., & Espinosa, A. (2002)	Volume 11 Number 1	pages 8–27
Paz-y-Miño, G., & Espinosa, A. (2002)	Volume 11 Number 4	pages 8–29
Dykhuizen, J. (2003)	Volume 12 Number 2	pages 74–87
Barnet, J. (2003).	Volume 12 Number 3	pages 68–73
Paz-y-Miño, G., & Espinosa, A. (2004)	Volume 13 Number 2	pages 44–63
Paz-y-Miño, G., & Espinosa, A. (2004)	Volume 13 Number 3	pages 64–81
Golden, B. (2005)	Volume 14 Number 1	pages 74–81
Kennedy, G. (2005)	Volume 14 Number 4	pages 48–61
Paz-y-Miño, G., & Espinosa, A. (2006)	Volume 15 Number 3	pages 20–37
Jonathan Miller-Lane, J. (2007)	Volume 16 Number 1	pages 64–81
Gauthier, M. (2010)	Volume 19 Number 1	pages 60–63
Suenaka, R., & Taylor, C. (2010)	Volume 19 Number 4	pages 64–83
Linden, P. (2011)	Volume 20 Number 2	pages 30–35
Paul, J. (2011)	Volume 20 Number 4	pages 36–51

Book and cover design by Via Media Publishing Company
Edited by Michael A. DeMarco, M.A.

Cover illustration

Artwork by Feodor Tamarsky
Email: feodor.tamarsky@gmail.com • www.artsglobe.com

ISBN: 978-1-893765-26-9

w w w . v i a m e d i a p u b l i s h i n g . c o m

contents

iv **Preface**
by Michael DeMarco, M.A.

CHAPTERS

1 Dichotomous Keys to Fundamental Attacks and Defenses in Aikido
by Guillermo Paz-y-Miño C., Ph.D. & Avelina Espinosa, Ph.D.

22 Aikido: The Art of the Dynamic Equiangular Spiral
by Guillermo Paz-y-Miño C., Ph.D. & Avelina Espinosa, Ph.D.

47 Tetsutaka Sugawara Discusses Aikido, Morihei Ueshiba and the Kagura-Kotodama Staff
by C. Jeffrey Dykhuizen, Ph.D.

62 Hiroshi Ikeda's Insights into Aikido Training
by Jay Barnet, M.A.

68 The Rhythm of Aikido, Part I
by Guillermo Paz-y-Miño C., Ph.D. & Avelina Espinosa, Ph.D.

94 Music Principles Applied to Aikido Techniques, Part II
by Guillermo Paz-y-Miño C., Ph.D. & Avelina Espinosa, Ph.D.

113 Using Aikido Principles for Conflict Resolution
by Bryan Golden, B.A.

123 Yoshimitu Yamada's Influence on Aikido in the West
by George Kennedy, M.A.

137 Optical Illusions in Aikido
by Guillermo Paz-y-Miño C., Ph.D. & Avelina Espinosa, Ph.D.

152 The Loyal Opposition and the Practice of Aikido
by Jonathan Miller-Lane, Ph.D.

170 Aikido as Myth
by Maurice Gauthier, M.Ed.

173 Aikido Defenses Against Real-World Attacks
by Roy Y. Suenaka and Chad Taylor, M.S.

192 Aikido and Body-Awareness Training for Peacemaking and Combat
by Paul Linden, Ph.D.

197 Teaching Aikido to Children with Autism Spectrum Disorders
by Josh Paul, M.A.

212 **Index**

preface

How can we fully understand aikido, or any other martial art for that matter, when we have only been exposed to part of it? While learning about the art, we can easily make assumptions and be tricked by false impressions. In most cases, even instructors do not have enough background to grasp the entirety of the art and are happy to work with part of it.

The content in this special two-volume anthology details the many facets of aikido as it was formulated by Morihei Ueshiba (1883–1969)—O-Sensei, the great teacher. Each chapter contributes to a piece of the aikido puzzle by providing historical details, insightful technical drills (bare handed and with weapons), and components that have flavored this art with a spiritual essence.

From the Ueshiba wellspring flows a number of streams—political splinter groups offering their own take on what aikido should be and how it should be practiced. Each branch may stand on its own, but a good number of scholars and practitioners prefer a more encompassing representation of what O-Sensei taught. So, chapters in these volumes help "put Humpty Dumpty back together again."

Volume I includes ten chapters and volume II another fourteen. The authors—twenty-three in all—present superb credentials as scholars and practitioners of aikido. On the academic side, you'll find chapters that detail aikido's philosophy, from ethical relationships and practical theory to the subtle spiritual dimension. A few authors highlight the circumstances regarding the transmission of aikido from teacher to student. Some authors show how culture influences the perception and understanding of aikido when it travels outside Japan.

Aikido is often practiced as a system of body movement encompassing a philosophy of peace and harmony. Others may focus on learning the art for its effective methods of self-defense. Composed of material previously published in the *Journal of Asian Martial Arts*, this two-volume anthology is heavy on the technical aspects of aikido that both teachers and students would benefit by reading. Training methods are discussed in detail, supported by hundreds of illustrations of attack and defense.

Whatever your primary interest is in aikido, *Aikido: O-Sensei's Sublime Synthesis* will prove to be a great reference for the scholar and practitioner. We hope this convenient collection of quality material dealing with Morihei Ueshiba's martial discipline will benefit your research and inspire the practice of this elegant art.

Michael A. DeMarco, Publisher
Santa Fe, New Mexico
March 2016

· 1 ·

Dichotomous Keys to Fundamental Attacks and Defenses in Aikido

by Guillermo Paz-y-Miño C., Ph.D., and Avelina Espinosa, Ph.D.

Photographs courtesy of A. Espinosa and G. Paz-y-Miño C.

Introduction

Novice practitioners in aikido arts are confronted with numerous challenges during training, including the difficulties of understanding the subtle aspects of mind and body coordination inherent to aikido and remembering basic strategies designed to evade or neutralize an attacker. A common problem for new aikido practitioners is the discovery of aikido "logic." Perhaps the first revelation after a few lessons is that "aikido looks easy until you try it; then, it turns into a humbling experience." Comprehending a simple attack or defense is not always intuitive for beginners who soon realize it may take years to master.

After exploring different methods aimed at teaching aikido to college students, who are usually eager to learn fast, efficiently, and with tangible outcomes ("good grades"), we decided to develop a simple tool to improve the communication of aikido principles in our *dojo* (school, training hall). Our previous experience as science educators facilitated the idea that a "dichotomous key," an organizational device commonly used by biologists to categorize species into groups according to similarities and differences, would assist aikido practitioners in learning and understanding the specific characteristics of the most frequent attacks and defenses.

We present two keys. One shows the most common attacks and another the defensive techniques used in aikido. Both keys are dichotomous and based on division of the attacks and/or defenses into distinct groups. Attacks for example, include grabs (i.e., to the wrist, elbow, shoulder) and strikes (i.e., open hand attacks, blows with the fist, kicks). Defensive techniques include evasive motions in which the defender moves out of the attacker's way or reach, as well as neutralizations of the attack by manipulation of the attacker's arm or wrist, or by manipulation of the attacker's torso or hips.

These keys may appear to contradict long-established organizational systems that have been preserved by instructors of numerous aikido styles, who remain loyal to historical nomenclature and the teaching legacies of their masters. However, our goal was to contribute to a deeper understanding of aikido by applying a method of identification designed to group the techniques according to resemblance and uniqueness. Attacks

Illustration by Oscar Ratti. © Copyright by Futuro Designs & Publications.
From a scene in the new book, *Tales of the Hermit Vol. 1 (2001)*.

and defenses are divided into groups that share structural and functional affinity (i.e., the overall appearance of a technique looks similar to other techniques) and relatedness (i.e., a group of techniques may have been derived from another technique), according to the effect that the techniques cause on the human anatomy. It is true that a dichotomous key is to some extent arbitrary and artificial. Nevertheless, this method encourages the student to focus on the similarities between the items so organized, in this case, the attacks and defenses of aikido.

After using the keys in our own aikido classes, we found that they allow practitioners to:

❶ Discover and quickly understand the logic of some attacks and defenses without the constant supervision of an instructor; a mentor of course is always needed.
❷ Improve the attacker's and the defender's efficiency in class and speed up the teaching process by enabling students to respond promptly to instructions.
❸ Learn a few technical terms, including some Japanese names.

We hope that this material will be as useful for others as it has been for us. The keys are by no means complete. No armed attacks, neutralization techniques against weapons, techniques from the kneeling position, or various types of pins are included. However, these techniques can be deduced from the information presented below. Terminology follows Ki Society Shin Shin Toitsu Aikido or Ki-Aikido (aikido with mind and body coordination), which differs from other aikido styles. However, not all the attacks or defenses are officially recognized or regularly taught by Ki Society. For example, some of the kicks and hip/shoulder projections are rarely discussed in Ki-Aikido classes. A glossary for the most important terminology is provided at the end of this chapter.

Difficulties in Constructing a Key

It is evident that the defender (*nage*) and the attacker (*uke*) have different perspectives while an aikido technique is in progress. Designing a key to the most frequent attacks used in aikido training is not particularly difficult, because the movements involved in aikido grabs or strikes are relatively simple and easy to define and/or describe. The attacker's perspective is clearly illustrated in the key itself. However, structuring a key in order to reflect the defender's point of view when executing a technique is not that obvious.

A general principle in aikido is that any defensive technique can be used against virtually all attacks, although attacks with weapons are an exception to this rule. This plasticity characteristic of aikido makes it difficult to consistently group the defenses into natural units based on a common functional design as is possible with the attacks. Here we discuss two examples regarding the difference in perspective between defender and attacker when interacting in aikido.

First, when a defender executes *kote oroshi*, a technique which bends the attacker's wrist and fingers in toward the attacker's center of balance while projecting the attacker back down onto the mat (Figure 1-A), the defender moves in a very different way than when he performs *shihonage* (Figures 1-B, C, and D). Here the defender turns completely around his own axis while twisting the attacker's wrist toward the attacker's shoulder, then projects the attacker backwards and down onto the mat (Figure 1-D). In each case, the defender feels his body moving in a very distinct manner. From the attacker's perspective, however, there is little difference besides a few adjustments concerning the position of the attacker's wrist at the moment of falling when kote oroshi or shihonage are applied to him (compare Figure 1-A with 1-B, C, and D).

Second, it is also possible for the defender to have a completely different effect on the attacker when the defender performs almost exactly the same physical motion. If the defender moves in a sort of "kote oroshi" fashion to counter a punch to the face, the defender can grab the attacker's wrist (same-side grab) and bend it in, toward the attacker's center of balance (same as in above), projecting the attacker back down onto the mat in a typical kote oroshi (Figure 1-A). However, if the defender grabs the attacker's wrist with the opposite-side hand and bends it out, toward the attacker's center of balance (this time mirroring the motion described in the previous sentence), then the defender will lead the attacker into a *nikkyo* neutralization, that is forward, face down onto the mat (compare Figures 1-A with 1-E). The outcome for the attacker in both cases is obviously different.

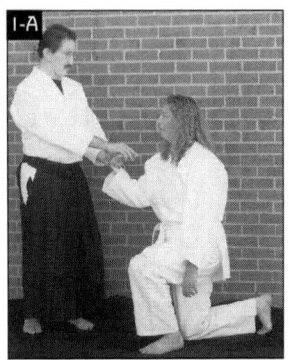

FIGURE 1:

The Defender's and Attacker's Different Perspectives.

1-A Defender (left) performs kote oroshi by bending the attacker's wrist and fingers in, toward the attacker's center of balance at the hips.
1-B Shihonage—another wrist technique where the defender (left) twists the attacker's wrist toward the attacker's shoulder.
1-C Close-up of shihonage. Compare wrist-hold in A with B and C.

I-D Defender (left) turns around his own axis while twisting the attacker's wrist toward the attacker's shoulder, projecting the attacker backwards and down onto the mat.

I-E Defender (standing) neutralizes the attacker by bending the wrist out and leading the attacker face down onto the mat (nikkyo).

These two different perspectives in perceiving aikido complicate the design of a dichotomous key that illustrates exclusively the defender's or attacker's viewpoints. For this reason, we present a "functional" or "artificial" key to the defenses, a sort of hybrid between natural dichotomies and practical dichotomies, which combines both the defender's and the attacker's experiences while sensing aikido. We acknowledge that the defenses would preferably be categorized based on the defender's perspective alone, since it is the defender who executes the defense. However, this is not always possible.

After cautiously studying aikido techniques and examining the literature that discusses them, it is evident that we, as well as most authors, have struggled when attempting to organize the fundamental defenses into distinct groups. In our opinion, this difficulty reflects:

1. The nature of aikido itself, where movement complexity builds synergistically on every previous action, generating multiple responses which are not easy to describe and/or categorize in a simple system.
2. The legitimate desire of several authors to discuss every defensive technique in respect to a huge number of attacks. Unfortunately, this encyclopedic method is more appealing to knowledgeable than inexperienced aikido practitioners.
3. The historical mode in which aikido has been taught from one generation to another. Here, "inertia" has played an important role; aikido's past is a living component of its present.

We propose that aikido defensive techniques should be taught to novice practitioners by emphasizing the overall characteristic similarities, that is, the effects on the attacker caused by the defender's reaction, rather than by presenting every defense in a series of infinite scenarios. We value the teaching importance of the multiple scenario system and consider it crucial for use with advanced students who already have a basic understanding of aikido principles. However, one of the disadvantages of this method is that it is usually communicated by means of multiple repetitions of a given technique, encouraging "muscle memory" rather than critical thinking. We believe that our dichotomous keys minimize this problem by helping the student to understand aikido concepts that can be critically and logically applied in diverse circumstances. Like all dichotomous keys, ours can certainly be improved.

How to Use the Keys

Here we show how a key should be formally structured. Concentrate your attention only on the format of this key; aikido terminology will be discussed later in this article. The keys below consist of a series of choices that lead the aikido practitioner to a definition and a name of a technique. "Dichotomous" means "divided into two parts." Therefore, in each step the keys give the user a clear choice between two alternatives. A first choice might be, for example, "key to the attacks" or "key to the defensive techniques." Another choice discussed here is "defender" or "attacker." An additional one is *irimi*, where the defender enters and positions himself in front of the attacker, or *tenkan*, where the defender turns and positions himself laterally or behind in respect to the attacker.

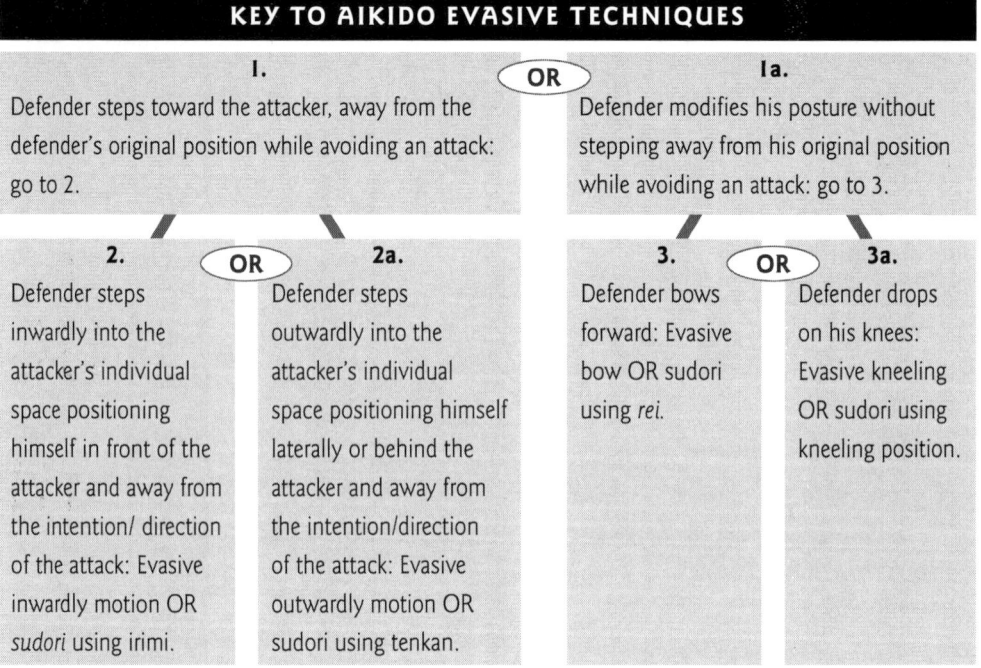

KEY TO AIKIDO EVASIVE TECHNIQUES

1. Defender steps toward the attacker, away from the defender's original position while avoiding an attack: go to 2.

OR

1a. Defender modifies his posture without stepping away from his original position while avoiding an attack: go to 3.

2. Defender steps inwardly into the attacker's individual space positioning himself in front of the attacker and away from the intention/ direction of the attack: Evasive inwardly motion OR *sudori* using irimi.

OR

2a. Defender steps outwardly into the attacker's individual space positioning himself laterally or behind the attacker and away from the intention/direction of the attack: Evasive outwardly motion OR *sudori* using tenkan.

3. Defender bows forward: Evasive bow OR sudori using *rei*.

OR

3a. Defender drops on his knees: Evasive kneeling OR sudori using kneeling position.

To use the keys presented here, the aikido practitioner should start at the beginning of either key and read the first pair of statements 1 and 1a (following the numerical order). Then, the user may decide which statement best describes the attack or defense in which he is interested. This will take the user of the key to the next pair of statements (i.e., 2 or 3). The procedure can be repeated until the technique is identified. If the user reaches a point in the selection of descriptive statements at which neither of the statements apply, he can work his way back through the preceding pairs of statements and reconsider the choices. In some cases, the user will find that he is unable to identify a particular technique; in a situation like that, the technique should be recorded as "unknown." Remember that only the fundamental attacks and/or defenses are included in the keys below. Some previous experience in aikido will help the student to understand and use the keys.

KEY TO ATTACKS — Illustrated in Figures 2-4 on next pages

1. GRABS (holds): go to 2.
1a. STRIKES (blows): go to 16.
2. Grabs aimed to control the arm (wrist, elbow, or shoulder/lapel): go to 3.
2a. Grabs aimed to control the torso or the neck (hugs or chokes): go to 13.
3. Wrist grabs: go to 4.
3a. Elbow or shoulder/lapel grabs: go to 8.
4. One-handed wrist grab: go to 5.
4a. Two-handed wrist grab: go to 6.
5. Same-side grab (*katate dori*).
5a. Cross-side grab (*katate kosa dori*).
6. Two-handed grab of the same wrist (*katate dori ryote mochi*).
6a. Two-handed grab of both wrists: go to 7.
7. From the front (*ryote dori*).
7a. From the back (*ushiro tekubi dori/ushiro ryokatate dori*).
8. Elbow grab: go to 9.
8a. Shoulder/lapel grab: go to 10.
9. From the front (*hiji dori*).
9a. From the back (*ushiro hijidori*).
10. One-handed shoulder/lapel grab: go to 11.
10a. Two-handed shoulder/lapel grab: go to 12.
11. Same side grab (*kata dori*).
11a. Cross-side grab (*kata kosa dori*).
12. From the front (*ryokata dori*).
12a. From the back (*ushiro ryokata dori*).
13. Bear hug: go to 14.
13a. Choke: go to 15.
14. From the front (*mae kara daki tsuku*).
14a. From the back (*ushiro dori*).
15. From the front. One arm around neck while the other holds the wrist/elbow (*mae kara katate dori kubi shime*).
15a. From the back. One arm around neck while the other holds the wrist/elbow (*ushiro kara katate dori kubi shime*).
16. Deceptive strikes: (*atemi* feints); numerous atemi exist in aikido, some of them are used as defensive techniques as well: go to 17.
16a. Deceptive/feints strikes (*atemi*).
17. Hand techniques: go to 18.
17a. Foot techniques: go to 20.
18. Open-hand strikes: go to 19.
18a. Closed fist strike (*munetsuki*).
19. Front open-hand strike (*shomen uchi*).
19a. Side/diagonal open-hand strike (*yokomen uchi*).
20. Strikes with the ball of the foot: go to 21.
20a. Strikes with the outside-edge of the foot or heel: go to 22.
21. Front kick (*mae keri*).
21a. Round kick (*mawashi keri*).
22. Strike with the outside-edge of the foot (*yoko keri*, side kick).
22a. Strike with the heel (*ushiro keri*, back kick).

Multiple combinations of attacks are also possible. For example, wrist grab and shoulder/lapel grab, wrist grab and front/side/diagonal strike (see page 10, Figure 4-C), shoulder/lapel grab and front/side/diagonal strike, wrist/shoulder/lapel grab and closed fist thrust strike, wrist/shoulder/lapel grab and front/round kick, etc. There is no need to include a specific key for hybrid attacks since they can be deduced from the material presented above. Combinations of attacks are limited only by the attacker's imagination.

FIGURE 2 — ATTACKS: wrist and elbow grabs.
2-A One-handed wrist-grab of the same side
(katate dori, technique corresponds to number 5 in Key to the Attacks).
2-B One-handed wrist-grab, cross-side wrist (katate kosa dori, 5a).
2-C Two-handed wrist-grab of the same wrist (katate dori ryote mochi, 6).
2-D Two-handed wrist-grab of both wrists, from the front (ryote dori, 7).
2-E Two-handed wrist-grab of both wrists, from the back (ushiro tekubi dori / ushiro ryo katate dori, 7a).
2-F Elbow-grab from the front (hiji dori, 9).
2-G Elbow-grab from the back (ushiro hiji dori, 9a).

FIGURE 3 — ATTACKS: shoulder/lapel grabs, bear hug, and choke.

3-A One-handed shoulder/lapel grab of the same side (*kata dori*, technique corresponds to number 11 in Key to the Attacks).

3-B One-handed shoulder/lapel grab, cross side (*kata kosa dori*, 11a).

3-C Two-handed shoulder/lapel grab from the front (*ryokata dori*, 12).

3-D Two-handed shoulder/lapel grab from the back (*ushiro ryokata dori*, 12a).

3-E Bear hug from the back (*ushiro dori*, 14a).

3-F Choke from the back (*ushiro kara katate dori kubi shime*, 15a).

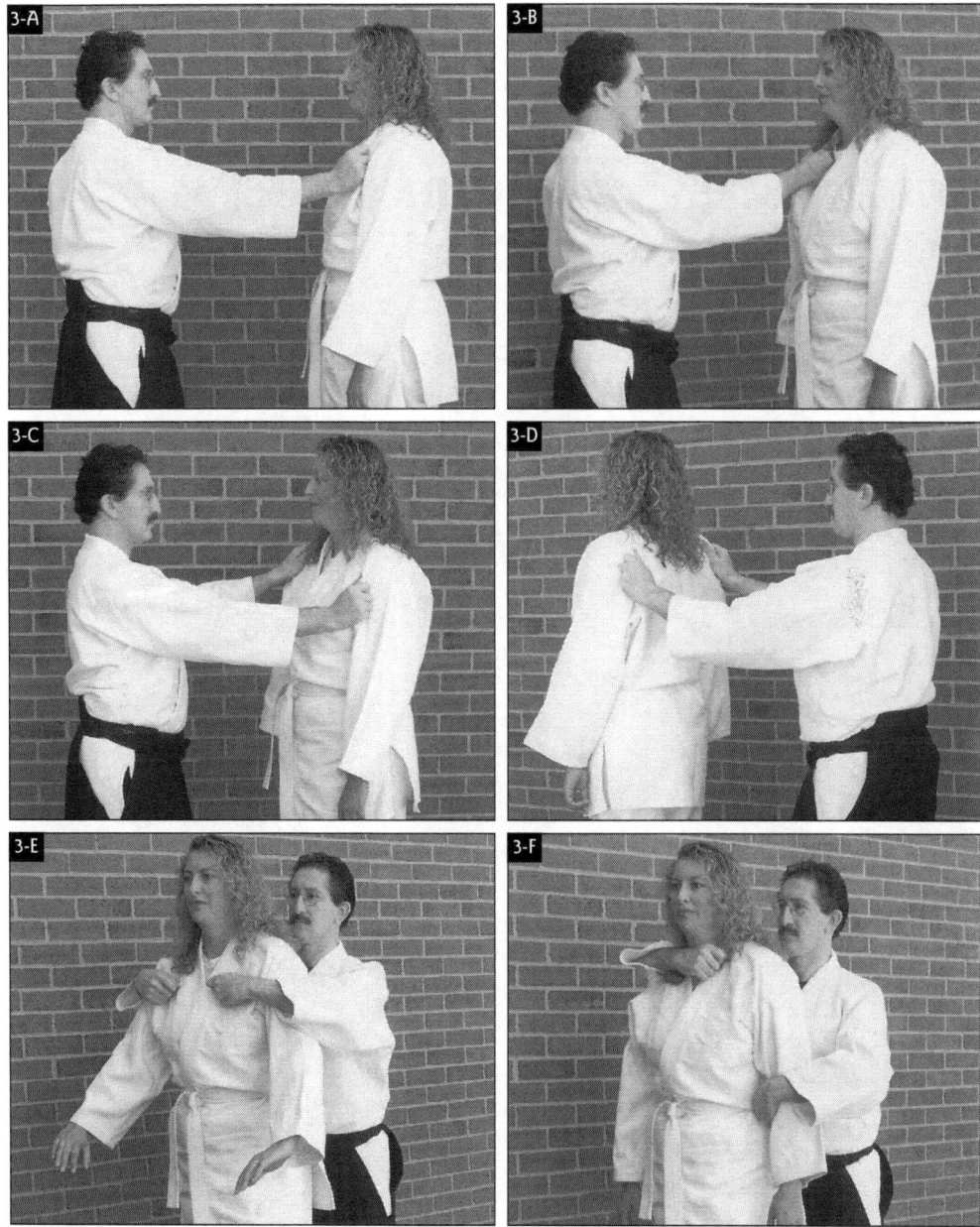

FIGURE 4 — ATTACKS:
deceptive strike or feint, open hand strike, punch, kicks, and combinations.

4-A Deceptive strike (atemi feint). Defender (left) neutralizes an open hand strike with his left hand and performs a counter deceptive attack with the right hand toward the face of the attacker (right), causing a hold-back reflex reaction on her (technique corresponds to number 16 in Key to the Attacks).

4-B Front open hand strike to the forehead (shomen uchi, 19).

4-C Side/diagonal open hand strike to the head/neck (yokomen uchi, 19a).

4-D Closed fist thrust strike to the torso (munetsuki, 18a).

4-E Front kick (mae keri, 21).

4-F Round kick (mawashi keri, 21a).

4-G Side kick (yoko keri, 22).

4-H Back thrust kick (ushiro keri, 22a).

4-I Combination attack: wrist-grab and front open hand strike to the head.

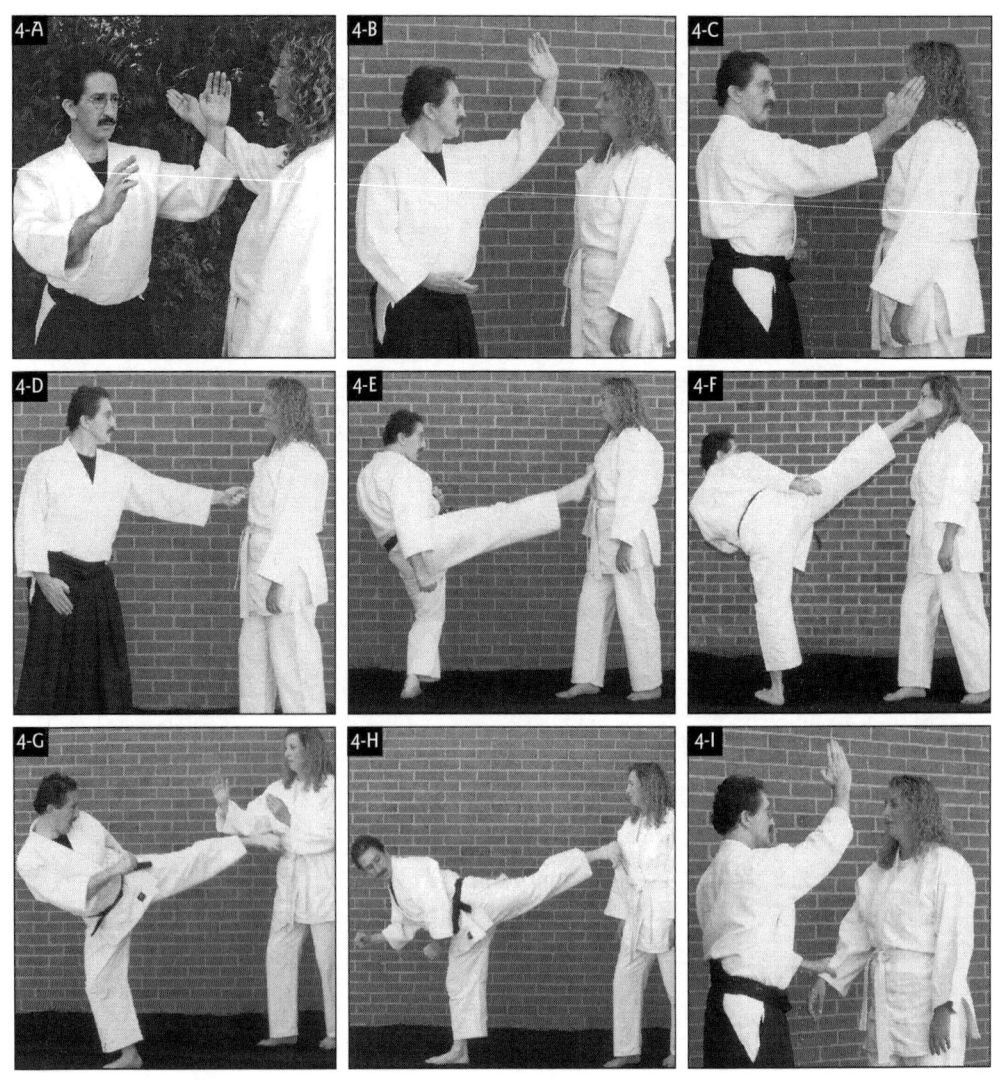

KEY TO DEFENSIVE TECHNIQUES — Illustrated in Figures 5-7 on next pages

1. **EVASIVE TECHNIQUES:** Defender avoids the attacker: go to 2.
1a. **NON-EVASIVE TECHNIQUES:** Defender neutralizes the attacker: go to 5.

2. Defender steps toward the attacker away from the defender's original position while avoiding an attack: go to 3.
2a. Defender modifies his posture without stepping away from his original position while avoiding an attack: go to 4.

3. Defender steps inwardly into the attacker's individual space positioning himself in front of the attacker and away from the intention/direction of the attack: Evasive inwardly motion OR sudori using irimi.
3a. Defender steps outwardly into the attacker's individual space positioning himself laterally or behind the attacker and away from the intention/direction of the attack: Evasive outwardly motion OR sudori using tenkan.

4. Defender bows forward: Evasive bow OR sudori using *rei*.
4a. Defender drops on his knees: Evasive kneeling OR sudori using kneeling position.

5. Neutralization of the attack by manipulation of the attacker's arm OR wrist: go to 6.
5a. Neutralization of the attack by manipulation of the attacker's torso/hips: go to 12.

6. Defender manipulates the attacker's arm: go to 7 (*ikkyo* group, all include *irimi* and *tenkan*; some of the *ikkyo* group techniques can end in a forward projection).
6a. Defender manipulates the attacker's wrist: go to 11.

7. Defender leads the attacker's arm up, in, and down, toward the attacker's center of balance, then locks the attacker's wrist/arm against the defender's shoulder (nikkyo; variations include locks with the defender's hand alone or around the defender's wrist).
7a. Defender leads the attacker's arm up, in, and down, toward the attacker's center of balance, projecting the attacker face down onto the mat. No lock is applied: go to 8.

8. Defender's one hand grabs the attacker by the fingers/hand or wrist (cross-side grab) while the other hand (particularly the thumb) supports the attacker's elbow from underneath: go to 9.
8a. Defender twists inwardly the attacker's fingers/hand making the attacker's arm bend at the elbow (the elbow points to the sky) while the forearm is positioned perpendicular to the mat: go to 10.

9. Defender's one hand (cross-side) grabs the attacker's fingers/hand (*ikkyo*).
9a. Defender's one hand (cross-side) grabs the attacker's wrist (*gokyo*).

10. Defender leads the attacker down by maintaining the twist of the hand and the bent position of the elbow (*sankyo*).
10a. Defender leads the attacker down by pressuring the radial nerve (external side of the attacker's forearm, about two inches from the wrist) with the base of the defender's index (*yonkyo*).

11. Defender bends attacker's wrist and fingers in, toward the attacker's center of balance, while projecting the attacker back down onto the mat (*kote oroshi*; variations include break fall).
11a. Defender turns completely around his own axis while twisting the attacker's wrist out and then bending it in, toward the attacker's shoulder, projecting the attacker backwards down onto the mat (*shihonage*, "four-directions throw"; includes *irimi* and *tenkan*).

12. Neutralization of the attack by projecting the attacker forward face down onto the mat (forward roll or break fall are possible): go to 13.

12a. Neutralization of the attack by projecting the attacker backwards, down onto the mat (back roll or break fall are possible): go to 17.

13. Defender leads the attacker into a standing position, just behind the defender, before projecting the attacker into a forward roll or break fall: go to 14.

13a. Defender leads attacker into a stooped position, just on front of the defender, before projecting the attacker into a forward roll (*kaitennage*, "harpoon throw"; includes several forms of *irimi* and *tenkan*).

14. Defender projects the attacker forward over the defender's body: go to 15.

14a. Defender does not project the attacker over the defender's body. Instead, defender turns his hips and torso to the side (while bowing forward) OR defender bows deeply forward before projecting the attacker into a forward roll: go to 16.

15. Over the defender's hips: zempo over hips (*koshinage*).

15a. Over the defender's shoulders: zempo over shoulders (*zempo seoinage*).

16. Defender leads the attacker (who usually attacks with a bear hug) by simultaneously opening the defender's arms (laterally, slightly forward, and almost parallel to the mat), stepping forward, then turning the hips and torso to the side (while bowing forward), so that the attacker is projected into a forward roll (*ushiro dori zemponage*).

16a. Defender leads the attacker (who usually grabs wrists or elbows) by simultaneously raising the defender's arms (perpendicular to the mat), stepping, then bowing deeply and lowering the arms (now parallel to the mat), so that the attacker is projected into a forward roll or break fall (*ushiro tekubi dori zemponage*; variations include stepping forward = *zenshin* or backwards = *koshin*).

17. Defender's one hand moves upwards on front of the attacker's face while the other hand is positioned behind the attacker's neck or lower back. Defender leads attacker to pass on front of defender's chest area while projecting the attacker back down to his rear (*kokyunage*, "breath" throw).

17a. Defender's one hand extends upwards (Heaven) while the other hand extends toward the mat (Earth). Defender leads attacker (who usually attacks from the front with a two-handed grab of both wrists) out and back down to his rear-diagonal side (*tenchinage*, "Heaven-Earth" throw, includes *irimi* and *tenkan*).

FIGURE 5 — DEFENSIVE TECHNIQUES: Evasive techniques (sudori).

5-A Defender (left) steps inwardly and positions herself in front of the attacker who performs a side/diagonal open hand strike (sudori using irimi; technique corresponds to number 3 in Key to the Defensive Techniques).

5-B Defender (right and in the background) steps outwardly and positions herself laterally or behind the attacker who performs a side/diagonal open hand strike (sudori using tenkan, 3a).

5-C Defender bows to avoid a side/diagonal open hand strike (sudori using rei, 4).

5-D Defender drops on her knees to avoid the attack (sudori using kneeling position, 4a).

5-E Variation of D, defender drops on her knees and forces the attacker to roll over her.

FIGURE 6 — DEFENSIVE TECHNIQUES:
Non-evasive techniques; manipulation of the attacker's arm or wrist.

6-A Defender (left) locks the attacker's wrist/arm against the defender's shoulder (nikkyo; technique corresponds to number 7 in the Key to the Defensive Techniques).

6-B Defender (left) grabs attacker's hand/fingers and supports elbow from underneath (ikkyo, 9).

6-C Defender (left) grabs attacker's wrist and supports elbow from underneath (gokyo, 9a).

6-D Close up of C. Compare B with C and D.

6-E Defender (left) twists the attacker's fingers/wrist making the attacker bend the arm at the elbow (sankyo, 10).

6-F Close up of E.

Glossary

- **atemi:** Strike to the body; stun by blow at a vital point. In Ki-Aikido atemi is not a real strike, but rather a 'touch and punch' where power is released through the fist in a spiraling motion. This action is supported by a unified connection to the body center (lower abdomen).
- **irimi:** Movement in which the defender enters and positions himself in front of the attacker.
- **koshin:** Stepping backwards.
- **nage:** Defender, person who transmits the technique.
- **rei:** Bow.
- **sudori:** Defender evades an attack by stepping away from it, bowing, or kneeling.
- **tenkan:** Movement in which the defender turns and positions himself laterally or behind the attacker.
- **uke:** Attacker, person who receives the neutralizing technique performed by the defender.
- **zempo nage:** Throw in which the attacker is projected into a forward roll.
- **zenshin:** Stepping forward.

6-A

6-B

6-C

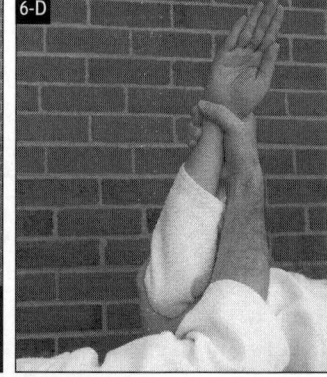
6-D

6-E

6-F

6-G Defender (left) leads the attacker down by pressing the radial nerve with the base of the defender's index finger (yonkyo, 10a).

6-H Close up of G. Arrow indicates how the base of the right index finger creates pressure on the radial nerve.

6-I Defender (left) bends the attacker's fingers and wrist in, toward her center of balance (kote oroshi, 11).

6-J Defender (left) turns around his own axis while twisting the attacker's wrist out and then bending it in, toward her shoulder (shihonage, 11a). Arrows indicate direction of defender's rotation.

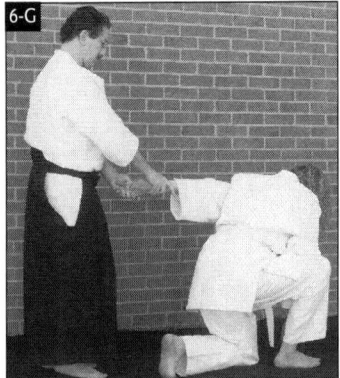

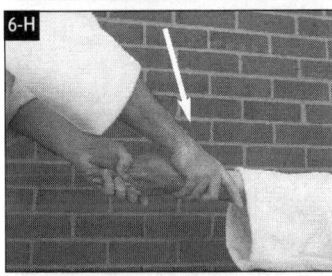

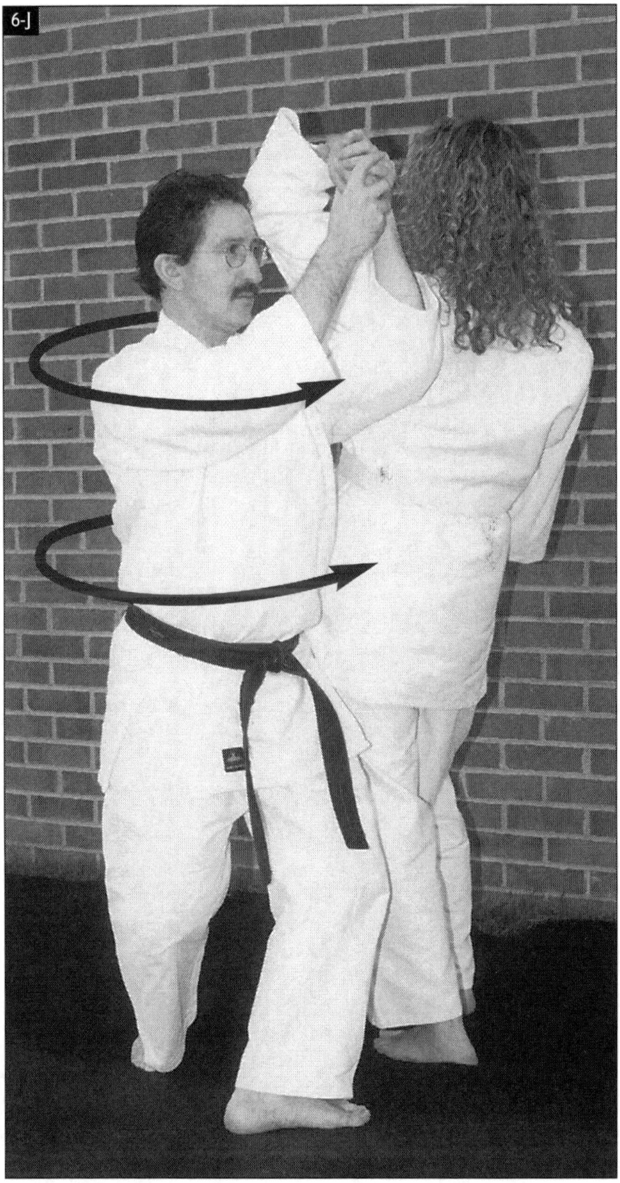

FIGURE 7 — DEFENSIVE TECHNIQUES:
Non-evasive techniques; manipulation of the attacker's torso/hips.

7-A Hip throw (koshinage; technique corresponds to number 15 in Key to the Defensive Techniques).
7-B Shoulder throw (zempo seoinage, 15a).
7-C Lateral/side throw, usually applied against a bear-hug attack (ushiro dori zemponage, 16).
7-D Similar to C, now showing a forward roll throw (16). A break fall is also possible.
7-E Defender (front) steps and bows deeply, projecting the attacker (top) forward (ushiro tekubi dori zemponage, 16a). This throw is usually used against two-handed wrist-grabs from behind.
7-F Projection into a forward roll from a stooped position (kaitennage, 13a).
7-G "Breath throw" (kokyunage, 17).
7-H Defender gently completes a "breath throw" (17).
7-I "Heaven and Earth throw" (tenchinage, 17a).

The experienced aikido practitioner might argue that aikido techniques are designed to move the attacker's body as a whole, rather than manipulating the attacker's arm or wrist alone, as we imply above. However, for teaching purposes it is important to indicate the specific area(s) of the body toward which the defender directs his neutralization technique. We acknowledge, of course, that any neutralization is intended to move the attacker's entire body. As with the attacks, multiple combinations of defenses are also possible. For example, the defender may lead the attacker, who usually grabs wrists or elbows, by simultaneously raising the defender's arms (perpendicular to the mat), stepping, then bowing deeply and lowering the arms (now parallel to the mat), so that the attacker is lead into a stooped position just "behind/on top" of the defender; then the defender turns completely around his own axis while twisting the attacker's wrist out and then bending it in, toward the attacker's shoulder, projecting the attacker back down onto the mat (*ushiro tekubi tori-shihonage*). There is no need to include a specific key for hybrid defenses since they can be deduced from the material presented above. Almost all the defensive techniques can also be performed from the kneeling position. Combinations of defensive techniques are limited only by the defender's imagination.

Concluding Remarks

Dichotomous keys are essentially designed for identification purposes. In this article, we grouped the attacks into two major categories: grabs and strikes; both categories include numerous subdivisions. Similarly, the defenses are grouped into two major categories: evasive techniques where the defender steps away from the attack or modifies his body posture to avoid the attack, and non-evasive techniques where the defender manipulates the attacker's arm/wrist or torso/hips; both defensive categories also include subdivisions.

Based on the comparative information that we gathered while constructing these keys, we propose a graphic representation of the relationships among the attacks (Figure 8) and among the defenses (Figure 9). Some similarities are obvious, like the ones detailed in the ikkyo group, i.e., neutralization of the attack by manipulation of the arm (Figure 9); see also Key to the Defensive Techniques 6, and Figures 6-A through 6-H), while others are arguable, like the comparison between kote oroshi and shihonage discussed earlier. Nonetheless, we hope that this initial attempt to illustrate the structural similarity of aikido techniques, from their simplest movement to the most complex combination of motions, might encourage martial arts' scholars to discuss our proposal, improve our methods, and hopefully even reevaluate their thinking about how aikido could be taught and, ultimately, how aikido techniques should be classified.

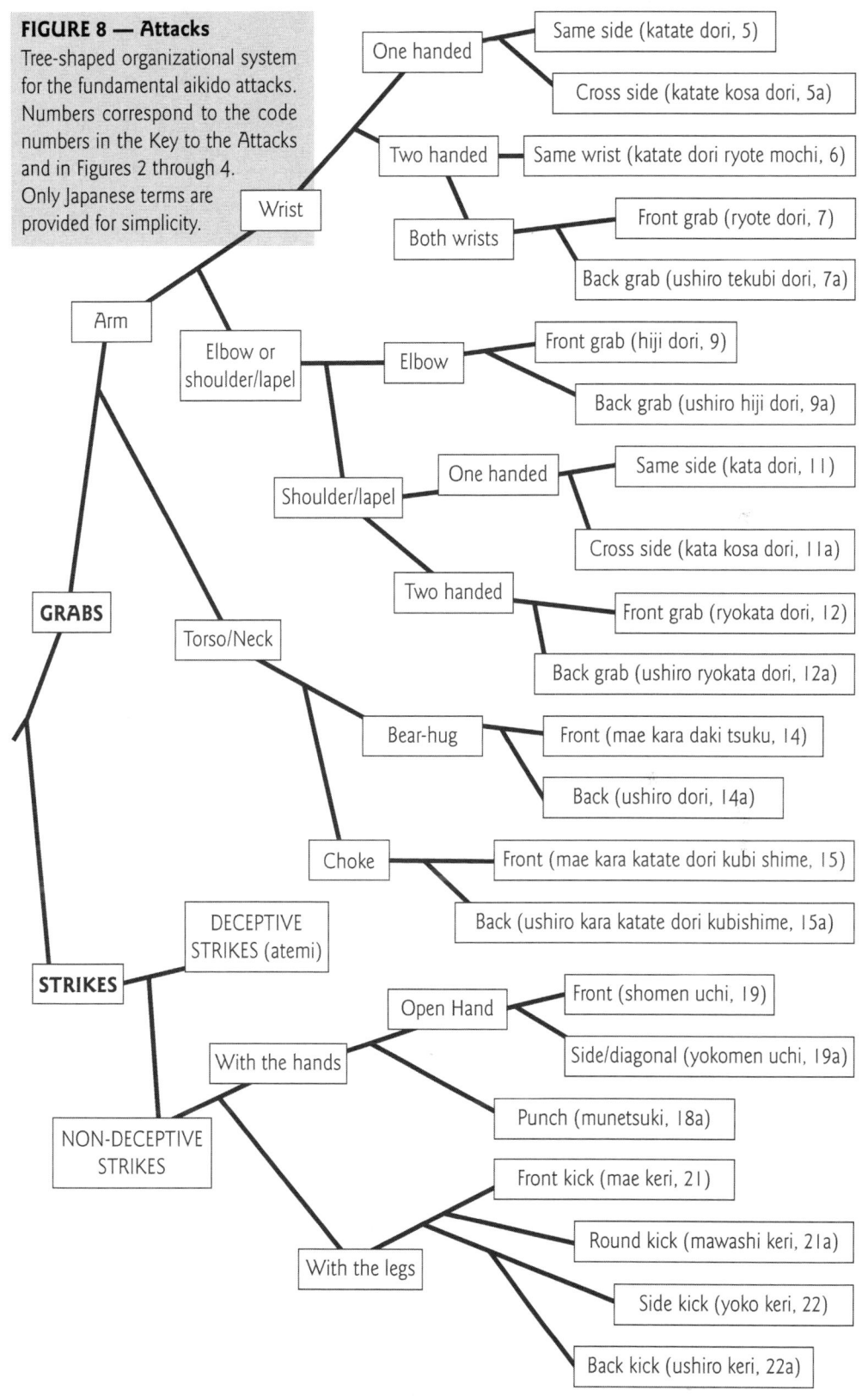

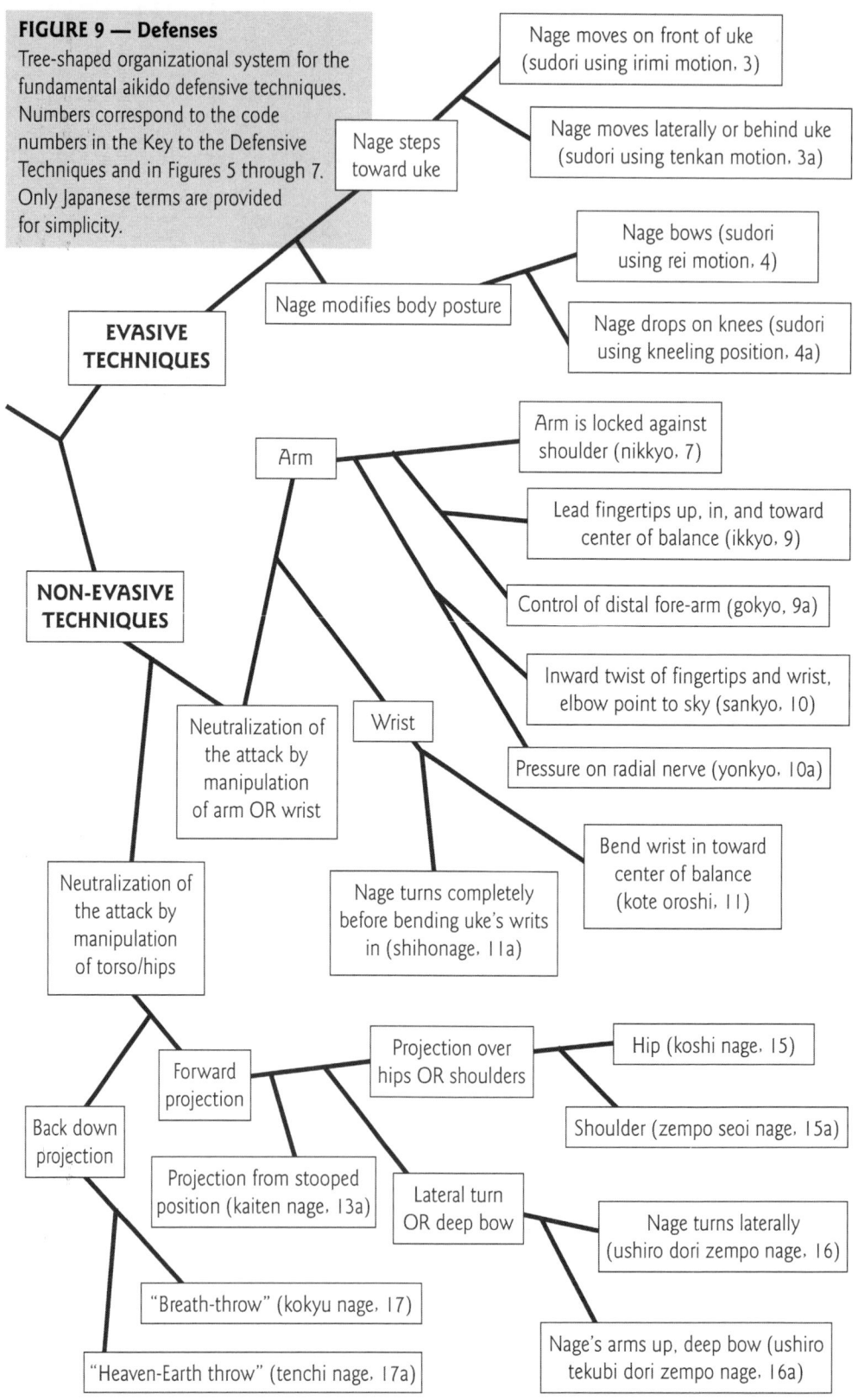

Bibliography

Curtis, C. (2001). *Ki-Aikido on Maui*, 3rd Ed. Maui, Hawaii: MAKS Publications.

Maruyama, K. (1984). *Aikido with ki*. Tokyo: Ki No Kenkyukai Headquarters.

Reed, W. (1999). *Ki: A practical guide for westerners*, 6th Ed. Tokyo: Japan Publications.

Reed, W. (1993). *Ki: A road that anyone can walk*, 2nd Ed. Tokyo: Japan Publications.

Shifflett, C. (1999). *Aikido: Exercises for teaching and training*. Merrifield, Virginia: Round Earth Publishing.

Shifflett, C. (1998). *Ki in aikido: A sampler of ki exercises*. Merrifield, Virginia: Round Earth Publishing.

Taylor, K. (2001). Ukemiwaza: The art of attacking in aikido. *Journal of Asian Martial Arts*, 10(2), 60–75.

Tohei, K. (2001). *The way to union with ki: Aikido with mind and body coordination*, 1st Ed. Tochigi: Ki No Kenkyukai Headquarters.

Tohei, K. (1998). *Ki in daily life*, 16th Ed. Tokyo: Ki No Kenkyukai Headquarters.

Tohei, K. (1974). *This is aikido*. Tokyo: Japan Publications.

Ward, B. (1999). Energy projection in aikido wrist-techniques. *Journal of Asian Martial Arts*, 8(1), 50–55.

Westbrook, A. & Ratti, O. (1999). *Aikido and the dynamic sphere*. Rutland, Vermont: Charles E. Tuttle Co.

Wolfe, R. (1999). The science of ukemi (rolls and breakfalls). *Journal of Asian Martial Arts*, 8(3), 54–75.

Acknowledgements

We dedicate this article to Mark Rubbert, William Reed, and Koichi Kashiwaya who have inspired us to explore the fascinating complexity of Shin Shin Toitsu Aikido (founder Koichi Tohei). Very special thanks to our mentor Mark Rubbert (Senior/Associate Instructor St. Louis Ki Society) and the St. Louis Ki Society members for continuous support and friendship. The Ki-Aikido students at the Student Recreation & Fitness Center, The University of Memphis (TUM), motivated us to develop the ideas discussed in this article. Jane Orcholski, Program Coordinator Campus Recreation Intramural Services, at TUM, helped us to initiate Ki-Aikido classes at TUM. We thank two anonymous reviewers for comments on the manuscript. The material discussed in this article is not necessarily endorsed by Ki Society or any of its affiliates. All photographs courtesy of C. Paz-y-Miño C., except for article cover photo and Figure 1-E that were taken by J. Dixon.

· 2 ·

Aikido:
The Art of the Dynamic Equiangular Spiral
by Guilermo Paz-y-Miño C., Ph.D., and Avelina Espinosa, Ph.D.

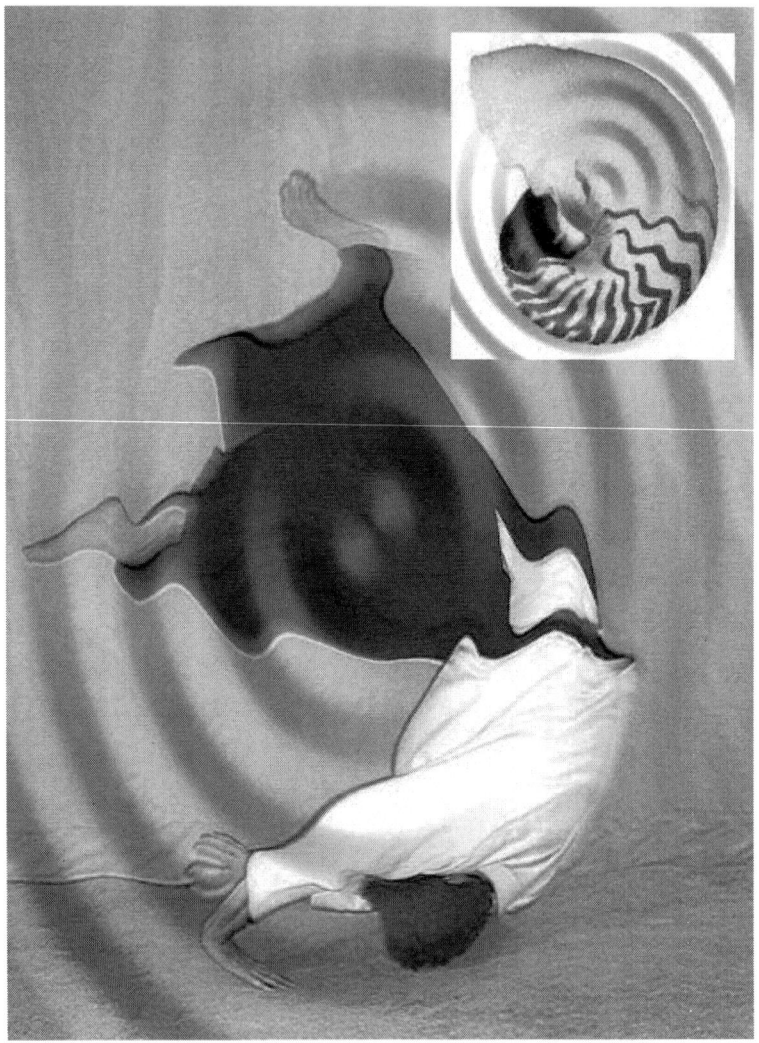

Photographs courtesy of A. Espinosa and G. Paz-y-Miño C.

The shell of Nautilus or snail... the elephant's tusk, the beaver's tooth, the cat's claws or the canary-bird's—all these show the same simple and very beautiful spiral curve... the equiangular spiral.
—Wentworth-Thompson, 1942

Introduction

D'Arcy Wentworth-Thompson (1860–1948), a British erudite in the physical and natural sciences, author of *On Growth and Form*, never imagined that his studies on the application of physical and mathematical principles to living forms could help us understand aikido (*aiki* = harmony, *do* = path, the way of). Aikido, a Japanese martial discipline, has been labeled the art of the dynamic sphere. Its techniques appear to move the body in a "circular" synchronized and aesthetic manner resulting in immobilization or projection of a partner. However, more than spherical motions, aikido techniques generate spiral ones. This distinction is not trivial because, when spiral movements are applied to aikido pins and throws, the techniques become much more efficient than when simple circular trajectories are used.

As the reader will discover in this article, perhaps a more accurate definition of aikido should be the art of the dynamic equiangular spiral. Here we discuss how the principles of the spiral can be applied to most aspects of aikido training, including stances and sitting postures, bows, stretching exercises, warm-ups, single-person routines to develop balance and mind/body coordination, rolling and falling, partnered techniques of neutralization, projections/throws, and weapons.

FIGURE I

The one-point or the body's center of balance/rotation.

The dynamic equiangular spiral originates in what aikidoists call the "one-point" (*seika-no-itten*), or the body's center of balance. In biophysical terms, the one-point is the body's center of rotation; it is located about two inches below the navel (Figure 1). When static, the body is stable as long as the one-point remains centered over its support, the feet. If this center of balance moves beyond its support, the effect of gravity creates a torque that may cause the body to fall, regardless of size, weight, or muscle. The aikidoist does not need to be constantly over his one-point to be balanced, but if off-center he will need a support, even an invisible one such as motion or inertia, to maintain stability. Aikido techniques are based on this principle. If the aikidoist remains as the center of any motion about himself (or about his one-point), he will be able to throw an attacker while maintaining himself in place.

FIGURE 2

2-A Belt coiled on itself illustrating a "tight" equable spiral of Archimedes.

2-B Entire Nautilus shell (external view).

2-C Sagital cut of a Nautilus shell (internal view). The chambers follow the design of an equiangular spiral of Descartes. The living animal resides in the newest and largest chamber.

2-D The elements of the spiral: point of origin or pole O, the radius vector r, and the traveling point P. The reader will count three equidistant whorls between O and P.

2-E The geometrical spiral of Descartes, or equiangular spiral. The reader shall count only one whorl between O and P even though the length of the radius r in E is similar to that of the radius in D.

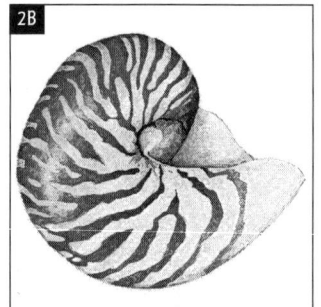

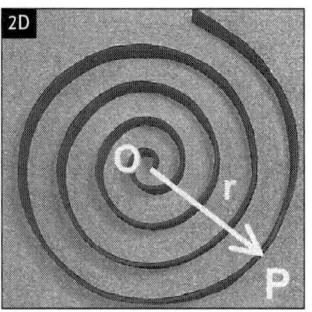
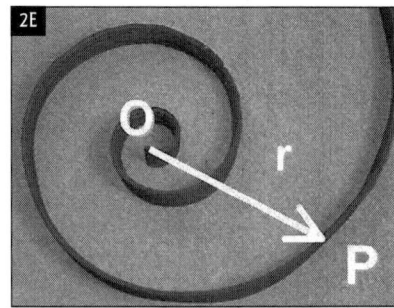

What Do the Nautilus Shell and Aikido Have in Common?

The equable spiral of Archimedes, illustrated by the way a martial artist coils his belt on itself (Figure 2A), although fascinating for its simple geometry, is as unusual in nature as it is unusual to find perfect spherical anatomical structures or circular motions (no matter how "circular" they may appear!). However, it helps us to understand the properties of its more popular relative, the equiangular spiral of Descartes, illustrated by the structure of a Nautilus shell (Figures 2B and 2C), a beautiful marine mollusk. All natural designs—such as the Nautilus shell, the human cochlea in the inner ear, our teeth and nails, the arrangement of scales in a pinecone, the movement pattern of a tornado, the bull's horn or deer's antler, as well as the aikido techniques discussed in this article—show the same equiangular design (see supplement 1). Why?

Supplement I: SPIRALS IN NATURE

To comprehend the bio-dynamics of aikido's spiral movements we need first to understand simple geometry and physics. Although the material discussed in this article is basic science, it may seem complex to those unfamiliar with these principles. Below, we paraphrase selected statements from Wentworth-Thompson's book and use them to explain how and why spiraling motions can be used in aikido to immobilize or throw an attacker.

A spiral is a curve which, starting from a point of origin (located in a center), continually diminishes in curvature as it recedes from that point, or whose radius of curvature continually increases. The elements of a spiral include (Figure 2D): ❶ the point of origin or pole (O), ❷ the radius vector (r) which is the straight line that, having its extremity in the pole, revolves about it, and ❸ the point (P) which travels along the radius vector, away from the origin, under definite conditions of velocity, thus describing the spiral curve.

Of the several mathematical curves, the two most important to illustrate this article are the equable spiral or spiral of Archimedes, and the equiangular spiral or logarithmic spiral of Descartes. The spiral of Archimedes might be illustrated by the way a martial artist often coils his belt around itself. As the belt is of uniform thickness, so in the whole spiral is each whorl of the same breadth as that which precedes and as that which follows it. If, while the radius vector revolves uniformly about the pole, a point P travels with uniform velocity along it, the curve described will be that called the equable spiral of Archimedes. The radius (r = OP), made up of the successive and equal whorls, will increase in arithmetical progression (see, for example, the three equidistant whorls between O and P in Figure 2D). The spiral of Archimedes might also be looked upon as a coiled cylinder.

In contrast, in the equiangular spiral of Descartes, the whorls continually increase in breadth, and in a steady and unchanging ratio. If, instead of traveling with a uniform velocity, the point P moves along the radius vector with a velocity increasing as does its distance from the pole, then the path described is called an equiangular spiral. Each whorl the radius vector intersects is broader than its predecessor in a definite ratio (Figure 2E); thus, the radius vector will increase in length in geometrical progression (note that in Figure 2E there is only one whorl between O and P, and that the distance from this whorl to O is shorter than the distance from it to P). As the spiral of Archimedes in our example of the coiled belt might be looked upon as a coiled cylinder, so the equiangular spiral might be looked upon as a cone coiled upon itself, like in the Nautilus shell (Figures 2B and 2C).

The Nautilus shell is an excellent example to illustrate why the equiangular spiral is an efficient way of growing. The presently existing structure is, so to speak, partly old and partly new. It has been formed by successive and continuous increments; each successive stage of growth, starting from the origin (the smallest chamber), remains as an integral and unchanging portion of the growing structure. The shell itself consists of dead material, old and smaller chambers used by the mollusk in earlier stages of its development.

Aikido techniques are designed exactly in the same fashion as the Nautilus chamber arrangement. A forward roll (such as the one illustrated on the cover page of this article), for instance, originates in a small swirl at the level of the aikidoist's hands, and continues in a geometric progression toward the feet. The entire body outlines an equiangular spiral where the feet move with a velocity increasing as does their distance from the hands. Just like the eye of a typhoon, which is always peaceful, so are the hands of the aikidoist while rolling forward, however, the feet move with great acceleration as they distance from the hands (see Supplement 2). Thus, the forward roll illustrates the essence of aikido's equiangular motions.

Supplement 2: THE PHYSICS OF THE EQUIANGULAR SPIRAL

If an aikidoist projects an attacker into a spiral path with the aikidoist's one-point as the center of the rotation, the attacker will fly off the center at a tangent to the aikidoist's body, describing an equiangular trajectory in respect to the aikidoist's one-point. After exerting an initial force to start the throw, the aikidoist will spin at a constant rate and, therefore, having no change in speed, he will have no angular acceleration (like the eye of the typhoon). In contrast, the attacker will experience significant centripetal force with a velocity increasing in relation to the distance from the aikidoist's one-point.* This can be described according to the equation:

$$F = m (v^2 / r)$$

Force = mass x (velocity squared divided by the radius of the spiral)

A 160-pound attacker being thrown by an aikidoist at 10 miles per hour, with a radius of 20 inches in respect to the aikidoist's one-point, will exert an impressive centripetal force of:

$$F = (72.72 \text{ kg}) (4.5 \text{ m/sec}^2 / 0.5 \text{ m}) = 2945 \text{ Newtons} = 661 \text{ pounds}$$

If falling out of control, the 160-pound attacker will hit the ground with a force equivalent to four times his normal weight. Do you see why aikidoists prefer to roll rather than to fall? This explains how a small individual can deflect, redirect, and project a far larger and stronger attacker. By staying offline, using the tools of leverage, rotation, and the power of the equiangular spiral, the smaller person—if moving properly—can have an advantage over a larger attacker.

* Note that, for simplicity, in this example we do not include all the factors that characterize the movement of an attacker such as his angular acceleration with respect to the aikidoist's one-point, his friction against the mat (or the aikidoist's body if contact occurs), or the inertia resulting from the technique applied to his body. For details, see Shifflett (1999), and Watanabe and Avakian (1997).

Thinking and Moving "Equiangularly"

Although the forward roll clearly illustrates the equiangular nature of aikido's motions, the application of this concept to other aspects of aikido training might not be that evident to most students. Realize that not only every arm lock, wrist bend or break fall, but also every posture, bow, stretch exercise, cut with a wooden sword (*bokken*) or poke with a wooden staff (*jo*), describe an equiangular trajectory. This is because, when the joints of the body interact and move in different directions, they simultaneously create small and large spirals. In consequence, there is not only one equiangular spiral at work when an aikido technique is in progress, but multiple ones interconnected in a three dimensional environment.

To improve the efficiency of aikido techniques the student should think and move "equiangularly." Here are some tips that may help you achieve this goal:

❶ discover the location of most of the equiangular spirals in both your and the attacker's anatomy, particularly where the centers of rotation of each spiral are located (i.e., the joints);
❷ understand how your own and the attacker's spirals are interconnected when in motion;
❸ determine the directions in which you should move or apply an aikido technique in respect to the attacker's movements (i.e., toward the spiral's point of origin or away from it); and
❹ allow your body to flow naturally in the direction that the dynamic spirals dictate.

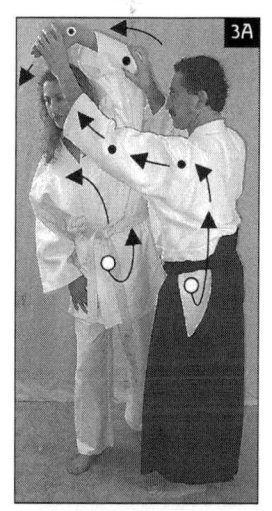

Figure 3 illustrates these points. Note that the relative position of the one-point in both aikidoists is indicated with a white circle (lower abdomen). Ultimately, the defender (right), whose one-point will become the center of the main equiangular motion, will assure control of both the technique and the attacker (left). The points of origin or centers of rotation/movement of the remaining minor (secondary) spirals are represented by black dots. The arrows indicate how those spirals must move harmoniously in relation to the defender's and also the attacker's one-points. In Figure 3A the defender redirects the attack (an open-hand strike to the forehead) downwards. Once the deflection is completed, the attacker's one-point moves to a lower level with respect to the defender's (Figure 3B). The neutralization of the attack is successfully accomplished if the defender remains at all times at the center of the spiral motion and his one-point is located (even slightly) above the attacker's one-point.

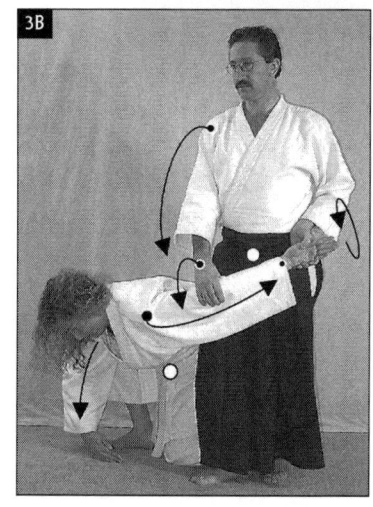

FIGURE 3

The equiangular spiral concept applied to aikido. A white circle indicates the location of the one-point, the center of the main equiangular spiral. Black dots indicate the centers of rotation/movement (the joints) of minor (secondary) spirals. Arrows point in the direction of movement.

The student will learn how to move in this spiral fashion only if he develops a clear mental image of the geometric progression of an equiangular trajectory. In most immobilizations and pins, for example, the aikidoist should curl the attacker's wrist, elbow or shoulder inward, toward the point of origin of the spiral. However, in numerous single-person routines, or even in projections, the aikidoist should first follow the opposite direction of the spiral, which is outwardly, toward the open course of the coil, in order to initiate big motions of the body and generate inertia for throwing. Then the aikidoist should bring the attacker toward the aikidoist's one-point to create the necessary equiangular direction and make the attacker fly off the center of rotation (centripetal force).

TECHNICAL SECTION

In the following figures we indicate how to apply the concept of the equiangular spiral to aikido stances, sitting postures, bows, stretching exercises, single-person routines to develop balance and mind and body coordination, rolling and falling, techniques of neutralization (mostly immobilizations), projections/throws, and weapons. The material presented below is by no means complete; nonetheless, it does cover essential aspects of aikido training. The photos illustrate cases where the equiangular spiral can be easily visualized. It will be up to the student, however, to detect equiangular motions in other training scenarios:

FIGURE 4 – Standing

4-A The aikidoist focuses his mind in the one-point (white dot), the body's center of balance. Centers of secondary spirals are shown at the shoulder level. The arms, with the elbows and hands slightly bent inward, naturally follow an equiangular direction (down/in).

4-B The aikidoist bows from the one-point (center of the main equiangular movement) and places the palms lightly over the thighs, close to the knees.

4-C Readiness posture, lateral view. The arms are partially extended following the direction of the equiangular spirals (centered in the shoulders) forward and upward. The entire posture relies on its connection with the one-point.

4-D Readiness posture, frontal view. The aikidoist "hides" himself behind the hands, protecting his face and torso.

FIGURE 5 – Sitting

5-A Seiza (formal aikido sitting posture). The equiangular direction of the arms is even more evident in seiza than in the standing posture shown in Figure 4-A (above). Black dots at the elbows and wrists indicate the centers of minor equiangular spirals.

5-B Seiza bow. A clear illustration of the equiangular direction followed by the torso, which always remains connected to the one-point (white circle). Note the centers of the secondary spirals in the shoulder and elbow (black dots).

5-C Cross-legged sitting, frontal view. The aikidoist feels the centers of the equiangular spirals not only in the forelimb joints but also in the crossed legs (particularly in the hip and knee-joints).

5-D Cross-legged sitting, lateral view. Note the directions followed by the numerous equiangular spirals. In relaxation, this pyramidal shape adopted by the aikidoist's body gives him great stability.

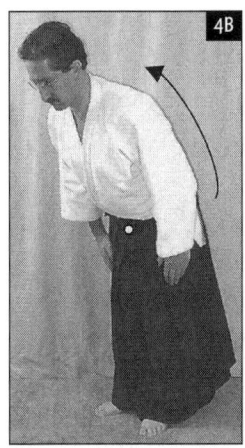
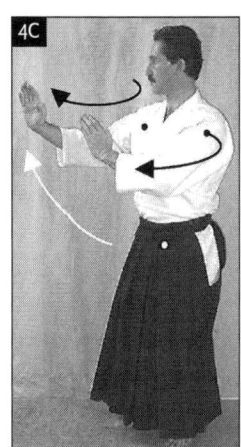

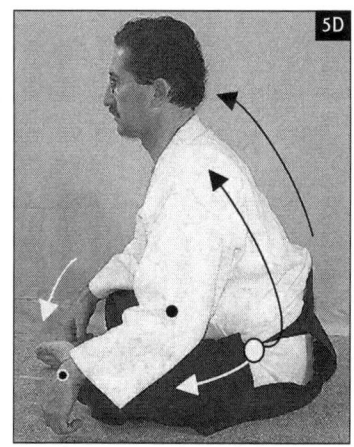

FIGURE 6 – Leg Stretches

6-A Open legs. Both legs have a very wide equiangular orientation centered in the one-point.

6-B The aikidoist bends forward from the one-point (not the shoulders!), keeping the back straight and the toes up; once in this position, he stretches the arms forward, feeling the centers of equiangular spirals first in the one-point, and then in the shoulders, elbows and wrists.

6-C Same as in B, but now the aikidoist brings his chest (not his head!) toward one of the knees and continues feeling the equiangular spirals in the shoulder, elbow and wrist.

6-D Legs extended, heels together. The aikidoist bends forward from the one-point, bringing the chest toward the knees. The equiangular motion should be smooth and the entire body must remain relaxed.

6-E Soles of feet in contact and drawn into the hips. Various equiangular directions are shown by the arrows.

6-F The aikidoist bends forward from the one-point, bringing the chest to the feet.

6-G Once in the position shown in F, the aikidoist stretches the arms forward. The diverse equiangular directions followed by the torso (forward), legs (out), and arms (forward/in), are indicated by the arrows.

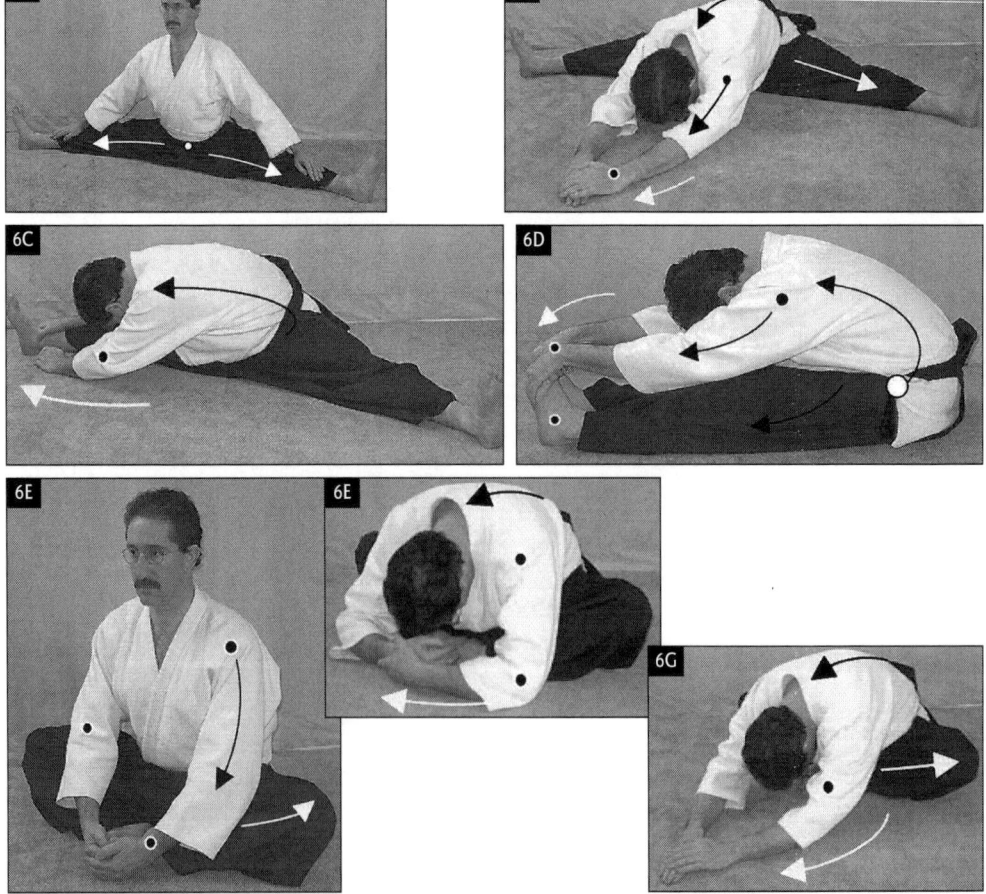

FIGURE 7 – Wrist Stretches From Seiza

7-A Sitting in seiza, the aikidoist stretches the wrists. The centers of the equiangular spirals are indicated by the white (one-point) and black (shoulder and wrist) dots.

7-B Keeping the elbows down and in complete relaxation, the aikidoist curls the fingers inward. The equiangular trajectory is obvious!

7-C The wrist remains close to the chest area while the fingertips point forward (elbows down). One hand grabs the edge of the other hand. Simple relaxation provides enough stretching of the joint in a natural equiangular direction.

7-D Fingertips up. Two equiangular trajectories are indicated by the arrows; if the aikidoist relaxes and allows both hands to fall toward the one-point, the stretch is safe and correct.

7-E By grabbing with one hand the edge of the other and by stretching both arms forward (shoulders down and elbows pointing out!), the aikidoist generates a pleasant equiangular rotation in the wrist.

7-F Elbow pointing to the sky and forearm perpendicular to the ground. The aikidoist stretches the wrist by turning it in. At least two equiangular spirals are evident here: one centered in the elbow and another in the wrist (black dots).

7-G Wrist stretch with the fingertips in the direction of the one-point.

7-H Same as in G, but the fingertips now point to the shoulder.

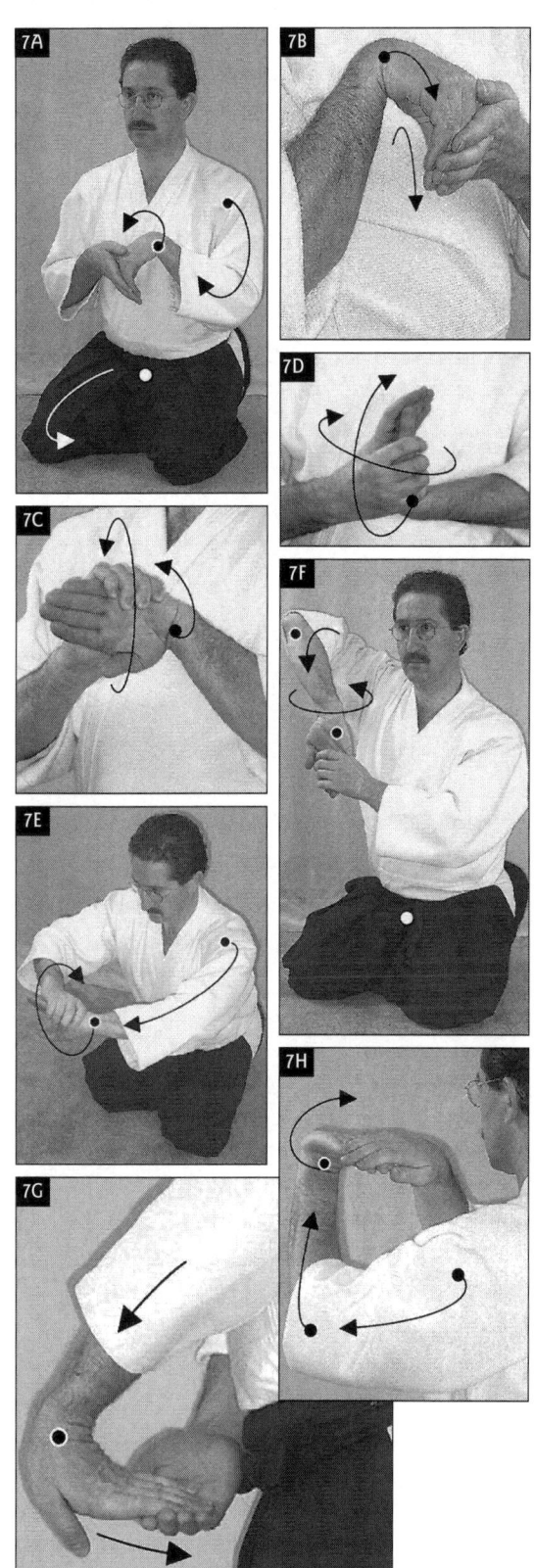

31

FIGURE 8 – Neck, Shoulders, Arms and Torso Stretches

8-A-D   Neck stretches (down, up, lateral and side). The centers of the equiangular spirals are located at the base of the cervical vertebrae.

8-E-F   From a standing position and with the arms wide open (relaxed shoulders as in E), the aikidoist rotates the torso from the hips toward one side (F) and then to the other. The equiangular trajectory (white arrow) is centered in the one-point and its plane of rotation is parallel to the mat. The arms form their own equiangular spirals.

8-G   Lateral stretch of the torso. Note how the torso and arm describe a clear equiangular spiral centered in the one-point.

8-H-I   Shoulder and arm stretches. The aikidoist grabs with one hand the dorsal side of the other and gently takes the elbow backward (H, frontal view), keeping the elbow close to the torso and the shoulders relaxed (I, lateral view). Ultimately, the one-point and the elbow remain connected and the aikidoist feels the spiral motion traveling from the one-point to the elbow and vice versa.

8-J-K   From a standing position and with the arms up (see the direction of the arm spiral in J), the aikidoist bends forward from the one-point, describing a long equiangular motion (K).

8-L-M   From seiza. Frontal (L) and posterior view (M) of a tight equiangular stretch of the shoulder joint.

8-N   From seiza. Long stretch. The equiangular spiral originates in the one-point and continues forward to the arms and fingertips.

8-O   From seiza. Long stretch backward. Equiangular spirals are evident in the one-point, the entire forelimb and, interestingly, the knee. Complete relaxation is required!

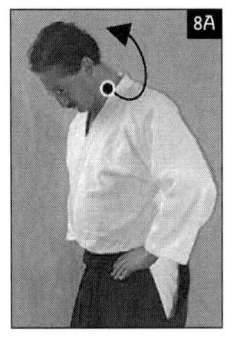
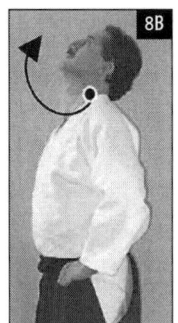

  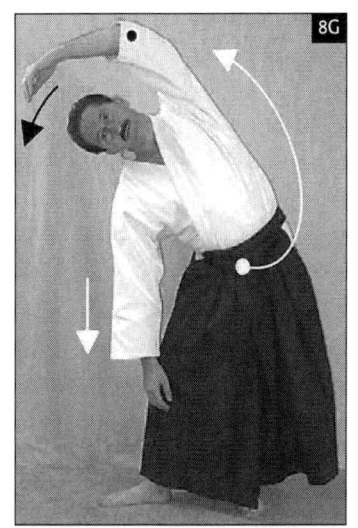
  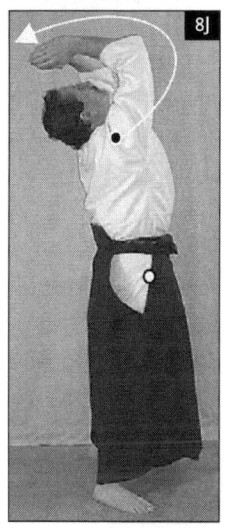 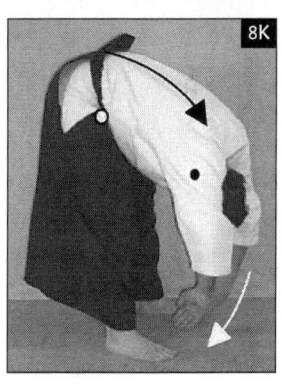
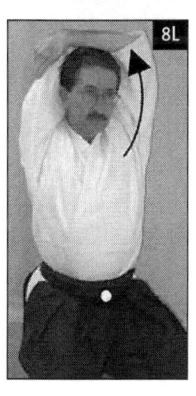 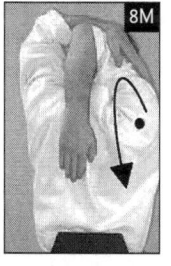 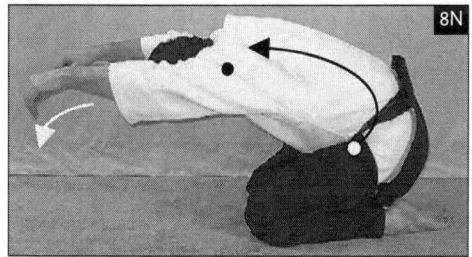
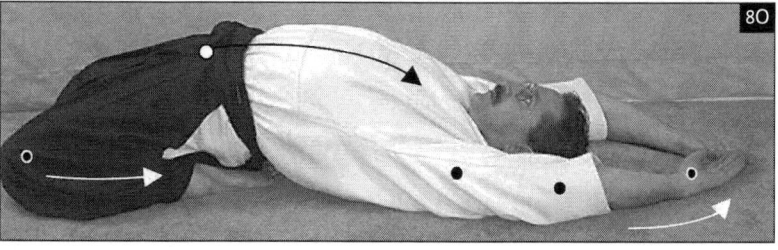

FIGURE 9 – Single Person Exercises to Develop Mind and Body Coordination from Seiza

The following exercises are performed in a completely relaxed state. These routines are designed to keep the mind focused on accurate, delicate movements. While keeping the body steady, the aikidoist feels the equiangular trajectories centered in the shoulders, elbows, and wrists. Series of up to eight repetitions are recommended.

9-A Arm "circles." In reality, the hand describes an elliptical trajectory. The arm itself is shaped as an equiangular spiral centered in the shoulder. The aikidoist allows the arm to fall with gravity, then he catches it when the hand reaches the knee level, and takes the arm up again.

9-B Same as in A, but with both arms in motion. The body remains calm while the arms move rhythmically. Both inward and outward motions should be practiced.

9-C-D Arms wide-open and equiangular spirals clearly visible on each side; fingertips point up (C). The aikidoist swings his arms to one side as in D, and then to the other (now, fingertips point down). The arms are moved gently but rhythmically while keeping the rest of the body calm, almost static.

9-E From the position illustrated in E, the aikidoist swings his arms to one side and then to the other. The equiangular trajectory of both arms should be clearly defined.

9-F-G From the position illustrated in F, the aikidoist moves his hands in and places them in front of the one-point, where they cross, as in G. The fingertips point in opposite directions.

9-H From F, the aikidoist swings his hands forward and up, placing them in front of the face.

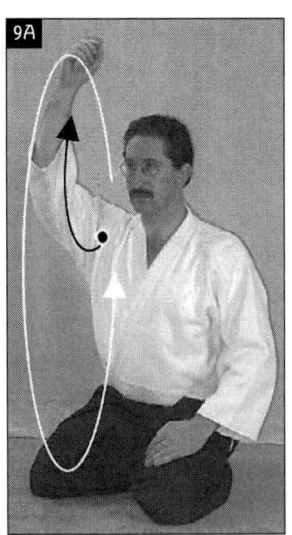
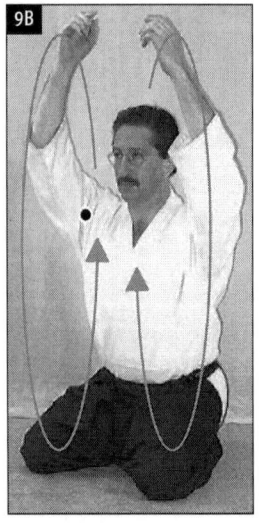

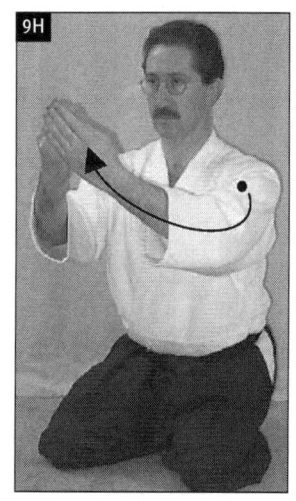

**FIGURE 10 – Single Person Exercises
to Develop Balance and Coordination, from a Standing Posture**

10-A-B Boat-rowing exercises. Hands touch the hips (A). The aikidoist shifts the hips forward while thrusting out the arms (B); then he goes back to the original position. The equiangular spirals are centered in the shoulders and continue along the arms toward the fingertips (pointing forward/down as in B).

10-C-D Arm-swing exercise. First, hands touch lightly the thighs (C), then the aikidoist shifts the entire body forward while swinging the arms forward and up; fingertips extended (D). The equiangular spirals are centered in the shoulders. The entire motion relies on its connection with the one-point.

10-E Both arms follow equiangular trajectories centered in the shoulders and continuing toward the fingertips, which point in opposite directions. The aikidoist turns his head to one side, in the same direction as the upper hand's fingertips; note how one of the feet also points in that same direction. Hands, head, and one-point should be vertically aligned.

10-F Similar to the exercise described in Figure 9-E, but now from a standing position. The aikidoist swings his arms to one side and then to the other. Note that one knee bends while the entire body drops slightly in the direction of the bent knee. The equiangular trajectory of both arms should be clearly visible. Additionally, the aikidoist feels an equiangular connection between his one-point, the bent knee, and the foot.

10-G-H From standing with the arms up (shoulders relaxed) and the wrists naturally bent forward (fingertips point forward/down), the aikidoist steps and bends from the one-point (H). The equiangular spiral originates in the one-point and continues forward to the arms and fingertips.

10-I "Front-kick" exercise. Two equiangular spirals are obvious, one centered in the one-point and the other in the knee; their combination generates impressive power in the technique. To maintain balance, the aikidoist keeps the head, shoulders, elbow, hand, hips (one-point), and supporting leg vertically aligned (white line). To show complete relaxation, he uses a "trick": the hands remain gently closed, next to the vertical alignment of the body, with the thumbs slightly touching the middle finger (see detail).

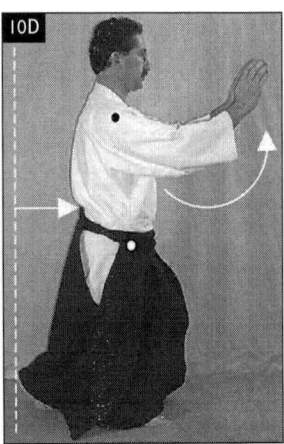

10-J-K Knee "walking." The aikidoist describes equiangular motions with each knee step (indicated by the white arrows); he pivots from side to side on alternating knees. Black arrows indicate the forward direction of the knee-walk.

10-L Aikido squats, a very demanding exercise. Sitting on his heels, the aikidoist jumps (arrows) while keeping the torso steady and relaxed. Legs must do all the work and knees should remain wide open (this is crucial!). Two equiangular spirals originate in the one point and depart in opposite directions toward the knees, where new spiral trajectories continue toward the feet. The angle of curvature of all these spirals changes when jumping.

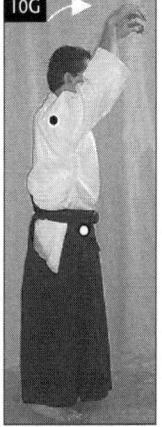

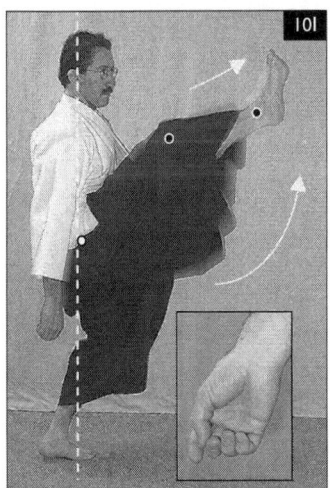
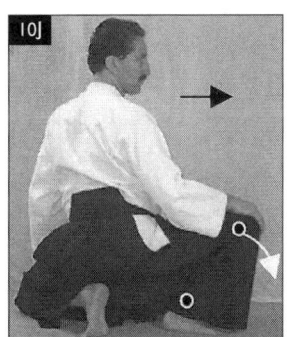
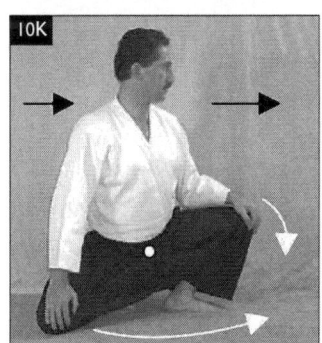

FIGURE 11 – Rolling and Falling

11-A   Wide-open aikido roll illustrating the equiangular spiral. Quiet rolls are an indication that the aikidoist is correctly performing an equiangular trajectory. The roll starts from standing and, after completion, the aikidoist recovers the standing posture or continues walking. Any deviation from the spiral geometrical progression of a roll will be revealed by the amount of noise the aikidoist makes when rolling.

11-B   Break fall. Once rolling as in A, the aikidoist could land on the mat (instead of standing up or continuing walking as indicated in A). Only if the body describes an accurate equiangular trajectory, is the break fall smooth, safe, and painless. Performing a "quiet" break fall, a task almost impossible to achieve, should be the ultimate goal of the student.

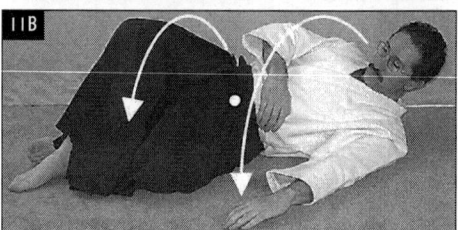

FIGURE 12 - Partnered Aikido Techniques of Immobilization

12-A   The arm contortion applied by the aikidoist (kneeling) follows an equiangular trajectory centered in the shoulder, which contributes to pin the attacker. Note how the attacker's arm remains perpendicular to the mat. The detail shows how the wristlock is performed; both the aikidoist's (top) and the attacker's wrists describe equiangular spirals.

12-B-C   The aikidoist (kneeling) holds the attacker's arm firmly against the mat (elbow grabbed) while bending the attacker's wrist/fingers toward her forearm. The equiangular spiral is centered in the wrist (B). A technique alternative to this lock is indicated in C, where the aikidoist holds the attacker's arm firmly against the aikidoist's knee while twisting the hand in the direction indicated by the arrows. In this case, the equiangular contortion takes place in a plane perpendicular to the forearm's axis (line).

12-D   Two equiangular spirals, one in the wrist and the other in the elbow, are shown in this elegant technique. The aikidoist controls the elbow and wrist while applying gentle pressure in the direction of the bent wrist.

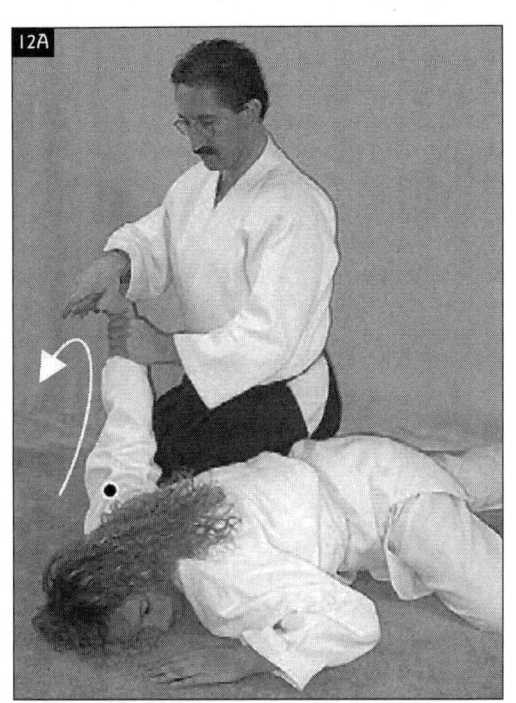
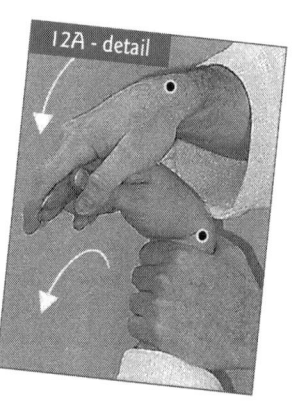

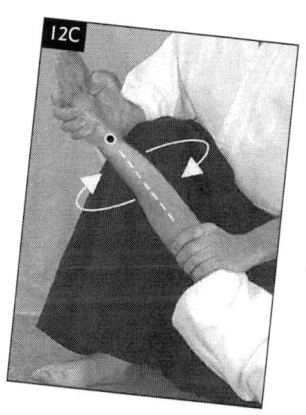
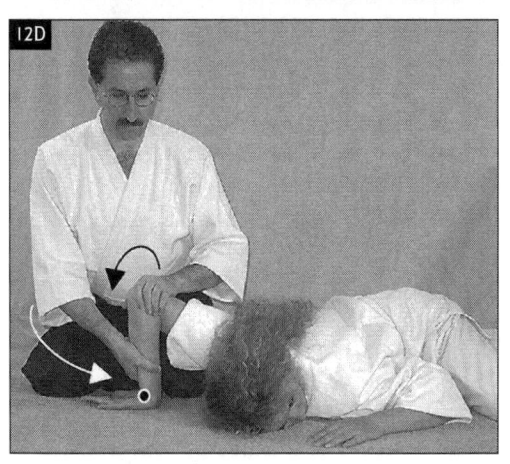
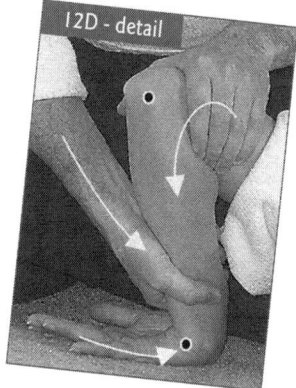

12-E   While keeping the attacker's fingers pointing up, the aikidoist bends the attacker's wrist toward her one-point. The equiangular trajectory of the technique, which connects the wrist with the elbow, shoulder and one-point, forces the attacker to kneel.

12-F   The aikidoist (standing) bends the attacker's wrist inward and down, in the direction of the one-point. The spiral motion centered in the wrist (detail) forces the attacker to fall.

12-G   Same as in F, but now after the attacker has been thrown into a break fall. Once the fall has been completed, the aikidoist (kneeling) continues bending the attacker's wrist in an equiangular trajectory (aimed to the attacker's one-point) to maintain the pin.

12-H   The aikidoist (standing) keeps the attacker's arm stretched and perpendicular to the mat while creating slight pressure down and in, toward the shoulder (center of the main equiangular spiral). The detail shows how the wrist should be twisted in a perpendicular plane (equiangular direction) with respect to the arm's axis.

12-I   "Three palms up" pin. This complex and beautiful aikido pin relies on, at least, three equiangular trajectories applied to the arm: one in the direction of each of the aikidoist's hands (down and in), and another in the direction of the attacker's shoulder. This is a sophisticated example of the equiangular concept applied to aikido: the three spirals converge into a major center of rotation, the attacker's shoulder.

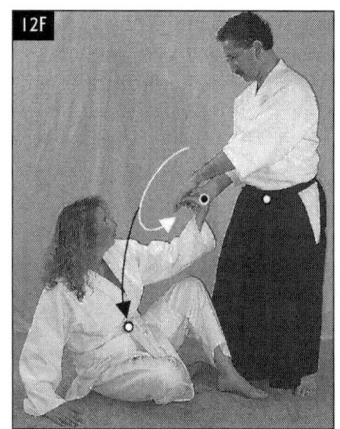
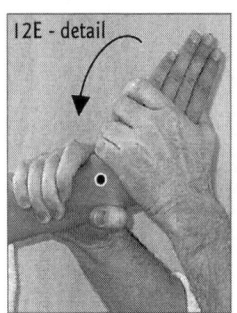
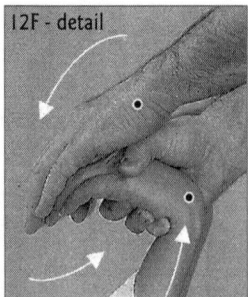
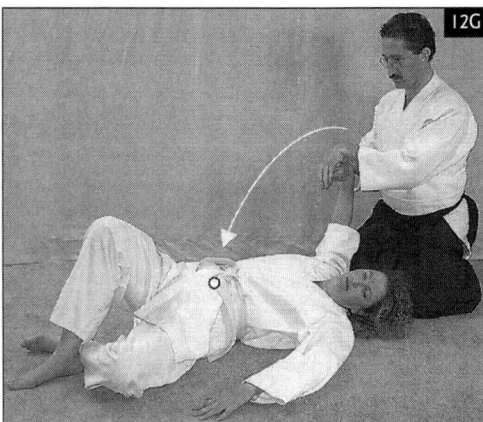

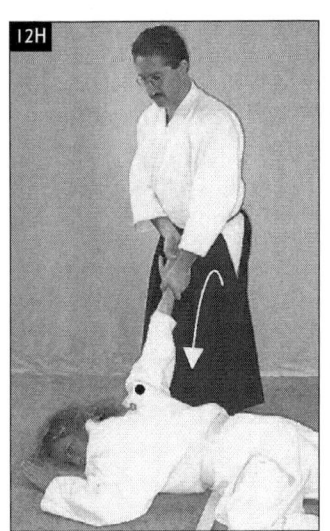

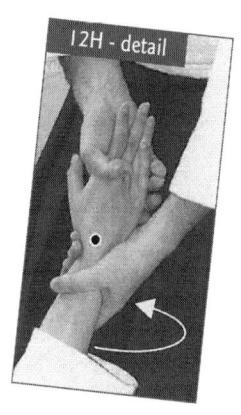

FIGURE 13 - Projections / Throws

13-A-C Harpoon-throw. The aikidoist (standing) leads the attacker into a stooped position (A) before projecting her into a forward roll (B) and a break fall (C). The roll and break fall describe equiangular trajectories similar to those shown in Figures 11-A and B, respectively. White arrows show the main equiangular trajectory. Note how the joints (black dots) are aligned according to the progression of the spiral motion (A-B). Black arrows indicate the direction of the projection.

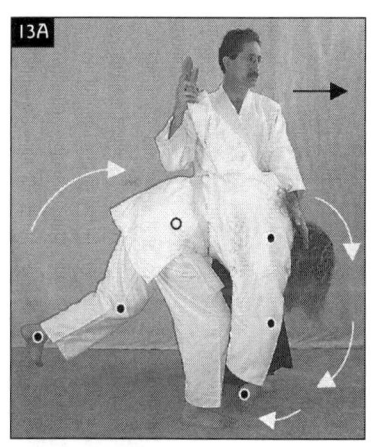
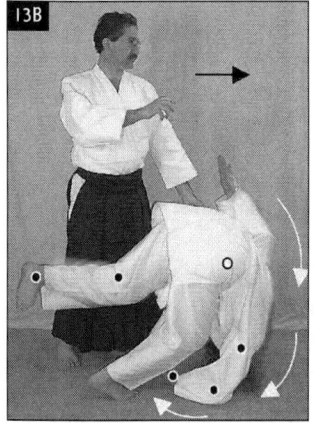

13-D-F   Wrist-bent-toward-shoulder throw. The aikidoist (right) bends the attacker's wrist toward her shoulder (D), leading her to sit (E), or projecting her backward down onto the mat (F). The bent arm describes an equiangular spiral centered in the wrist (see detail). The effectiveness of this technique relies on the connection between the bent wrist, the shoulder and the one-point. When rolling backward (F), the attacker's entire body follows the equiangular trajectory initiated in the wrist.

13-G-J   Breath-throw. The aikidoist (left) leads the attacker to pass in front of his chest area (G) while projecting the attacker back down onto the mat. In this powerful projection, the center of the main equiangular motion is located in the upper torso (black dot). The attacker's entire body pivots at this point (H). A backward roll (I) or a break fall (J) are possible outcomes of this technique.

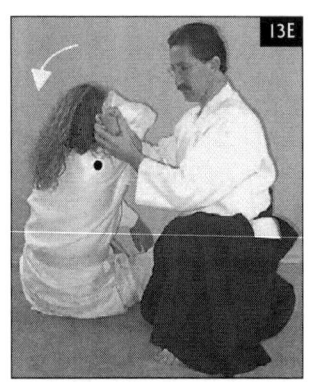
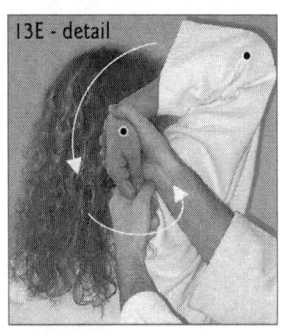
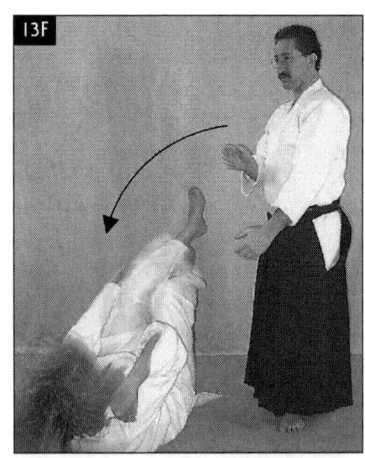

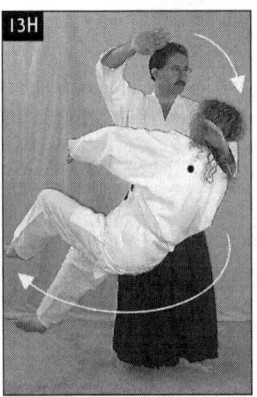

FIGURE 14 - Weapons

14-A *Bokken* (wooden sword). Upper-level readiness posture (tip of the bokken pointing to the sky). The aikidoist maintains an equiangular connection between the one-point and the weapon; secondary equiangular trajectories are also evident in the forelimbs. Similar connections should be maintained with a short-reach weapon, such as the wooden knife (*tanto*, right), or without a weapon (open hand, left).

14-B When a bokken-cut is performed, it should describe a wide-open equiangular trajectory centered in the one-point. Note how the same principle is applied with an open-hand cut (no weapon, left).

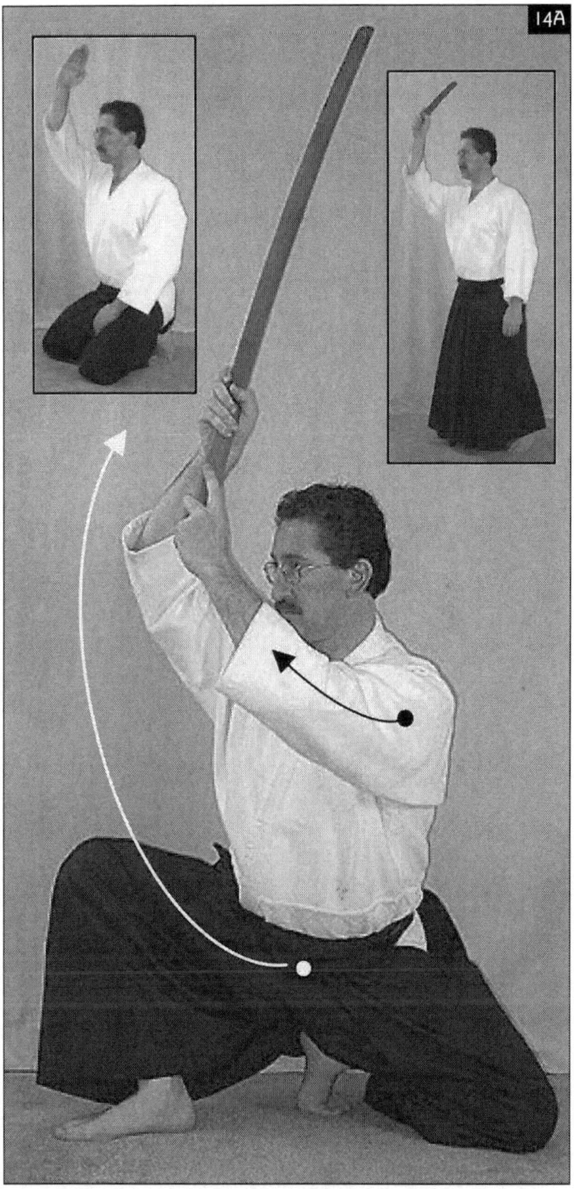

14-C Tanto poke. After completing an upward/forward arm swing (first equiangular motion), the aikidoist is ready to poke with the wooden knife (second equiangular motion).

14-D Thrust with the tanto illustrating a wide-open equiangular movement centered in the shoulder and connected to the one-point.

14-E Upper-level block/strike/poke with a *jo* (wooden staff). A wide-open equiangular motion centered in the shoulder and connected to the one-point is executed.

14-F Side/diagonal strike with the jo. The spiral motion is parallel to the mat and centered in the shoulder.

14-G Down/back block and/or backward poke with a jo; the spiral is clearly shown.

14-H Long and deep frontal thrust with the jo. Even though in this technique the aikidoist appears to perform a perfectly "straight-line" poke, the overall body motion describes an equiangular trajectory centered in the shoulder and connected to the one-point.

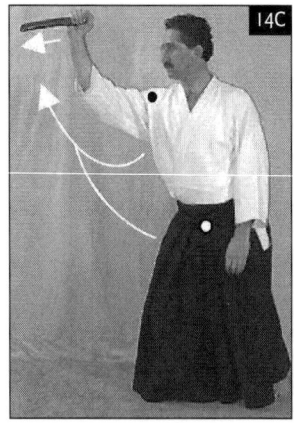
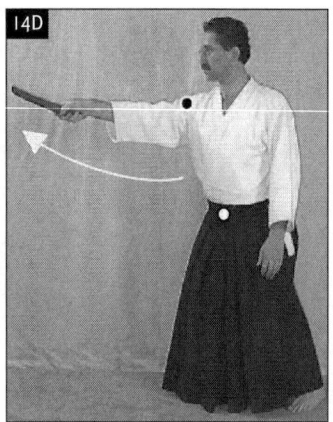

Concluding Remarks

The concept of the equiangular spiral is not restricted to aikido. Most martial arts, like judo and karate, or even swordsmanship (*kendo*) or archery (*kyudo*), include equiangular motions in their techniques, even though practitioners of these disciplines may not be aware of it. The human joints are designed, in conjunction, to follow spiral pathways that can be so wide-open that they appear to have strictly straight-line trajectories (i.e., a poke with a jo like the one shown in Figure 14-H) or so narrow and close that their spiral nature is difficult to detect (e.g., the twist of a finger). It is true that—as the inquisitive reader may well argue—some individual joints move in only two directions like, for example, the flexion and extension of the knee joint, which does not describe an equiangular trajectory. However, this joint can interact with others, like the femur-hipbone joint and the ankle joint, generating the equiangular trajectory followed by the entire leg in a front kick (Figure 10-I). It is because of aikido's nature, with its evident swirling movements in throws, rolls and break falls, that it is perhaps appropriate to call aikido the art of harmonizing equiangular spirals. Nonetheless, numerous martial arts routines in other disciplines can also be explained according to the physics and dynamics of the equiangular spiral.

Bibliography

Curtis, C. (2001). *Ki-Aikido on Maui*. 3rd Ed. Maui, Hawaii: MAKS Publications.

Maruyama, K. (1984). *Aikido with ki*. Tokyo: Ki No Kenkyukai Headquarters.

Paz-y-Miño C., & Espinosa, A. (2002). Dichotomous keys to fundamental attacks and defenses in aikido. *Journal of Asian Martial Arts, 11*(1), 8–27.

Reed, W. (1993). *Ki: A road that anyone can walk*. 2nd Ed. Tokyo: Japan Publications.

Reed, W. (1999). *Ki: A practical guide for westerners*. 6th Ed. Tokyo: Japan Publications.

Shifflett, C. (1998). *Ki in aikido: A sampler of ki exercises*. Merrifield, Virginia: Round Earth Publishing.

Shifflett, C. (1999). *Aikido: Exercises for teaching and training*. Merrifield, Virginia: Round Earth Publishing.

Taylor, K. (2001). Ukemiwaza: the art of attacking in aikido. *Journal of Asian Martial Arts, 10*(2), 60–75.

Tohei, K. (1974). This is aikido. Tokyo: Japn Publications.

Tohei, K. (1998). *Ki in daily life*. 16th Ed. Tokyo: Ki No Kenkyukai Headquarters.

Tohei, K. (2001). *The way to union with ki: Aikido with mind and body coordination*. 1st Ed. Tochigi: Ki No Kenkyukai Headquarters.

Tözeren, A. (2000). *Human body dynamics: Classical mechanics and human movement*. New York: Springer-Verlag.

Ward, B. (1999). Energy projection in aikido wrist-techniques. *Journal of Asian Martial Arts, 8*(1), 50–55.

Watanabe, J. & Avakian, L. (1997). *The secrets of judo: A text for instructors and students*. Rutland, Vermont: Charles E. Tuttle Co.

Westbrook, A. & Ratti, O. (1999). *Aikido and the dynamic sphere: An illustrated introduction*. Rutland, Vermont: Charles E. Tuttle Co.

Wentworth-Thompson, D. (1942). *On growth and form*. 1st Ed. Cambridge, England: Cambridge University Press.

Wolfe, R. (1999). The science of *ukemi* (rolls & breakfalls). *Journal of Asian Martial Arts, 8*(3), 54–75.

Acknowledgments

We dedicate this chapter to Mark Rubbert, William Reed, and Koichi Kashiwaya who have inspired us to explore the fascinating complexity of Shin Shin Toitsu Aikido. Very special thanks to our mentor Mark Rubbert and the St. Louis Ki Society members for continuous support and friendship. The Ki-Aikido students at the Student Recreation and Fitness Center, The University of Memphis, motivated us to develop the ideas discussed in this article. Jane Orcholski, former Program Co-ordinator Campus Recreation Intramural Services, and Steve Whistler, current Recreation Services Coordinator, at TUM, helped us to initiate and continue with Ki-Aikido classes at TUM. We thank an anonymous reviewer for comments on the manuscript. The material discussed in this article is not necessarily endorsed by Ki Society or any of its affiliates.

· 3 ·

Tetsutaka Sugawara Discusses Aikido, Morihei Ueshiba, & the Kagura-Kotodama Staff
by C. Jeffrey Dykhuizen, Ph.D.

Tetsutaka Sugawara. All photos courtesy of Tetsutaka Sugawara.

Introduction

Tetsutaka Sugawara was born in 1941 and began training in aikido in 1960. He was an in-house student (*uchideshi*) of aikido founder Morihei Ueshiba for a year and a half from 1961 to 1962 in Ibaraki Prefecture. He is a 7th-degree black belt.

In addition to aikido, Sugawara has studied Katori Shinto-ryu, a Japanese weapons style that incorporates long and short staff, glaive (*naginata*), sword drawing (*iaido*), and sword training. He began training under Risuke Otake in 1975, and received a teacher's license (*kyoshi*) from Yasusada Iizasa of Tenshin Shoden Katori Shinto-ryu Headquarters in 1986. He also has over fifteen years training in Okinawan Goju-ryu karate-do, beginning under Yasuichi Miyagi, and receiving a master's license in 1992. Sugawara has also studied taijiquan and other Chinese martial arts under Professor Xing Yanling of Fujian University since 1989.

Sugawara has published several books on the martial arts, particularly in the area of aikido and weapons training. In addition to teaching in Japan, he regularly teaches aikido and Katori Shinto-ryu in the United States, Finland, Spain, the Philippines, Canada, and Russia. He has organized and sponsored martial arts exchange programs and demonstrations between Japan and China since 1992.

Some members of Tetsutaka's aikido training hall.

Mr. Sugawara has actively explored the breadth and depth of martial arts principles and their application in his 42 years of martial arts study. He has incorporated techniques and principles from all the other arts he has studied into his aikido movements and techniques, producing an effective blend of martial arts training.

In addition to frequent informal discussions, three formal, two-hour interviews were conducted with Sugawara in July and August 2001 and January 2002. Our discussions have been consolidated to focus on the most salient of the many topics discussed. An introductory section relates a few of Sugawara's experiences and duties as Morihei Ueshiba's in-house student. The bulk of this article concerns a matter that impressed Sugawara greatly during his time training under aikido's founder: the kagura-kotodama routine performed by Morihei Ueshiba (whom Sugawara frequently referred to as "O-sensei," "Great Teacher") early each morning at the Aiki shrine in Ibaraki. A final section outlines a few of Sugawara's perspectives on martial arts training.

INTERVIEW

合氣道

SUGAWARA'S START IN AIKIDO

■ How did you become a live-in student of Morihei Ueshiba?

When I first came to Tokyo, I entered one of the religious institutes. I stayed there, and Ueshiba sometimes visited. I really didn't have any connection to that religion, but my sister was staying there. She was a member, and I was poor at that time, so I stayed there. That is how I could meet Ueshiba. He started to teach aikido at the religious center. Then, gradually fewer and fewer members of the religious center continued training, until there was only me. So I started to visit the aikido headquarters to train. And I trained there for about one year. Then the head of the religion told me that I was a special person. He said: Your only job should be to learn martial arts. That should be your mission.

■ The leader of the religion told you this?

Yes. There is no need for you to learn the religion, he told me. He told me about Morihei Ueshiba. He said that only once every 700 years does such a person come along. He told me that he is a very important person, and that is why I should go and study aikido with him.

■ What was Morihei Ueshiba's aikido like at that time?

At that time, Ueshiba's aikido was not so hard. He had a very soft touch. And he always flowed.

On the first day I entered the main dojo for training, I asked, "How do you do?" He replied, "Aikido is triangle, square, and circle in layers, with breathing." This is what he said [laughs]. I could not understand it. And that was his first teaching: Aikido is a triangle, square, and circle, with breath [laughing]. I thought that in the future, maybe I would be able to understand, so I will always remember this teaching. So this is always a question that remains in my body. That is why I will never forget that teaching.

■ How did you become an in-house student?

The head of the religion talked to Ueshiba. Usually it is very difficult to become an in-house student. You need a guarantor. But I had the head of the religion as my guarantor.

■ What does it mean to be an in-house student?

It is when you stay at the teacher's house and work. We did not only do aikido training, but also farming. We had to make our own food, by ourselves. We worked in the rice fields everyday [laughing]. We were farmers; and a farmer's actions with a hoe can be the same as sword work.

■ WHEN YOU WERE STAYING IN IBARAKI AS THE FOUNDER'S STUDENT, WHAT WAS DAILY LIFE LIKE?

For almost half of the month, Ueshiba was gone. The founder went out to teach at the aikido headquarters and other places. At those times, I trained by myself, or with Morihiro Saito.* Saito's house was next door. He came to the dojo and taught. He was working all night, you know. So when he came back in the early morning, he would sleep. Then we would train and talk about aikido at the evening class.

_{* Morihiro Saito was an 8th-dan instructor in Aikikai aikido, and one of the founder's earlier live-in students. He was guardian of the Aiki shrine in Ibaragi Prefecture until his death in 2002. Many considered him to be the leading aikido expert with the wooden sword and short staff (jo) in aikido. He also wrote a series of books on aikido, published by Sugawara's publishing company.}

■ WHEN THE FOUNDER WAS THERE, WHAT WAS DAILY LIFE LIKE?

I would try to sleep until 7:00. Every morning the founder would wake up at about 5:00. About 5:00! That's why I couldn't sleep [laughing]. I usually I tried to sleep until 7:00, but I felt … afraid [laughing]. He was very strict.

■ SO WHEN YOU WOKE UP, WHAT WOULD YOU DO?

After waking up, I had to get food and present it to the Shinto gods. You know, I would prepare rice, water, and salt in some bowls. Then Ueshiba came, and I would go with him. I carried it very carefully [laughing]. We went to Ueshiba's [Aiki] shrine. But before going to that shrine, we had to pray at the training hall [dojo] shrine. We prayed to the god of the shrine, and the ancestors at the altar. Always when he prayed, I sat behind and remain bowed.

He prayed a very long time. He prayed the names of many gods, and the names of many high mountains. Miyogi-san and Nantai-san; every mountain had a god. I forget them, there are so many. So many mountain names. But [laughing] I only listened. I was very young.

After praying at the dojo shrine, he would go outside and pray to the gods of the four directions. Then we went to the Aiki Shrine, and he prayed there. Every morning we spent about one hour in this type of ritual.

■ SO AT THIS POINT IN HIS LIFE, UESHIBA WAS A VERY RELIGIOUS MAN.

Yes. In his home he wore white clothes, a white hakama. He always tried to keep unclean things away from his body, both internally and externally. He was concerned with this, even when taking a bath. I had to heat the water using a wood fire, but I could not even put my hand in the water. But I needed to check the water temperature, so I used a board to stir the water, then a scoop to take some water out to check the temperature. Once while checking the temperature, he asked me, "Are you putting your hand directly into the water?" I said, "No teacher, I never do that.

I stirred it using the wooden cover. Then I scooped some out and checked the temperature using my hand. Then I pour that water out." Then he said. "Yes, that is good. You are smart; a good student." Like that, he was always thinking about keeping his body pure. That's why he didn't usually eat meat or even fish.

■ JUST VEGETABLES AND RICE?
Yes. That is why I was a little worried about him. We need fish or meat sometimes. I tried sometimes to give him some *niboshi*. It is a small dried fish; we sometimes make soup with it. I used this and gave it to him. And sometimes he ate this fish. Because I was a little scared for him. His body, you know, where did his energy come from?

■ HE HAD A LOT OF ENERGY?
[Hesitating] When I was his in-house student, he wasn't so young, so he wasn't so strong.

THE KAGURA - KOTODAMA STAFF ROUTINE

■ IT IS APPARENT THAT RELIGIOUS THOUGHT AND SPIRITUAL PRACTICES WERE A LARGE PART OF MORIHEI UESHIBA'S LIFE. ONE RELATED PRACTICE IS HIS PERFORMANCE OF A "KAGURA-KOTODAMA" STAFF ROUTINE, ONE THAT HE DESIGNED AND PERFORMED IN FRONT OF THE AIKI SHRINE EACH MORNING.

Ueshiba created this routine based upon his knowledge of a Shinto dance form known as "kagura" and the systematic use of utterances known as *kotodama* from the Omoto-kyo religion.

When we went to the shrine, after formal praying, Ueshiba sometimes prayed using a small spear or staff. He performed a kind of kagura, which also included some kotodama training. His movement was very natural, so that every time the performance was a little bit different.

■ WHAT IS KAGURA?
Kagura is a sacred Shinto dance performed to please the gods. Young women perform it at shrines. There is a repetition of movements, circling three times to the left, three times to the right. In the actual Shinto kagura, they use a bell and other decorations on the staff, and the performers were women. That style was somewhat different from [Ueshiba's]. Ueshiba probably copied that, but he also adapted it with his own ideas. But when Ueshiba was doing this, I think he probably got the image from these dance forms.

■ AND SO UESHIBA ADDED KOTODAMA TO THIS KIND OF DANCE TO CREATE THE ROUTINE?
Yes. Kotodama is a practice from the Omoto-kyo religion. But from the kagura base, he gradually created his own staff routine. I watched him do this everyday. Just the two of us were there. He performed in front of the shrine while I sat and watched. He thought that the kotodama sounds were very important. Each sound represents a different type of friction, each is a way that intrinsic energy [ki] moves, and a different way of moving in the martial arts. So this is where aikido came from. This kind of thing recognizes natural movement and how one form changes into another. Out of one thing, many things are born. This kind of natural change is creation. The creative aspect is very important. That is why the martial arts are not only for killing. We need to make life. That's why Ueshiba stressed *takemusu* ["inexhaustible fount"]. *Umu* means "to be born." Ueshiba's ideas were different from other martial arts teachers. Some other martial arts, like judo, have become like games. This is only competition. Ueshiba said, Yin and Yang together make something. There is creation.

■ DID THE KAGURA-KOTODAMA ROUTINE CONCERN KI?
Yes, in the four directions, yes. It was a way of purifying ki.

■ COULD YOU EXPLAIN THAT PLEASE?
I think that Ueshiba's thinking again concerned a triangle, square, and circle. These shapes represent forms of movement, forms of ki, or how it moves. They are also associated with the sounds of kotodama. At first, there are only the sounds *ah* and *oh*. These are like the two ends of a staff. Ah and *oh* are the ends of a staff, like the poles on a battery. And when movement begins, there is interaction, and technique is produced.

■ UESHIBA USED THIS AS A WAY OF PURIFYING HIMSELF? OF PURIFYING KI?
Yes, yes. But it wasn't done; it happened. There is no way that humans can do anything to ki. The universe is completely natural; humans can't impose anything on ki. You simply have to feel it. First you open yourself and meet ki, then, penetrating... Ah and *oh*, there comes to be a natural separation of the quality of ki.

The *ah* is the clean ki. The *oh* is the unclean, the heavy ki. Saying unclean is not exactly correct, but rather heavy. These forms of ki have naturally separated into heaven and earth. The heaven is the clean ki and earth is the heavy ki. And, between the two of them, there is communication, continual communication. If there is no communication, there's nothing.

■ WHAT THEN IS THE MEANING OF THE KAGURA-KOTODAMA ROUTINE?
The routine the founder created is an expression of this type of communication.

After realizing a distinction through the *ah* and *oh* sounds, the movements are the start of communication. The sounds move from *ah* [heaven] to *oh* [earth] to *uooo*. And the *uooo* is the *uooo* sound characterizing the universe. This is what Ueshiba said. *Uooo* is the universe; being inside, with the communication of the universe.

■ SO THE "AH" AND "OH" BRING ABOUT DISTINCTION, AND THE "UOOO" AGAIN BRINGS UNIFICATION....

The distinction, then movement, yes. The movement of the routine is the communication. Any type of movement is this way. Of course, all the movements in the martial arts are this way. Really, all communication is this way. This kind of communication, the natural interaction between *ah* and *oh*, no one can change this. If you are open and understand this type of communication and move naturally, there is no enemy that can ever be a match for you. If you move naturally, blending [using aiki] with the other, no one can beat you. To state the matter simply, there is no enemy.

■ HOW IS THIS ROUTINE RELATED TO THE PRINCIPLES OF AIKIDO?

If there is no communication, no blending of ki, there can be no aiki. If someone comes at you, attacking, and you think, Okay, I'm going to get you, this is not aiki. There must be natural relaxedness, a sensitivity. That is the final form of the martial arts. That is what Ueshiba was saying: you have to be natural. That is why he always emphasized aiki.

• • •

Sugawara explained how Morihei Ueshiba incorporated the sounds of Omoto-kyo's kotodama with the staff movements to create the kagura-kotodama routine. Sugawara also pointed out that in Shintoism and other Asian religious traditions there exists the belief that these and other utterances are deeply significant, that they embody spiritual power. This is, of course, exemplified in the kotodama of Omoto-kyo, which has a historical foundation in Shintoism.

Just outside Shinto shrines throughout Japan, a pair of guardian lion-dog statues (*komainu*) can be found protecting the entrance to the sacred area. Typically, the one on the right has its mouth slightly open, symbolizing the utterance of the *ah* sound, while the one on the left has its mouth closed, symbolizing an *ummn* sound. These sounds, respectively the first and last characters of the Japanese phonetic alphabet, represent the beginning and the end, the coming into and going out of being, the dynamic energy of totality. When *ah* and *oh* are uttered fluidly, the result is reminiscent of the well-known *ah-um* of Tibetan Buddhism. Within the Tibetan tradition, the "Aum" chant represents the essential, underlying reverberation of the universe. The elemental sounds of this chant, in the same order, are voiced during the performance of the kagura-kotodama routine.

THE KAGURA-KOTODAMA ROUTINE

"Aikido is a triangle, circle and a square."
—Morihei Ueshiba

#1: The beginning posture for the kagura-kotodama: The body is naturally relaxed and centered, the staff is held at its midway point, hands positioned at the body's center.
Inset: One settles into stillness at this point.

#2: The staff is slowly moved straight upward as the "ahhh" sound is emitted from the belly (*hara*).
Inset: There is recognition of and directional focus on manifesting the ki of heaven, a triangle pointing upward.

#3: At the vertical peak, the staff begins to descend vertically toward the earth. At the same time, the "ahhh" kotodama sound is transformed into an "ohhh" sound. **Inset:** There is a recognition of and directional focus on manifesting the ki of earth, a triangle pointing downward.

#4: Upon completion of the vertical heaven-earth recognition and manifestation, the staff is swung horizontally, parallel to the earth while performing a 360-degree pivot. Three complete rotations are typically performed. As this movement occurs, the "ohhh" sound is transformed into a reverberating "Uooo" sound, which is maintained throughout the circular movements.
Inset: The circularity represents the dynamic communication of the various forms of ki, a manifestation of the productive movement of the universe. The "uooo" sound is a verbal manifestation of this dynamic energy.

#5-9: When the circular actions and "uooo" sound are completed, parries and strikes are performed in the four directions. These movements are performed silently. **Inset:** Parries and strikes are performed in the four directions. These movements are represented as a square. The center of the performer is the fifth direction.

Comment: Having been a student of Sugawara's for the past five years, I was somewhat surprised that he chose to center our discussions on spiritual or religious matters. My surprise arose because the focus of aikido training with Sugawara is typically upon martial utility. Sugawara tends to emphasize speed and precision in the execution of a movement, which makes the martial application of aikido techniques very clear. Additionally, one third of each session is spent training with the wooden sword (*bokken*) and staff routines that Sugawara has created by blending Katori Shinto-ryu sword and staff techniques with aikido weapons work. As an eclectic martial artist, Sugawara embodies a perspective that is an interesting blend of grounded, martial practicality, and spiritual vastness.

A running theme throughout the interview was Sugawara's belief that training should be on-going, and that study of other martial systems is useful, even necessary, for eventual mastery. He pointed out that aikido's founder engaged in the study of various arts, martial and otherwise, and incorporated this knowledge into the development of aikido technique and philosophy. Sugawara teaches that while training in a single art has worth, training for mastery requires a fuller exploration of the various martial systems. This sentiment is a fitting testimony to how well Sugawara absorbed the training principles taught by Morihei Ueshiba.

Sugawara's Perspective on Training

■ CAN YOU DISCUSS THE DEVELOPMENT OF SKILLS IN AIKIDO TRAINING?

Ueshiba always wanted to teach us how fast we can move if we move naturally. When someone strikes at you, if you begin to move after they have begun to strike, you will get hit. You must move with the strike; if you think, it's too late. The way that humans move has become unnatural. It is too slow. As much as possible, it is best to think and move naturally.

So I return to basics when I teach now. What is standing? What is walking? What is running? At first I never thought about this. I only moved or turned if another person struck. But the founder told me, "Sometimes you when are pushing, you are trying too hard." He wanted to explain the natural way to stand, to sit, and how to put ki into movement. He wanted to teach us how to use ki. There are many ideas included in aikido: the three dimensions, the relationship between the triangle, square, circle and breathing, and how they relate to martial arts movements. So the founder wanted us to continue to study more and more deeply.

When a person starts training, there is a lot of wasted movement. With training, this wasted movement is dropped. Because of that, the person becomes quicker and quicker, because they learn to move more naturally. People who are just beginning want to do everything fast. They try and try. They breath hard and gasp until their hearts might stop. With training though, they will become settled and quiet. Then they start to do things slowly, naturally. As they progress, they will become quicker. They become faster, but they are still doing things slowly, because they are quiet. Mentally they have quieted, and their movements become natural. So there are no wasted movements.

It is not necessary to train so hard that you pant. If you think in terms of winning, of fighting, you will pant. Ueshiba taught that it is important to quiet the mind. If you first learn this, you will learn to move naturally.

■ IN YOUR THINKING, WHAT IS AIKIDO?

For me, what is most interesting about aikido is its spirit. I think the techniques are wonderful too, but more than that, the spirit. In aikido, there are no contests with a winner and a loser; there is more cooperation in aikido.

The way that Ueshiba talked about aikido, he wanted it to embody martial principles, not just be another school [ryu-ha]. He created aikido as an expression of these principles. One principle he emphasized in creating aikido was *aiki*: that you should move by blending with the other person's ki.

By focusing on the ki, the intention of the other and naturally blending with it, you can apply techniques freely, and the movements will still be aikido. If you wish, you could add karate techniques to aikido, you can add them freely. You can freely add Katori's techniques also. Of course, if you do nothing but blend with the other's movements, that can become a problem too. But really, aiki doesn't depend on technique. It is simply a principle, a method in the martial arts. But the most important thing is blending the ki of heaven and earth. At the highest level, that is what we aim for. But you have to continue researching and training.

I think that I have to study more for myself, study various arts. Ueshiba was the same way. All the martial arts are okay. So try them out. But, if you go too far in any one of them, you may forget aikido. That isn't good either. It is best to learn other arts, but bring them back to your study of aikido. Everything you study and learn will become aikido. That is what aikido is. It has a very broad meaning, a very large concept. If you study and learn everything, it will all become your own, conceptually and technically. There really is no borderline.

■ WHY DID YOU BECOME INTERESTED IN KATORI SHINTO-RYU AND WEAPONS TRAINING?
Weapons training is very useful for mastering aikido. Ueshiba trained with weapons everyday. You learn timing, how to read the other person, where the best place to strike is, breathing. You can learn many things from weapons training. For instance, if this is a weapon [he grabs a pen from the desk], the movement of the hand is very slow, but the speed at the tip is very fast. So by weapons training, you learn to become quiet. Because if you are excited you will focus on the part that can hurt you, the tip of the sword. But after training with weapons, you watch only the source of the movement, and you can see that it is slow and can be blended with. So weapons training is mental training. Weapons training is a natural form of settling.

Actually, as in aikido and the kagura–kotodama routine, the same way of *ah-oh* thinking exists in Katori: *yin* and *yang*, defend and attack, the one changes to the other, and back again. That is why I teach that it is so important to develop feeling. Heaven and earth do not touch. It is just ki. There is nothing to see, but there is communication. This is in nature. I know it is difficult to put into practice in martial situations, this communicating. But really, understanding and practicing that is all that is needed to become a master.

■ WHAT DO YOU THINK IS THE MOST IMPORTANT THING FOR A BEGINNING STUDENT TO LEARN?
I think the most important thing to learn is how to change body position [*tai no henka*]. This is a basic principle. For example, if you hold a ball, whenever a strike comes in and hits the surface, there can be a turning, a redirection of the force. The turning is natural. You simply keep your center, and turn, this way or that way, naturally. There are times, of course, when the strike comes directly at the center. In that case, there is a dead point. If someone pushes or strikes you there, you must change your own center.

Aikido students learn this well, but they are usually not so good at maintaining proper distance [*maaii*] or timing. Compared to people who train in weapons, they are not so good in terms of those skills.

The history of martial arts is very long and deep. There have been many great people. To only think one way about these things is too narrow. Yet there are people who do this, and in aikido, often technique becomes a form of dance. Now this is very interesting and it has benefit, but it is not really a martial art. There needs to be realistic movement. It can be beautiful, like dance. I think that can be good in itself, but it doesn't really have a martial application.

Some instructors might think that weapons training is not necessary. Perhaps they have the impression that weapons are used for fighting. They might say, "In aikido there is no fighting. Aikido does not use weapons." Some people are satisfied with that, and that is okay. I have no problem with that. But if someone attacks with a weapon, what will they do? If someone attacks using a karate style, what will they do? That is why I think it is important to learn various martial arts. That is why I try to, little by little, incorporate other techniques into training. I use Katori techniques in aikido. I bring some Goju-ryu techniques to aikido. Some taijiquan. And this is possible because aikido is free, open.

But even in training for martial mastery, fighting is not necessary. Those who think of it as a fight, as competition from the beginning, they don't understand the martial arts. In martial arts training, game-like competition isn't needed. Training is for mastery, not winning. If you only train to win, you will never master martial arts.

Comment: One thing that distinguishes Sugawara from many of the other aikido instructors with whom I have trained and whom I have observed, is not simply his proficiency in such a broad range of arts, or the depth of his knowledge of the principles guiding martial movements. It is rather his on-going enthusiasm for learning and training. When he teaches, for example, there is an eagerness, an intensity that seems to stem from his desire to pass on to his students all that he knows. He is by no means a stingy teacher. His frustration is apparent when we do not get it quickly enough. In these instances, he sighs and states bluntly, "Keep training."

■ How do you view the physical, mental, and spiritual aspects of aikido practice?

Young people all want to become strong. Eventually, they will overcome that desire themselves. Like climbing a mountain, they will discover that there is more to it than strength. Strength is needed, of course; if you don't become strong, you cannot gain any spiritual strength. Now some company employees studying aikido say, "We do not need the techniques; just teach us the spiritual stuff." But that cannot be done. Spiritual benefits are not possible if you do not train. Even for spiritually strong people, it is no good for them to have weak bodies. Their ki will be reduced. The spirit and the physical body are not separated. There has to be connection, communication, and harmony.

■ Do you think that anyone can become a master?

The founder thought so. I do not think, however, that anyone can fulfill 100% of his or her potential. For example, I have only fulfilled about 20% of mine. Some of the religious masters, their level of development is much, much higher. But their methods of training are different. I do not know about that in too much detail. I have focused my training on the martial arts.

TECHNICAL SECTION: STANDARD TECHNIQUES

SERIES #1: Four-direction throw from wrist grab (*katate tori shihonage*).
1) Your partner grabs your wrist.
2) Grasp your partner's wrist with your free hand while redirecting your partner's momentum, taking him off-balance.
3) Step in diagonally and pivot, keeping your hands at forehead level. Lead with the hand that has been grabbed, moving in a fluid, circular motion.
4) The technique is completed with your partner off-balance, his initial grabbing momentum now behind him. Continuation of this momentum results in a throw.

SERIES #2: Four-direction throw from wrist grab.

Practical Application: Avoiding a counter-punch.

1) Stepping in without redirection leaves an opening for your partner to strike.
2) Blending with your partner's initial grabbing motion, redirect his momentum taking him off-balance and minimizing the possibility of a counter-strike.
3) Similarly, bringing your hands up to forehead level helps minimize a counter-strike by protecting your head.

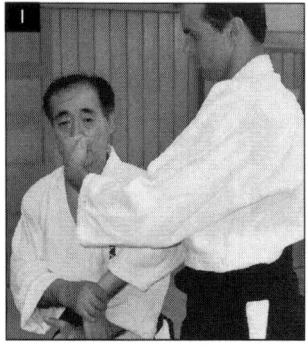
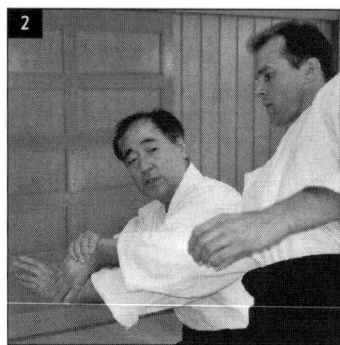

SERIES #3: Heaven and earth throw from a double wrist grab (*ryote tori ten-chi nage*).

1) Your partner grabs both your wrists.
2) Redirect your partner's grabbing motion, splitting his momentum by moving one hand up (toward heaven) and the other down (toward earth).
3) As you step forward behind your partner, bring the hand that has redirected your partner's momentum upward back down behind your partner to join with the hand that directed your partner's momentum down. Your partner will be off-balance; continuation of this motion results in a throw.

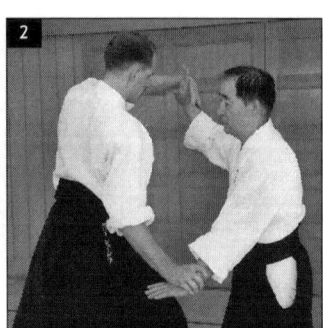
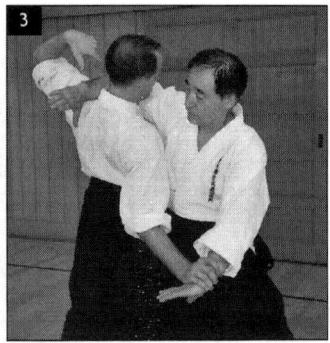

SERIES #4:
Heaven and earth throw from double wrist grab.

Position of hands in greater detail (pictures 1-3).

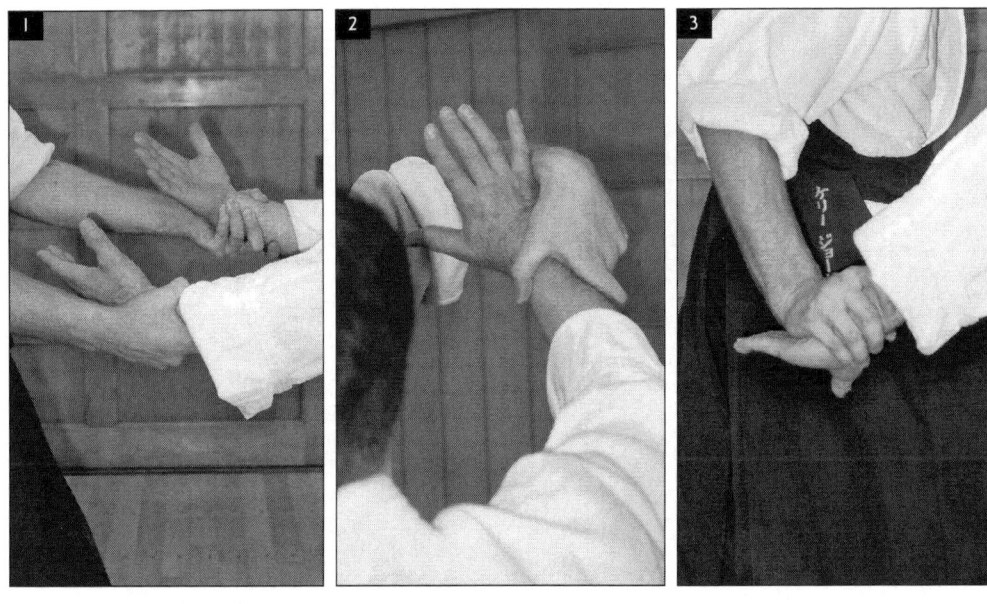

SERIES #5:
Heaven and earth throw from double wrist grab.

Movements demonstrated without partner (pictures 1-3).

Special Thanks To
Joseph Kelley for his assistance with the technical section.

· 4 ·
Hiroshi Ikeda's Insights into Aikido Training
by Jay Barnet, M.A.

The goal is one movement... that continuously unfolds until completion.
Photo by Jun Akiyama.

Introduction

Hiroshi Ikeda is the founder and chief instructor of Boulder Aikikai, Inc., a thriving school of aikido in Boulder, Colorado, USA. He currently holds a 7th-degree ranking through Mitsugi Saotome and the Aikido World Federation (Honbu Dojo). Mr. Ikeda also manages the operations of Bu Jin Design, his martial arts supply company. He travels extensively as a guest instructor, conducting aikido seminars at studios in the U.S. and abroad. Information for this article was obtained during some of Mr. Ikeda's seminars. The following brief reflections are shared as they have helped many aikido students to get more out of their training.

Mindset

Before a student can progress in aikido, it is necessary to align one's mindset with the reality of training in an aikido dojo. But what is the "correct mindset"?

As in most martial arts schools, aikido students are tested to evaluate proficiency and to assign rank. In current times, most aikido students are warned in advance of their test date, and as the big day approaches it is common to see students making a special effort to prepare for the techniques they will be asked to demonstrate.

There is only now.
Photo by Cheryl Moore.

In a traditional dojo, students are not informed of their test in advance. The understanding is that every moment in the dojo is important, and that they may be tested at any time. There is no room for saving one's best effort for some special event. There is only now. This is the proper mindset for training.

Prepare for Combat

Every moment on the mat is preparation for combat. Focus and concentration are essential to prepare for real life situations where you do not face a cooperative training partner and there won't be a "second try."

Your Aikido Must Fit You

Each individual must develop an aikido that fits his or her unique body and personality. We have all seen martial artists demonstrate techniques that are very powerful and complete. But it is a mistake to try too hard to do it "their way." A person's technique is powerful because they have adapted it to fit their own unique attributes. Each individual must find this for themselves.

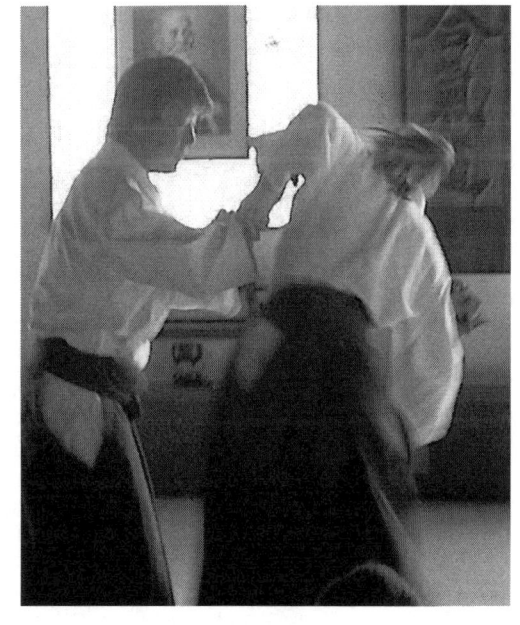

Connection.
Photo by Michael Braden.

Don't Put Up a Wall – Welcome and Lead Your Opponent

Some people deal with attacks by putting up a wall of strength to stop the attacker's progress. It may work if you have an untrained attacker who is weaker than you are. But that is not aikido, and there is always the potential for someone stronger or better trained to break down your wall.

Instead of putting up a wall, connect with your opponent. Don't "fight back" against their strength. Lead their strength to weakness. Then you can control the outcome.

Look for Weak Points

Training is the opportunity to look for weak points. That is why we welcome a strong, committed attack from our training partner. By exposing weakness, your partner helps you to refine your instincts and to focus your mind and body. Don't gloss over weakness with speed or incomplete technique. Slow down and search for your weak points. Hold them up to the light and understand them. Then focus your training to strengthen the weakness you discover.

Everyone has vulnerable points. If they are in your opponent, learn how best to exploit them. Lead the force of their attack into a position of weakness, and then move through their weakness to control their center. If they are within you, deal with them through self-improvement.

Lead your opponent's strength to weakness, then you can control the outcome. *Photo by Jun Akiyama.*

The goal is one movement... that continuously unfolds until completion.
Photo by Jun Akiyama.

Check your technique by noting the position of the attacker.
Photo by Cheryl Moore.

Go Beyond the "Correct Movement"

Beginning students start out by learning the "correct movement", without too much concern for the ultimate objective of overcoming any attack and controlling the outcome. Gradually the focus shifts from learning a prescribed movement to achieving the result the movement is designed for. At this stage there is awareness and connection to one's opponent. There is balance, centering, and moving in harmony with our physical nature, breath, relaxation, and the power of ki. Truly, the work of a lifetime. The more we focus on these fundamental elements—rather than simply moving our body in a certain way—the more advanced our training can become.

One Movement

A technique should have no stop points. These become openings for an opponent to regain balance or reverse your technique. The goal is one movement that continuously unfolds until completion. It can be short or long. It can be "oooooooooonnnnnne". It can be "one!" But in no case should there be break points in the connection to your opponent or in the flow of movement.

When you train, be a human being.
Photo by Michael Braden.

Pay Attention to Where You Are, and Where Your Opponent Is

When it is most effective, aikido anticipates the attack, draws the attacker off balance, and then controls the outcome. These are difficult things to execute. It is tempting to simply move through a technique without fully engaging with the fundamental objectives.

Check your technique by noting the position of the attacker. Is he or she really off balance? Is there truly an opening to execute your technique? Have you connected with the attacker's center? Is the attacker standing upright when you want them off balance? Are you moving an opponent's hand or arm but not their entire body? Are they positioned where you are safe and they are vulnerable? Or are you exposed? If this were actual combat, would you survive?

Be a Human Being

When you train, be a human being. A machine is built to do the same technique over and over again in exactly the same way, regardless of the circumstances. People are not machines. We adapt to circumstances and rely on a set of powerful human attributes to survive.

Human beings connect to the world through the five senses, through awareness, through intellect and through spiritual powers. These inherent human attributes are at the core of the warrior's code (*budo*): our self-awareness, our connection to others, our ability to make enlightened choices that lead to favorable outcomes. Aikido elevates and channels our humanity into a powerful martial art.

What is the essence of beautiful aikido?... Simplicity. *Photo by Jun Akiyama.*

Beauty

Each individual expresses the principles and techniques of aikido in their own unique way. The result can be beautiful, but—just as in the world of art—one also finds "ugly aikido."

What is the essence of beautiful aikido? Simplicity. One cut flower, alone in a vase, expresses the essence and inspires the soul. If it were one in fifty, its beauty might be lost. So too, the most beautiful aikido often consists of very little.

A Final Reflection

Mr. Ikeda speaks of the need for each individual to develop his or her own aikido. In martial arts, as in life, each of us is responsible for our own progress. Hopefully, these insights from Hiroshi Ikeda will help the reader to train hard and reap the maximum rewards.

· 5 ·

The Rhythm of Aikido: Part I

by Guillermo Paz-y-Miño C., Ph.D. & Avelina Espinosa, Ph.D.

Abstract

In this two-part article, we discuss how some music principles can be applied to various aspects of aikido training: Part I—including stretches, single-person routines to develop balance and mind-body coordination, rolling and falling; Part II—partnered techniques of neutralization, projections/ throws, weapons, breathing exercises, and meditation. We use simple music notation and a percussion instrument to explain aikido's natural rhythm. Our goal is to provide students and instructors with novel tools for learning and teaching aiki arts. Not only aikido but every martial art—or physical discipline—has its own pace, which the student should discover. Learning to move according to this rhythm will allow the martial artist to adequately match an attack, blend and flow with it, and finally neutralize it.

> The real work of a musician is to reveal the way of the universe through music. The calligrapher and artist do the same using a brush. Is not [Ki-] Aikido an art designed to reveal the way of the universe through movement?
>
> Time has its own flow. It is very important ... to have an accurate grasp of the flow of the universe. In order to achieve this, [we] must have a sense of the rhythm of the universe. This is something [we] know with [our] body, not [our] intellect.
>
> —Tohei Koichi (Reed, 1992: 299, 285)

Introduction

Aikido and music have numerous similarities. Both are arts because they allow us to create and express beauty in movement or sound. They are also science because aikido and music principles can be organized systematically in a body of knowledge susceptible to testing. Like music, aikido consists of "elements" (the techniques) ordered according to spatio-temporal relationships that have unity and continuity. For example, an attack and its corresponding neutralization technique occur in a given location and time and are governed by the laws of physics. Aikido (*aiki* = harmony; *do* = path, the way of) depends on rhythm and harmony. A technique's flow of movement and rate of speed, as well as the congruent and pleasant arrangement of body motions, define aikido's rhythm and harmony.

All photos courtesy of A. Espinosa & G. Paz-y-Miño C.

FIGURE 1

A floor tom-tom drum or any other percussion instrument with a loud low-frequency vibration can be used to mark aikido's tempo. A plastic barrel and a short broomstick will also work!

In this two-part article, we discuss how some music principles can be applied to various aspects of aikido training: PART I—including stretches, single-person routines to develop balance and mind-body coordination, rolling and falling, PART I—partnered techniques of neutralization, projections/ throws, weapons, breathing exercises, and meditation. We use simple music notation and a percussion instrument, the floor tom-tom drum (Figure 1), to explain the natural rhythm of aikido.

Discovering Aikido's Rhythm

FIGURE 2

Electronic metronomes offer a variety of options to indicate the tempo of "aikido music." A large, old-fashioned alarm clock can replace the metronome; however, you will not be able to adjust its tempo to a pace slower and/or faster than sixty clicks per minute.

An essential component of aikido's rhythm is its tempo. We define aikido tempo as the rate of speed of an aikido technique or routine. It is possible to mark aikido's tempo by counting, or chanting, numbers at specific intervals. A more precise method is to use a metronome, a device that produces clicks and/or light flashes over a prearranged time interval (e.g., per second) to indicate the tempo of music (Figure 2). We recommend adjusting the metronome to 60 beats per minute (one second equals one unit of aikido music; see Supplement); this pace induces appropriate mind and body coordination during aikido practice. Slow and gentle training will let the student discover when to speed up.

Be patient! The ultimate goal should be to feel the rhythm in your "one-point" (*seika-no-itten*), or your body's center of balance. In biophysical terms, the one-point is the body's center of rotation; it is located about two inches below the navel. If the one-point moves rhythmically, the entire body will also move rhythmically. Aikido practitioners devote much effort to mastering the appropriate coordination between the overall body movements and the one-point motions.

SUPPLEMENT: BASIC AIKI MUSIC NOTATION

Like in music, the duration of aikido techniques can be indicated by different types of notes (**Figure 3**). Here we arbitrarily assign the following duration to these notes: whole note = four seconds; half note = two seconds; quarter note = one second; and eighth note = half a second. The unit of aikido music is the quarter note. In consequence, one whole note equals two half notes, one half note equals two quarter notes, and one quarter note equals two eighth notes (**Figure 3-A**; there are also other notes in music, like the sixteenth, thirty-second and sixty-fourth notes; they are too fast to illustrate the aikido principles discussed in this article). All notes have their corresponding rests or pauses (**Figure 3-B**) which in music indicate silence. In aikido, however, there is no silence, just pause.

Aikido music is divided into equal parts called measures (**Figure 3-C**); bar lines indicate the beginning and end of a measure. Two dots, placed between double bars, indicate repetition of the aikido sequence within one or more measures. Double bar lines show the end of an entire aikido routine, which may include numerous measures.

Time signatures and note values: Time signatures are placed at the beginning of a sequence of aikido music. The most common time signature is 4/4 which consists of four quarter notes per measure (one per second; **Figure 3-A**). The top number shows the number of beats on the drum or the number of vocal counts chanted by the aikido practitioner (i.e., one, two, three, four...) in each sequence of aikido techniques. The bottom number simply specifies that the note in each beat corresponds to a quarter note.

In **Figure 3-D**, the 4/4 time signature indicates one arm circle per second, which is represented by the four quarter notes. The aikido practitioner shall count out loud each number, matching the rhythm kept by a drummer or a metronome.

3A: Types of notes used in aiki music.

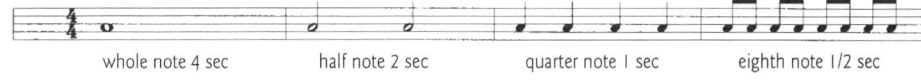

3-B: Rests or pauses.

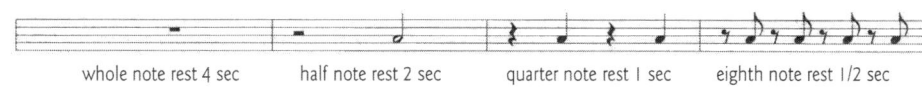

3-C: Measures and their notation and symbols.

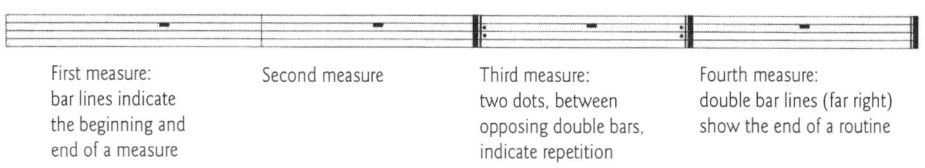

First measure: bar lines indicate the beginning and end of a measure

Second measure

Third measure: two dots, between opposing double bars, indicate repetition

Fourth measure: double bar lines (far right) show the end of a routine

3-D: Arm "circles."

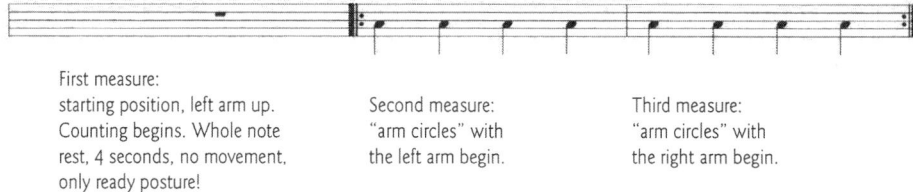

First measure: starting position, left arm up. Counting begins. Whole note rest, 4 seconds, no movement, only ready posture!

Second measure: "arm circles" with the left arm begin.

Third measure: "arm circles" with the right arm begin.

FIGURE 3

This apparently simple exercise is the foundation of numerous aikido routines, particularly wrist techniques like the one shown in **Figure 4**. Rather than "arm circles," the aikido practitioners perform elliptical trajectories with their hands, while the shoulders remain relatively immovable. The practitioners allow their hands to fall with gravity and catch them when the hands reach the lowest point in the elliptical trajectory; then, they take their hands up again. The student on the right matches this point in the trajectory with the rhythmic beating of the drum (left) and uses an excellent learning/teaching tool, the finger tap (borrowed from music) to accurately match her physical action with the rhythm (inset).

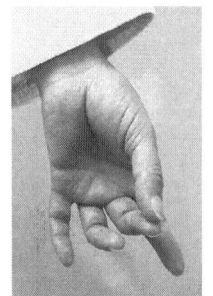

Note that each down movement of the arm circle corresponds to a drum beat (or a finger tap). Every time that the arm is up, the drum stick is also up. In correct aikido music this "up" should be chanted as "an." Therefore, the aikido practitioner shall count "one an, two an, three an, four an," emphasizing the down part of each arm circle and matching it with the count of the number. The up portion of the arm circle should be gentle while it matches the "an" part of the chanting. Because a quarter note equals one second (above), the "an" is chanted half second apart between two counts (i.e., one an two an three an four an). This simple method gives aikido practitioners an even better sense of timing (i.e., no unequal gaps or silence—pauses—between counts: e.g., one...... two... three............ four...). This principle also helps us indicate how fast a technique should be performed. For example, leg stretches (**Figures 5-6, 13-18**) are usually practiced at a frequency of one every half second (time signature 2/4), which corresponds to eighth notes (above). In contrast, knee walking (**Figure 21**) is usually performed at slow tempo: one every second (quarter note).

Aikido implies a harmonious dialogue between the attacker and defender. The defender must learn to detect the attacker's rhythm, match it, and blend with the attack's intrinsic speed. Knowing when to pause (= music rest, see Supplement) and when to continue determines the outcome of this dialogue. Here are some tips that will help you achieve this goal while training in a controlled environment:

1) Let the metronome at 60 beats per minute or count out loud "1 an, 2 an, 3 an, 4 an," again "1 an, 2 an, 3 an, 4 an," (time signature 4/4, see Supplement for details) at approximately this tempo (the assistance of a drummer beating a floor tom-tom would be ideal).
2) Both attacker and defender must move according to this rhythm: in essence "follow the music."
3) The attacker executes "one-handed wrist grab, cross-side wrist" (Fig. 4).
4) The defender locks the attacker's wrist and neutralizes the attack as shown in Figures 4 A-E.
5) Practice this routine numerous times at this slow pace (60 beats/minute) until you can perform it in a completely relaxed manner. If you do this long enough, you will discover aikido's natural rhythm.
6) Once you have mastered the slow tempo, you might feel confident to speed up (time signature 2/4, as shown in Fig. 4), without jeopardizing relaxation, accuracy, or performance: "jazz-time."

FIGURE 4

Starting position from standing (pause). **4-A**: Attacker (right) performs one-handed wrist grab, cross-side wrist. Out-loud counting begins (time signature 2/4, see Supplement for details): one an... two an... **4-B one**: Defender locks the attacker's wrist by gently placing the defender's free hand on top of the attacker's hand (inset). At the same time, the defender executes a finger tap with the fingers of his lowest hand. The finger tap is an excellent tool for learning and teaching how to accurately match physical actions with an attack's intrinsic rhythm (see Supplement). **4-C an**: Defender leads the attacker's arm up. **4-D-E two**: Defender leads attacker down, projecting her face down onto the mat. **4-F an**: Defender neutralizes the attacker with a classical aikido pin: twisting the attacker's wrist and elbow in the direction indicated by the arrows and preventing her from standing up by pressuring her thorax with the knee. This wrist technique relies on the principles of the "arm-circle" exercises discussed in the Supplement and also in **Figure 3**.

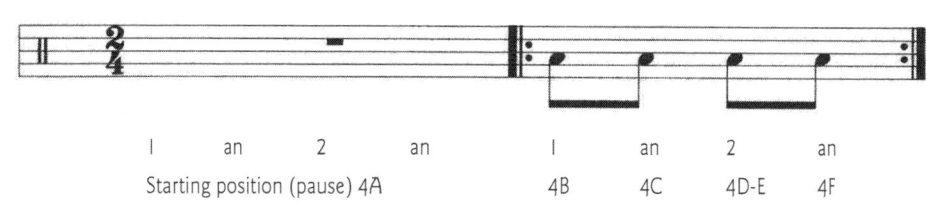

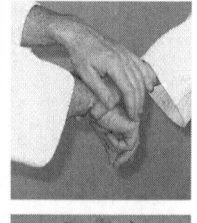

4B - detail

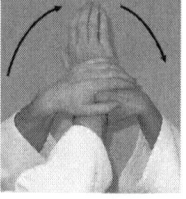

4C - detail

TECHNICAL SECTION

In the following figures, we indicate how to apply basic music principles to diverse aikido routines. Adopt the starting position ("pause") as indicated in every figure before proceeding to chant out loud the aikido tempo (set the metronome at 60 beats per minute and/or make sure your drummer partner beats the drum at this pace). Only relaxation will allow you to discover aikido's natural rhythm.

STRETCHES

Here we encourage students to practice numerous aikido routines with a 4' wooden staff (*jo*). The jo is an extraordinary tool for teaching and learning mind and body coordination.

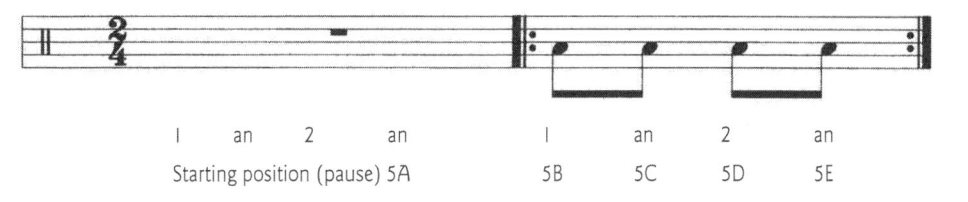

FIGURE 5: Leg stretches, "feet together"

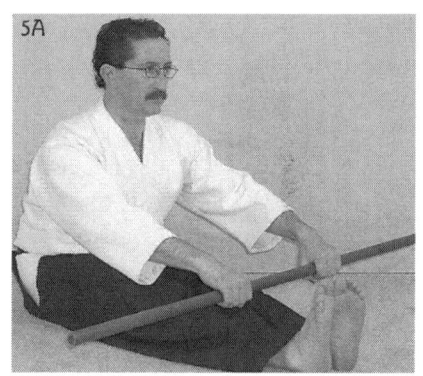

5-A: Starting position (pause): legs extended, heels together, hold the staff with both hands and place it slightly above the shins (without touching), relax. Out-loud counting begins (time signature 2/4). **5-B one:** Bend forward bringing the chest (not the head) toward the knees and gently touch the soles of the feet with the staff. **5-C an:** Return to the starting position. **5-D two:** stretch again as in B. **5-E an:** Finish in starting position. Repeat this series twice (= four music measures, see Supplement).

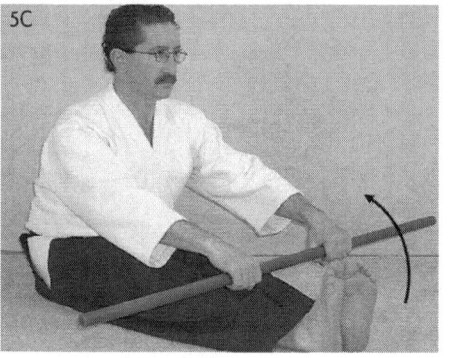

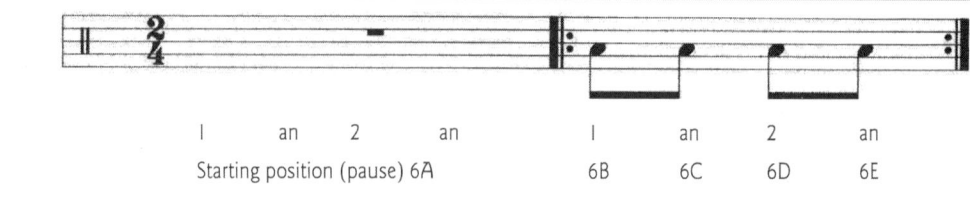

| an | 2 | an | | | an | 2 | an |
Starting position (pause) 6A   6B   6C   6D   6E

FIGURE 6: Leg stretches, "one leg in"

6-A: Starting position (pause): left leg extended, right leg bent (heel close to the groin), hold the staff with both hands (separated at a comfortable distance), shoulders relaxed. Out-loud counting begins (time signature 2/4). **6-B one**: Bring your chest (not the head) toward the left knee and gently touch the shins with the staff. **6-C an**: While returning to the starting position, switch the position of your feet. **6-D two**: Stretch toward the right knee. **6-E an**: Finish in starting position. Repeat this series twice.

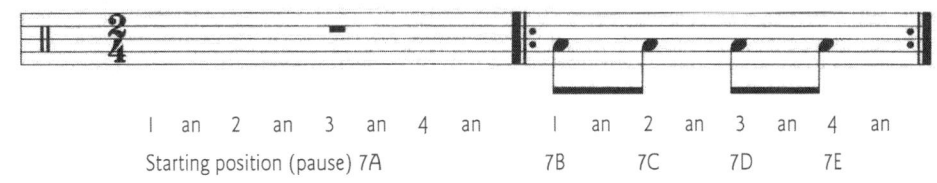

I	an	2	an	3	an	4	an			
Starting position (pause) 7A										
I	an	2	an	3	an	4	an			
7B		7C		7D		7E				

FIGURE 7: Leg stretches, "open legs"

7-A: Starting position (pause): open legs, hold the staff with both hands (separated at a comfortable distance) and raise it to chest level. Out-loud counting begins (time signature 4/4). **7-B one an:** Bring your chest (not the head) toward the left knee and gently touch the shins with the staff. **7-C two an:** Bend forward (back straight). **7-D three an:** Stretch toward the right knee. **7-E four an:** Finish in starting position. Repeat this series twice.

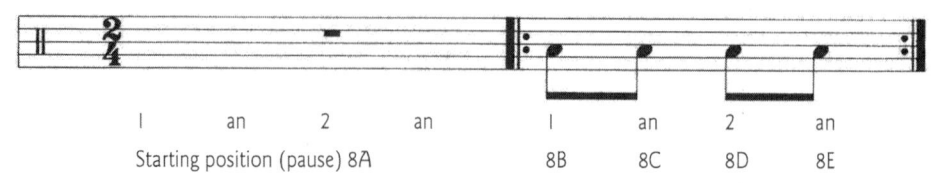

FIGURE 8 : Turning upper-body to the side, arms at chest level

8-A: Starting position (pause): formal aikido sitting posture (*seiza*), hold the staff with both hands (separated at a comfortable distance) and raise it to chest level. Out-loud counting begins (time signature 2/4). **8-B one:** Turn gently toward the left side. **8-C an:** Return to starting position. **8-D two:** Turn gently toward the right side. **8-E an:** Finish in starting position. Repeat this series twice.

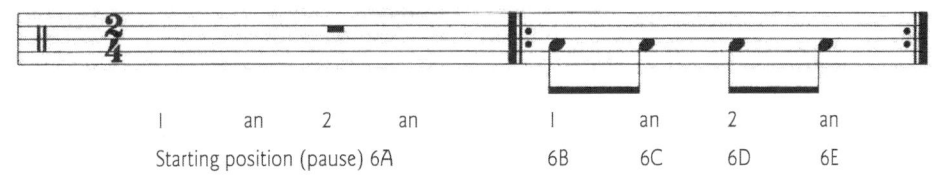

I	an	2	an		I	an	2	an
Starting position (pause) 6A					6B	6C	6D	6E

FIGURE 9: Bending upper body laterally

9-A: Starting position (pause): sitting *seiza*, hold the staff with both hands (separated at a comfortable distance) and raise it up (arms stretched, shoulders relaxed). Out-loud counting begins (time signature 2/4). **9-B one**: Bend gently laterally to the left side. **9-C an**: Return to starting position. **9-D two**: bend gently to the right side. **9-E an**: Finish in starting position. Repeat this series twice.

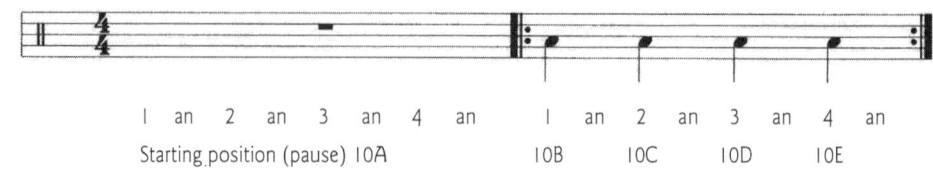

| an 2 an 3 an 4 an | 1 an 2 an 3 an 4 an |
Starting position (pause) 10A   10B 10C 10D 10E

FIGURE 10: Shoulder stretches: rotation

10-A: Starting position (pause): sitting *seiza*, hold the staff with both hands (separated at a comfortable distance), staff slightly rests on thighs. Out-loud counting begins (time signature 4/4). **10-B one an**: Raise the right arm while keeping the left arm and particularly the left hand in place (do your best!). **10-C two an**: The movement continues backwards using the right shoulder joint as a rotation point until the staff is positioned behind the hips (be careful!). **10-D three an**: Raise the left arm while keeping the right arm and particularly the right hand in place. **10-E four an**: Finish in starting position. Repeat this series twice. With practice, this routine should be performed in only two counts (time signature 2/4).

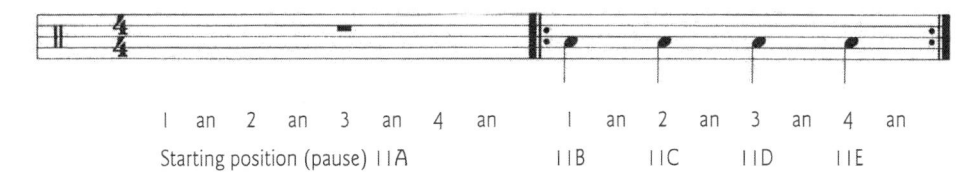

| an 2 an 3 an 4 an | 1 an 2 an 3 an 4 an |
Starting position (pause) 11A | 11B 11C 11D 11E

FIGURE 11:

Shoulder stretches: back and front

11-A: Starting position (pause): take formal aikido sitting posture, hold the staff with both hands separated at a comfortable distance, staff slightly resting on thighs. Out-loud counting begins (time signature 4/4). **11-B one an:** Raise both arms. **11-C two an:** The movement continues backwards using the shoulder joints as a rotation point until the staff is positioned behind the hips (be careful!). **11-D three an:** Return to B. **11-E four an:** Finish in starting position. Repeat this series twice. With practice, this routine should be performed in only two counts (time signature 2/4).

SINGLE-PERSON ROUTINES TO
DEVELOP BALANCE & MIND-BODY COORDINATION

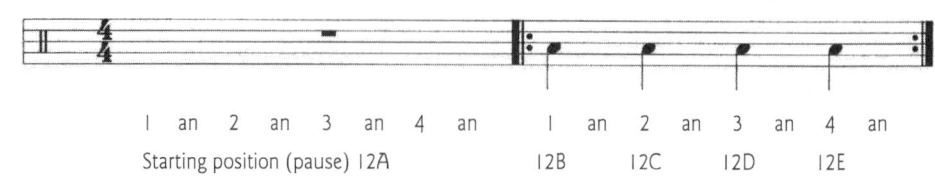

FIGURE 12: Sitting and standing

12-A: Starting position (pause): take formal sitting posture. Out-loud counting begins (time signature 4/4). **12-B one an:** Raise your hips and sit on your heels, toes touching the mat. **12-C two an:** Stand up perpendicularly to the mat and keep your balance (most of the bodyweight should rest on the toes). **12-D three an:** Return to B. **12-E four an:** Finish in starting position. Repeat this series twice. With practice, this routine will help you develop not only stability but also powerful legs.

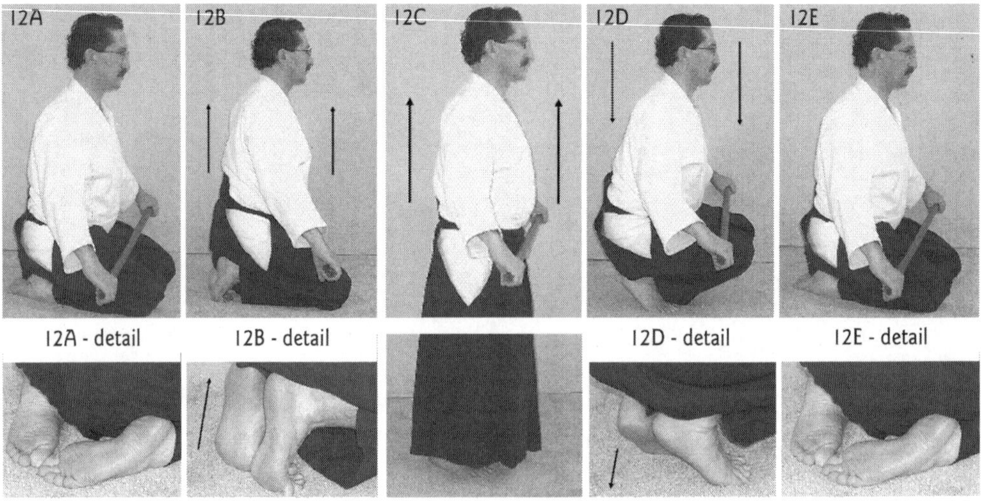

FIGURE 13 - Leg stretch, forward

13-A: Starting position (pause): standing, hold the staff with both hands and use it as a support for this routine: left hand keeps one end of the staff close to the armpit while the right hand maintains it perpendicular to the mat. Out-loud counting begins (time signature 2/4). **13-B one:** Raise your left leg as high as you can (be careful!), leg stretched. **13-C an:** Return to the starting position calmly. **13-D two:** Raise your leg again. **13-E an:** Return to starting position. Repeat this series twice and alternate sides. Keep your balance and relax.

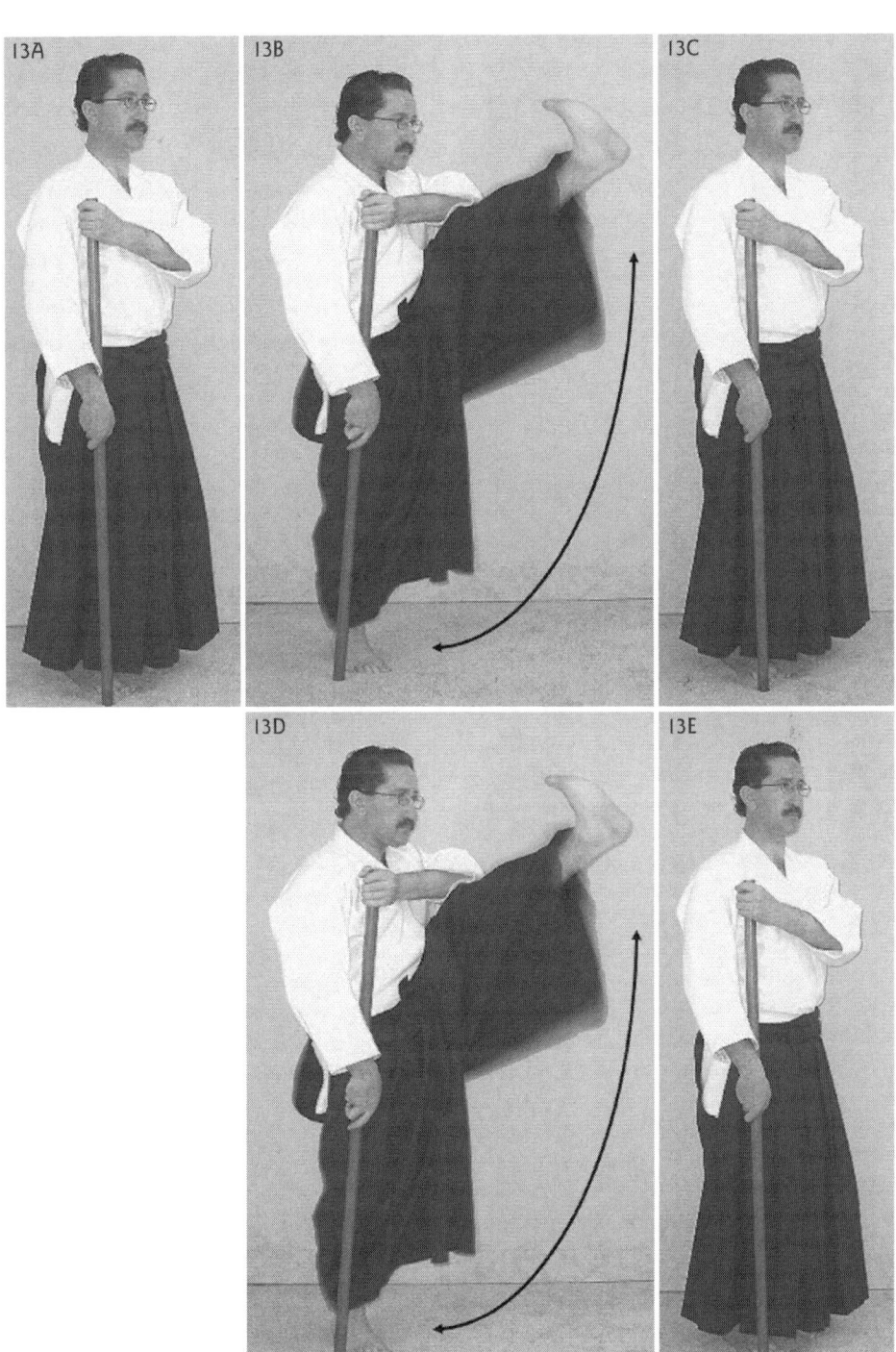

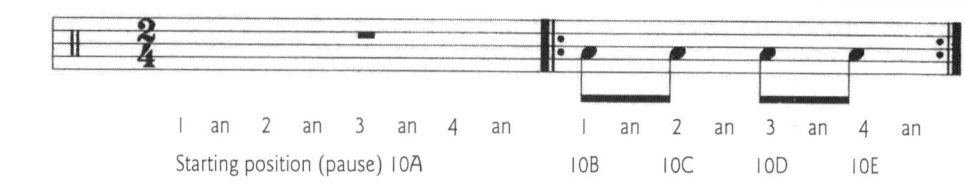

| an 2 an 3 an 4 an | 1 an 2 an 3 an 4 an |
Starting position (pause) 10A   10B   10C   10D   10E

FIGURE 14: Leg stretch, forward and in "arc"

14-A: Starting position (pause): standing, left leg forward, left arm forward and parallel to the mat, hold the staff with the left hand. Out-loud counting begins (time signature 2/4). **14-B one:** Raise the right leg and reach your left hand with the inside edge of the right foot. This movement should describe an arc trajectory (front view). **14-C an:** Return to the starting position calmly. **14-D two:** Raise your leg again. **14-E an:** Return to starting position calmly. Repeat this series twice and alternate sides. To maintain relaxation and balance, the aikido practitioner uses a trick: the right hand remains gently closed, next to the vertical alignment of the body, with the thumb slightly touching the middle finger (see detail).

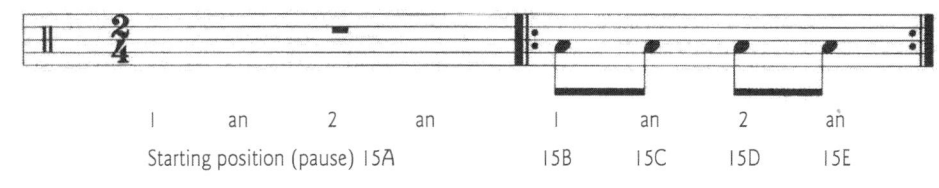

	an	2	an		an	2	an
Starting position (pause) 15A				15B	15C	15D	15E

FIGURE 15: "Walking" over the staff

15-A: Starting position (pause): standing (one leg forward), hold the staff with both hands separated at a comfortable distance. Out-loud counting begins (time signature 2/4). 15-B one: Raise one knee up. 15-C an: "Walk" over the staff so that you position the staff between your legs. 15-D two: Return to B. 15-E an: Finish in starting position. Repeat this series twice with each leg.

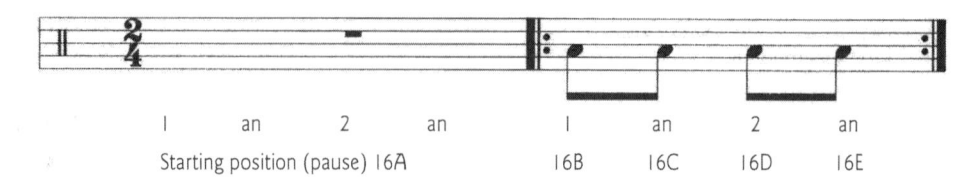

1 an 2 an 1 an 2 an
Starting position (pause) 16A
16B
16C
16D
16E

FIGURE 16: Leg stretch, back

16-A: Starting position (pause): standing, hold the staff with both hands and use it as a support for this routine. Out-loud counting begins (time signature 2/4). **16-B one:** raise your left leg to the back, toes pointing down. **16-C an:** Return to the starting position. **16-D two:** raise your leg again. **16-E an:** Return to the starting position. Repeat this series twice with each leg and alternate the position of your hands when holding the staff.

16A
16B
16C
16D
16E

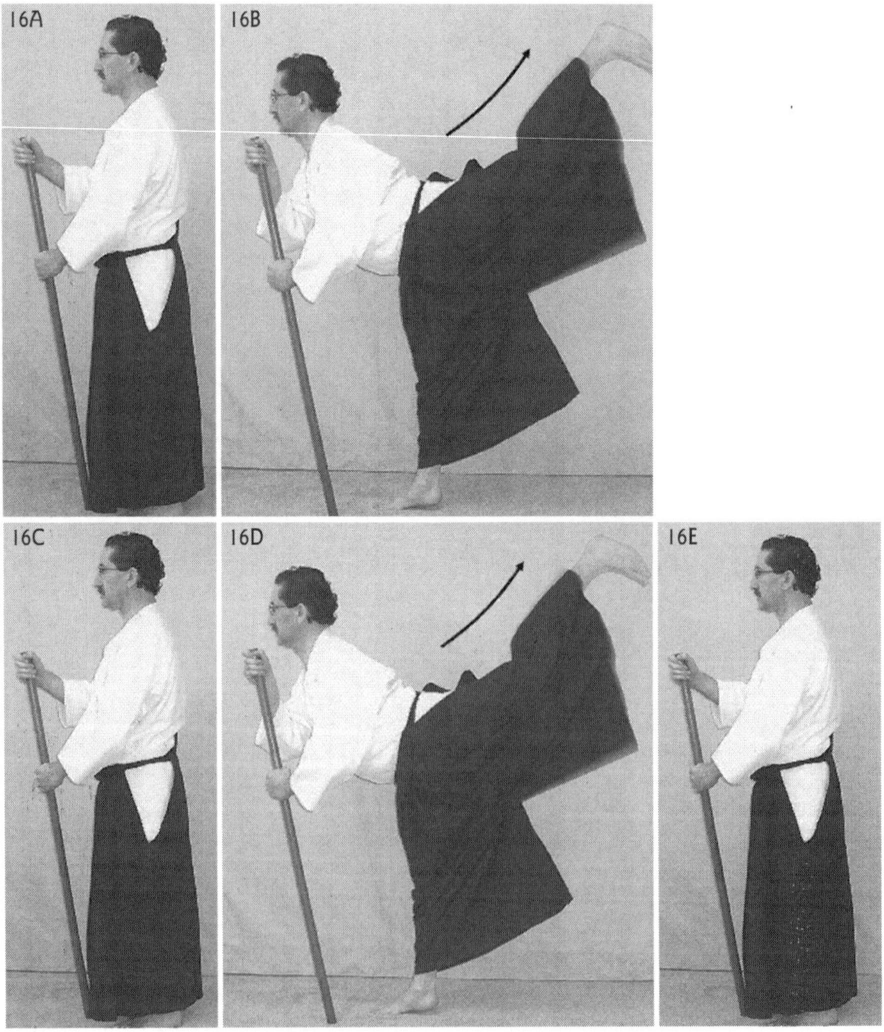

1 an 2 an 1 an 2 an

Starting position (pause) 17A 17B 17C 17D 17E

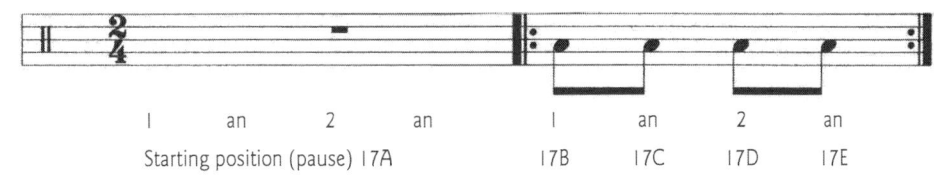

FIGURE 17: Leg stretch, lateral

17-A: Starting position (pause): standing, hold the staff with both hands and use it as a support for this routine. Out-loud counting begins (time signature 2/4). **17-B one**: Raise your left leg to the side. **17-C an**: Return to the starting position. **17-D two**: Raise your leg again. **17-E an**: Return to the starting position. Repeat this series twice with each leg and alternate the position of your hands when holding the staff.

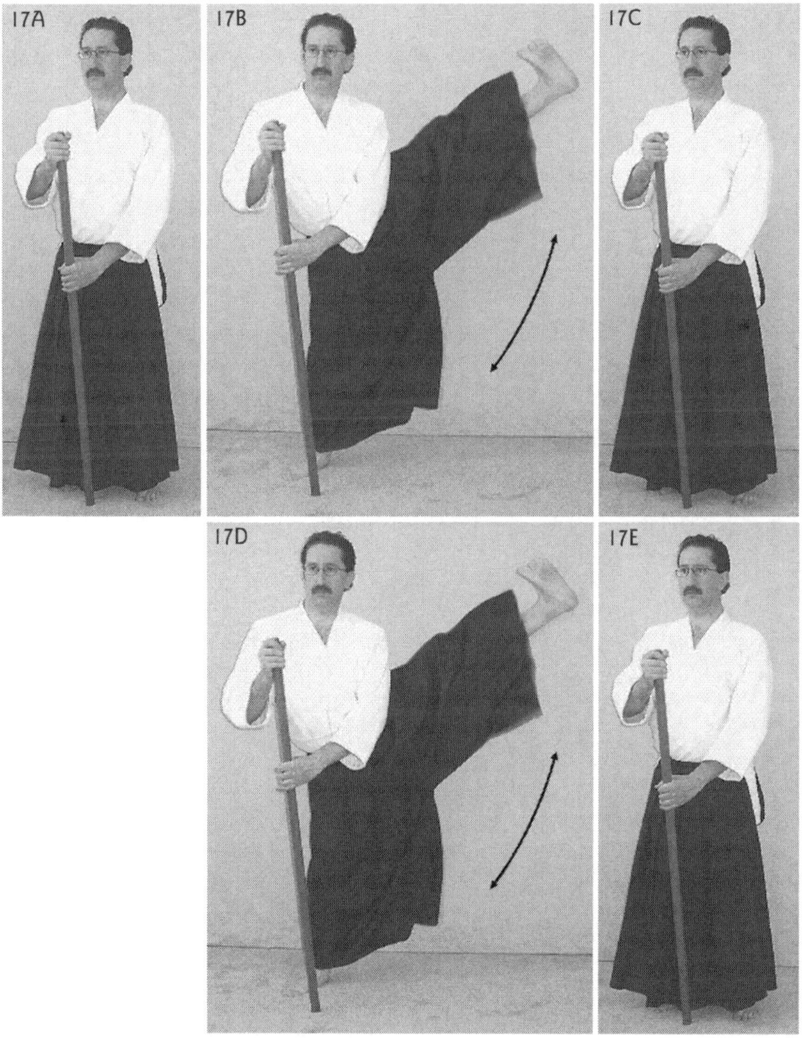

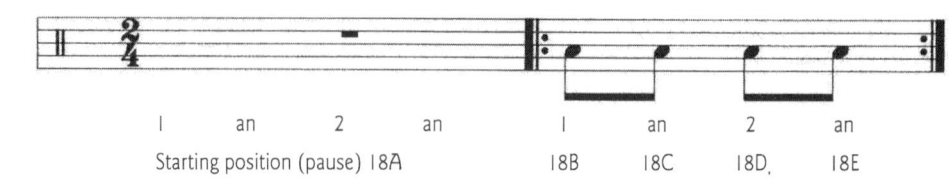

	an	2	an		an	2	an
Starting position (pause) 18A				18B	18C	18D	18E

FIGURE 18: Kick over the staff

This exercise requires speed and good mind and body coordination (practice it away from windows!). **18-A**: Starting position (pause): standing (left leg forward), hold the staff with the right hand and stabilize it perpendicularly to the ground. Out-loud counting begins (time signature 2/4). **18-B one**: Once the staff is steady, release it carefully so that it remains in balance for at least one second. Right after you release the staff, kick over it describing an elliptical trajectory with your right foot: up, out, down, in. Be fast! Use a short staff at first and/or ask a partner to hold it for you (inset) until you become skillful with this exercise. To maintain relaxation and balance, the aikido practitioner uses the same trick explained in **Figure 14** (hand relaxed with the thumb touching the middle finger; see detail). **18-C an**: Quickly regain control of the staff by grabbing it with the opposite hand (left) before it falls. **18-D two**: Once you re-stabilize the staff, release it again and kick over it describing with your foot an elliptical trajectory in opposite direction to the one described in **B** (i.e., up, in, down, and slightly out). **18-E an**: Finish in the starting position. Repeat this series twice with each leg. To the observer, this routine should seem easy. Complete relaxation will help you give that impression.

ROLLING & FALLING

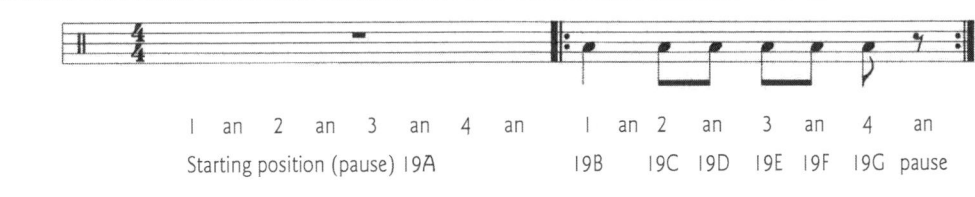

1 an 2 an 3 an 4 an	1 an 2 an 3 an 4 an
Starting position (pause) 19A	19B 19C 19D 19E 19F 19G pause

FIGURE 19: Backward half-roll from a formal sitting posture (*seiza*)

19-A: Starting position (pause): formal sitting posture. Out-loud counting begins (time signature 4/4). **19-B one an**: Lean forward and cross your legs (inset) while gently touching the mat with your fists. **19-C two**: Backward half-roll begins; allow the body to roll naturally. **19-D an**: Legs reach perpendicular alignment in respect to the floor. **19-E three**: Smooth return forward; allow gravity to take the weight of your legs down. **19-F an**: Gain momentum and return to the position described in **C**. **19-G four an**: Finish in formal sitting posture. Backward half-rolls should be practiced constantly, aiming to perform them with little effort. Backward half-rolls and complete forward rolls (**Figure 20**) are excellent—perhaps the best—solo exercises that will help you understand the natural rhythm of aikido.

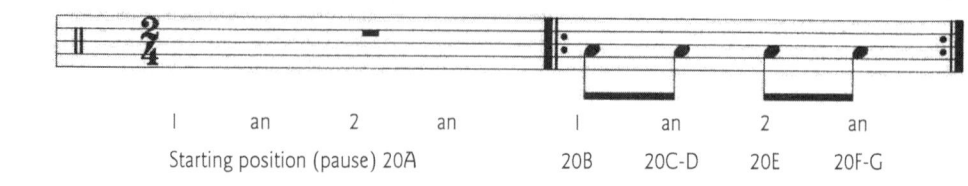

1 an 2 an
Starting position (pause) 20A
1 an 2 an
20B 20C-D 20E 20F-G

FIGURE 20 – Forward roll from a formal sitting posture (*seiza*)

20-A: Starting position (pause): formal sitting posture. Out-loud counting begins (time signature 2/4). **20-B one**: Raise your body up and forward and "throw" yourself into a classical aikido forward roll (this motion needs full commitment, therefore, mind and body coordination). **20-C-D an**: Continue rolling. **20-E two**: Slow down and prepare yourself to "knee walk." **20-F-G an**: "Knee walk" one step and finish in seiza. This modality of rolling should be practiced on both sides of the body.

20A
20B
20C
20D
20E
20F
20G

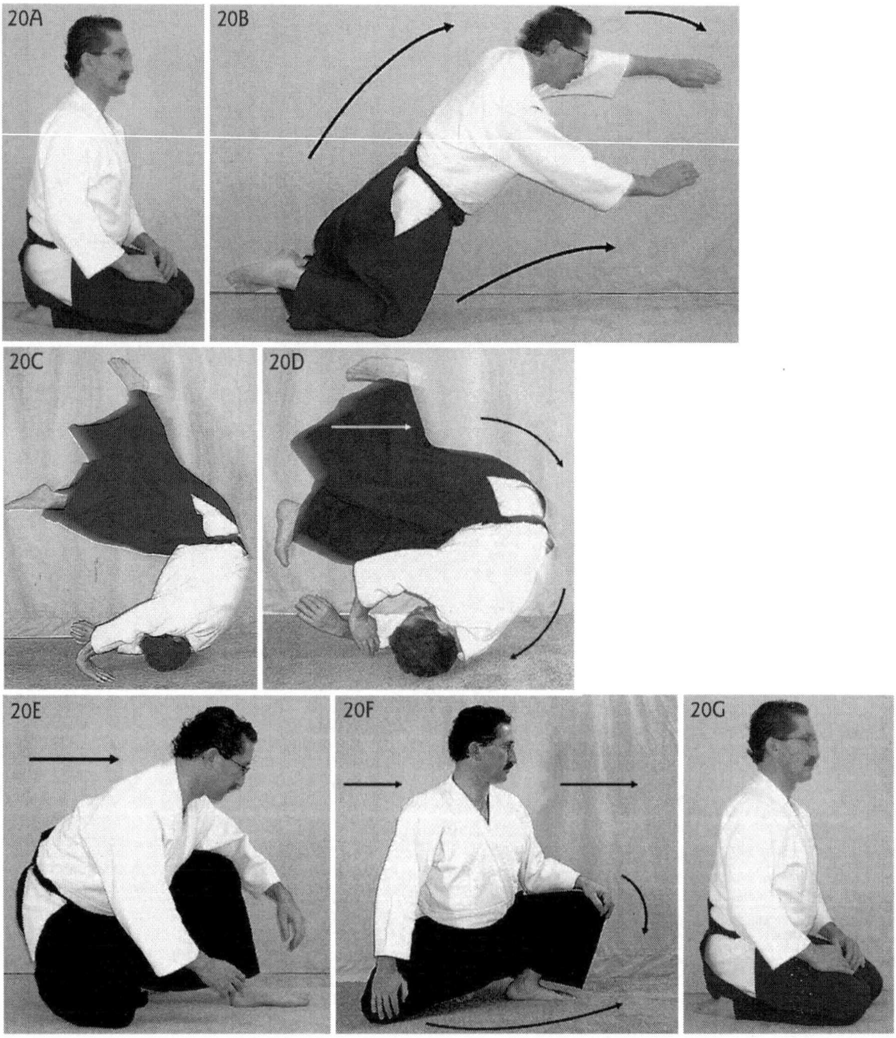

| 1 an 2 an 3 an 4 an | 1 an 2 an 3 an 4 an |
Starting position (pause) 21A | 21B 21C 21D 21E-F 21G

FIGURE 21 – Knee "walking" and break fall

21-A: Starting position (pause): formal sitting posture. Out-loud counting begins (time signature 4/4, two measures). **21-B one an:** Perform one "knee-step" with the right knee. **21-C two an:** Second knee-step with the left knee. **21-D three an:** Third knee-step with the right knee. **21-E-F four:** The fourth knee-step with the left knee turns into a short forward roll. **21-G an:** End with a break fall. Practice the break fall on both sides of the body. For this you should alternate the side with which you initiate knee-walking.

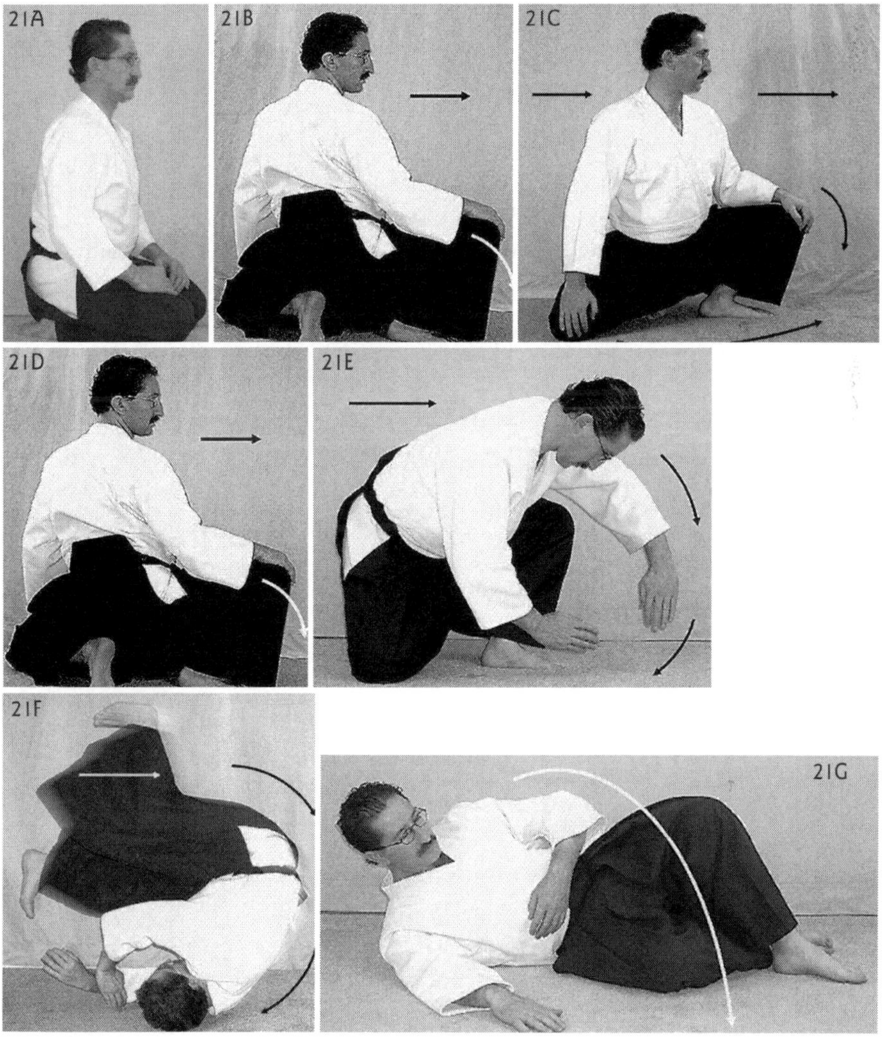

Illustration courtesy of Oscar Ratti.
©2000 Futuro Designs & Publications.

Concluding Remarks

Not only aikido but every martial art—or physical discipline—has its own rhythm ("music"), which the student should discover. Learning to move according to this natural "tick" should be an important goal of training. This will allow the student to adequately match an attack, blend and flow with it, and finally neutralize it.

In this article, we have shown how music notation can help us "write" and understand the "rhythm" inherent to aikido. Keep in mind that aikido practitioners are just like musicians: at some point in their development, they want to interpret aikido's rhythm in unique manners. Some learn to move fast, others emphasize motions in specific parts of a sequence (accentuating the expression of an "aikido note" or "pause"), and a few improvise by simplifying or prolonging the components of the "song." They all are, however, governed by the laws of physics that impose a natural pace to the movements of their common human anatomies. In part two of this article, we will discuss how music principles can be applied to partnered techniques of neutralization, projections-throws, weapons, breathing exercises, and meditation.

Bibliography

Curtis, C. (2001). *Ki-Aikido on Maui*, 3rd Ed. Maui, Hawaii: MAKS Publications.

Feldstein, S. & Black, D. (1990). *Alfred's beginning drumset method*. Van Nuys, California: Alfred Publishing Co.

Maruyama, K. (1984). *Aikido with ki*. Tokyo: Ki No Kenkyukai Headquarters.

Paz-y-Miño C., G., & Espinosa, A. (2002). Dichotomous keys to fundamental attacks and defenses in aikido. *Journal of Asian Martial Arts, 11*(1), 8–27.

Paz-y-Miño C., G., & Espinosa, A. (2002). Aikido: The art of the dynamic equiangular spiral. *Journal of Asian Martial Arts, 11*(4), 8–29.

Reed, W. (1992). *Ki: A road that anyone can walk*, 2nd Ed. Tokyo: Japan Publications.

Reed, W. (1999). *Ki: A practical guide for Westerners*, 6th Ed. Tokyo: Japan Publications.

Shifflett, C. (1998). *Ki in aikido: A sampler of ki exercises*. Merrifield, Virginia: Round Earth Publishing.

Shifflett, C. (1999). *Aikido: Exercises for teaching and training*. Merrifield, Virginia: Round Earth Publishing.

Stewart, D. (1999). *The musician's guide to reading and writing music*. San Francisco, California: Miller Freeman Books.

Tohei, K. (1962). *What is aikido?* Tokyo: Rikugei Publishing House.

Tohei, K. (1974). *This is aikido*. Tokyo: Japan Publications.

Tohei, K. (2001). *Ki in daily life*. Tokyo: Ki No Kenkyukai Headquarters.

Tohei, K. (2001). *The way to union with ki: Aikido with mind and body coordination*. Tochigi: Ki No Kenkyukai Headquarters.

Acknowledgments

We dedicate this article to Mark Rubbert, William Reed, Kashiwaya Koichi, and Andrew Tsubaki, who have inspired us to explore the fascinating complexity of Shin Shin Toitsu Aikido (founder Koichi Tohei). Very special thanks to the St. Louis Ki Society and Kansas Ki Society members for continuous support and friendship. The material discussed in this article is not necessarily endorsed by Ki Society or any of its affiliates.

· 6 ·

Music Principles Applied to Aikido Techniques: Part II
by Guillermo Paz-y-Miño C., Ph.D. & Avelina Espinosa, Ph.D.

Abstract

In Part I of this article (Paz-y-Miño C. & Espinosa, 2004) we discussed how some music principles can be applied to various aspects of aikido training, including stretches, single-person routines to develop balance and mind-body coordination, rolling and falling. Here we expand on this idea and discuss how these principles can also be applied to partnered techniques of neutralization, projections-throws, weapons, breathing exercises, and meditation. Our goal is to provide students and instructors with novel tools for learning and teaching aiki arts.

Introduction

In Part I of this two-part article, we indicated that *aikido* (*aiki* = harmony; *do* = path, the way of) and music have numerous similarities, particularly rhythm and harmony. We stated that a technique's flow of movement, its rate of speed, and the congruent and pleasant arrangement of body motions define aikido's rhythm and harmony. Simple music notation and a percussion instrument (see Supplement) were used to discuss how music principles can be applied to various aspects of aikido training, including stretches, single-person routines to develop balance and mind-body coordination, rolling and falling. Here we expand on this idea and discuss how these principles can also be applied to partnered techniques of neutralization, projections-throws, weapons, breathing exercises, and meditation. Not only aikido but every martial art—or physical discipline—has its own pace, which the student should discover. Learning to move according to this rhythm will allow the martial artist to adequately match an attack, blend and flow with it, and finally neutralize it.

The Concept of Tempo in Aikido

An essential component of aikido's rhythm is its tempo. We define aikido tempo as the rate of speed of an aikido technique or routine. It is possible to mark aikido's tempo by counting, or chanting, numbers at specific intervals. A more precise method is to use a metronome, a device which produces clicks (e.g., every second) to indicate the tempo of music (see Supplement). We recommend adjusting the metronome to 60 beats per minute (one second = one unit of aikido music); this pace induces appropriate mind and body coordination while practicing aikido. Slow and gentle training will let the student discover when to speed up.

SUPPLEMENT: BASIC AIKI MUSIC NOTATION

Like in music, the duration of aikido techniques can be indicated by different types of notes (**Figure 1**). Here we arbitrarily assign the following duration to these notes: whole note = four seconds; half note = two seconds; quarter note = one second; and eighth note = half a second. The unit of aikido music is the quarter note. In consequence, one whole note equals two half notes, one half note equals two quarter notes, and one quarter note equals two eighth notes (**Figure 1-A**; there are also other notes in music, like the sixteenth, thirty-second and sixty-fourth notes; they are too fast to illustrate the aikido principles discussed in this article). All notes have their corresponding rests or pauses (**Figure 1-B**) which in music indicate silence. In aikido, however, there is no silence, just pause.

Aikido music is divided into equal parts called measures (**Figure 1-C**); bar lines indicate the beginning and end of a measure. Two dots, placed between double bars, indicate repetition of the aikido sequence within one or more measures. Double bar lines show the end of an entire aikido routine, which may include numerous measures.

Time signatures and note values: Time signatures are placed at the beginning of a sequence of aikido music. The most common time signature is 4/4 which consists of four quarter notes per measure (one per second; **Figure 1-A**). The top number shows the number of beats on the drum or the number of vocal counts chanted by the aikido practitioner (i.e., one, two, three, four...) in each sequence of aikido techniques. The bottom number simply specifies that the note in each beat corresponds to a quarter note.

In **Figure 1-D**, the 4/4 time signature indicates one arm circle per second, which is represented by the four quarter notes. The aikido practitioner shall count out loud each number, matching the rhythm kept by a drummer or a metronome.

A floor tom-tom drum or any other percussion instrument with a loud-low-frequency vibration can be used to mark aikido's tempo.

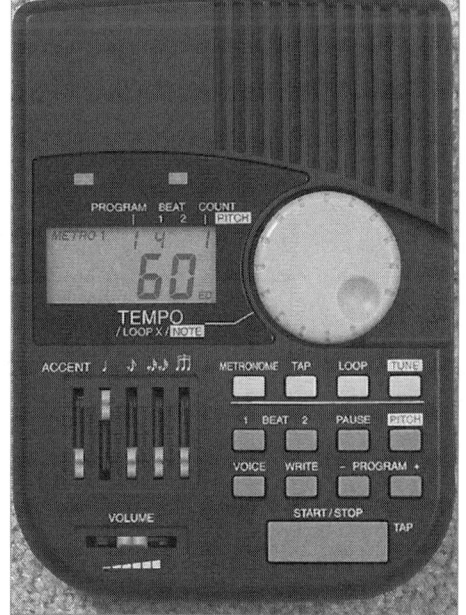

Electronic metronomes offer a variety of options to indicate the tempo of "aikido music."

All photos courtesy of
A. Espinosa & G. Paz-y-Miño C.

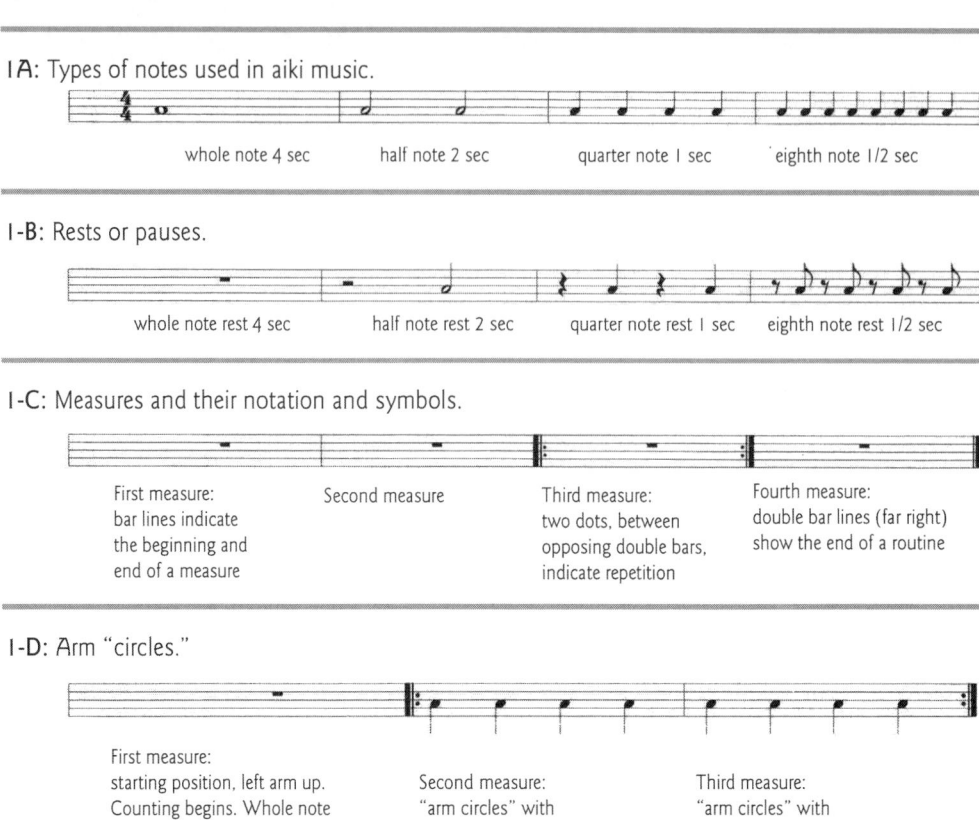

FIGURE 1

This apparently simple exercise is the foundation of numerous aikido routines, particularly wrist techniques like the ones shown in **Figures 2-6**. Rather than "arm circles," the aikido practitioners perform elliptical trajectories with their hands, while the shoulders remain relatively immovable. The practitioners allow their hands to fall with gravity and catch them when the hands reach the lowest point in the elliptical trajectory; then, they take their hands up again. The student on the right matches this point in the trajectory with the rhythmic beating of the drum (left) and uses an excellent learning/teaching tool, the finger tap (borrowed from music) to accurately match her physical action with the rhythm (inset).

Note that each down movement of the arm circle corresponds to a drum beat (or a finger tap). Every time that the arm is up, the drum stick is also up. In correct aikido music this "up" should be chanted as "an." Therefore, the aikido practitioner shall count "one an, two an, three an, four an," emphasizing the down part of each arm circle and matching it with the count of the number. The up portion of the arm circle should be gentle while it matches the "an" part of the chanting. Because a quarter note equals one second (above), the "an" is chanted half second apart between two counts (i.e., one an two an three an four an). This simple method gives aikido practitioners an even better sense of timing (i.e., no unequal gaps or silence—pauses—between counts: e.g., one...

... two... three............ four...). This principle also helps us indicate how fast a technique should be performed. For example, techniques with weapons (**Figures 7-9**) are usually practiced at a frequency of one every half second (time signature 2/4), which corresponds to eighth notes (above). In contrast, breathing exercises or meditation (**Figure 11-12**) are usually performed at slow tempo: one every sixteen (4 whole notes) or one every second (quarter note), respectively.

TECHNICAL SECTION

In the following figures we indicate how to apply basic music principles to diverse aikido routines. Adopt the starting position ("pause") as indicated in every figure before proceeding to chant out loud the aikido tempo (set the metronome at 60 beats per minute).

PARTNERED NEUTRALIZATION TECHNIQUES

Projections & Throws

In this section, we divide all aikido techniques into various components—discrete steps—that match the specific counts of a time signature, either 4/4 or 2/4. With practice, however, all these techniques should be performed in one continuous motion.

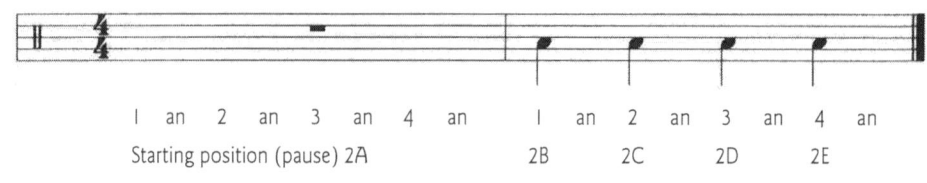

| an 2 an 3 an 4 an | 1 an 2 an 3 an 4 an |
| Starting position (pause) 2A | 2B 2C 2D 2E |

FIGURE 2: Lateral projection from *seiza*

2-A Starting position: sitting seiza, attacker (right) performs two-handed wrist grab of both wrists. Out-loud counting begins (time signature 4/4). **2-B one an**: defender (left) moves right hand upwards, fingertips pointing to sky. **2-C two an**: defender's left hand mirrors the initial motion of the right hand and then he leads the attacker out and back down to her rear diagonal side. Note how the defender's right knee rises up and how he twists the attacker's wrist with his right hand at the same time that the left hand addresses the direction of her movement. **2-D three an**: attacker turns completely over her hip and break falls. **2-E four an**: defender finishes with a neutralization: knee over the attacker's head and continuous twisting of her arm.

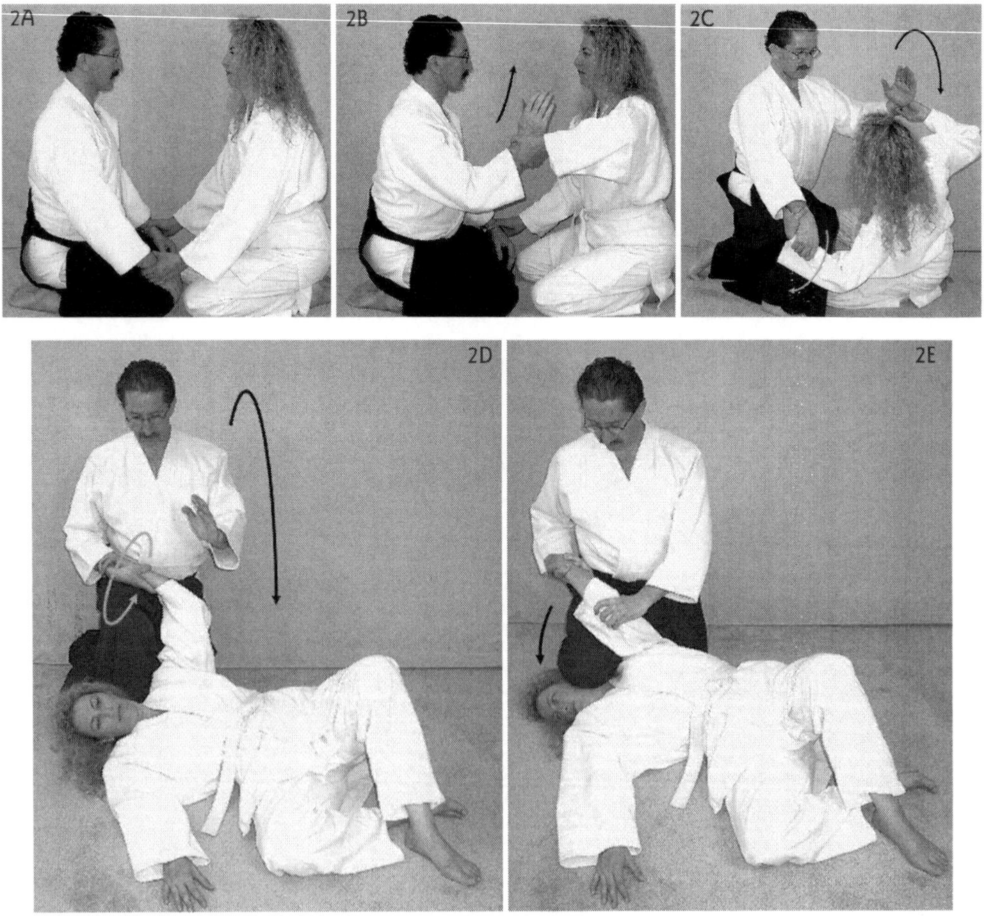

1	an	2	an	1	an	2	an
Starting position (pause) 3A				3B	3C	3D	3E

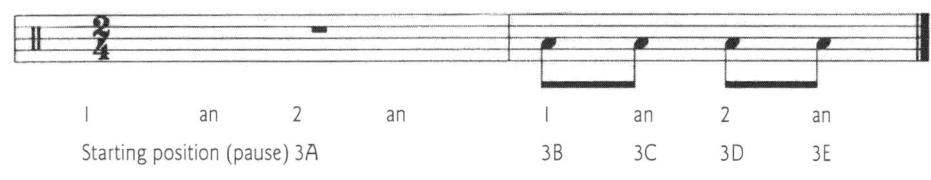

FIGURE 3: Backward projection from standing: "Heaven-Earth" throw

3-A starting position: standing, attacker (left) performs two-handed wrist grab of both wrists. Out-loud counting begins (time signature 2/4). **3-B one**: defender (right) moves right hand upwards (Heaven), fingertips pointing to sky, while the other hand remains extended toward the mat (Earth). **3-C an**: defender steps in (short step with the right foot) and raises his right hand even further. **3-D two**: defender steps even further with the right foot while leading the attacker back down. **3-E an**: attacker falls backward onto the mat.

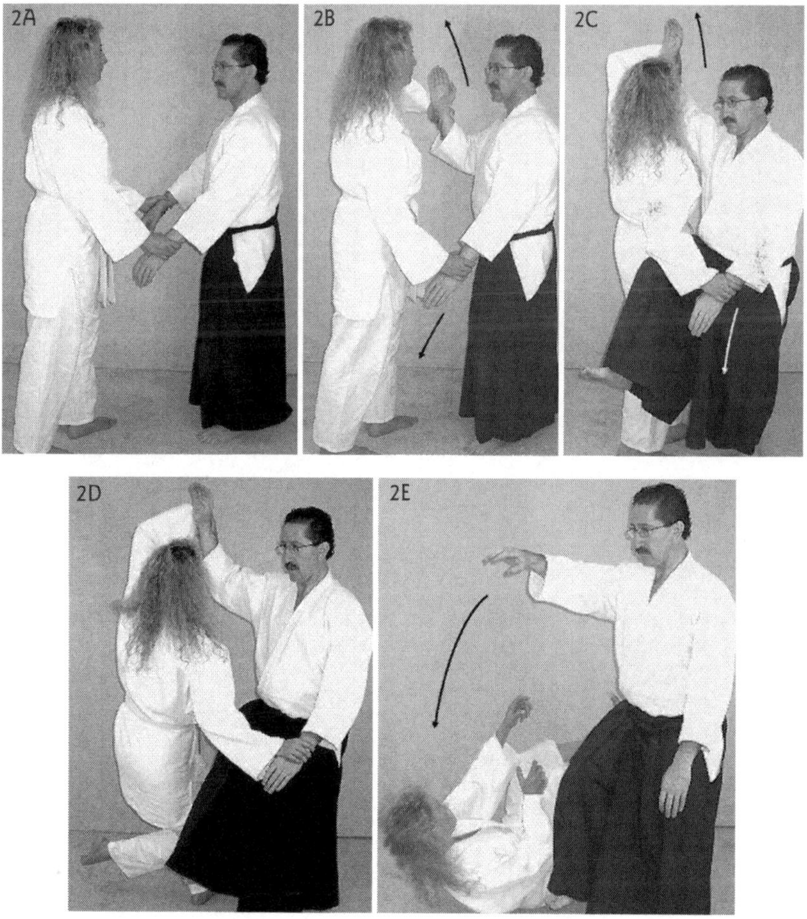

1 an 2 an 3 an 4 an 1 an 2 an 3 an 4 an

Starting position (pause) 4A 4B 4C 4D 4E

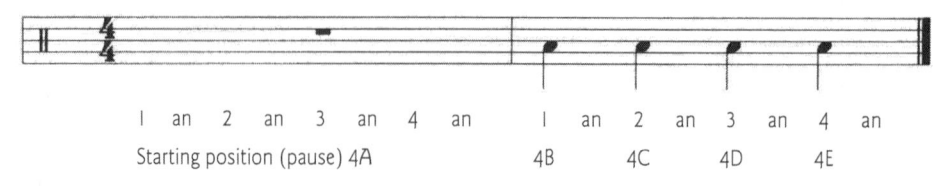

FIGURE 4: Neutralization of a punch to the face

4-A starting position: attacker (left) and defender face each other. Out-loud counting begins (time signature 4/4). **4-B one an:** attacker (left) strikes with a punch to the face. At the same time, defender leads the attack up and slightly out. **4-C two an:** defender enters with the right foot at the same time that hooks the attacker's striking arm with the left hand and projects her down to her diagonal side. **4-D three an:** as the attacker is falling onto the mat, the defender strikes the jaw with his open hand. **4-E four an:** defender leaves the attacker's individual space. With practice, this routine should be performed fast (time signature 2/4).

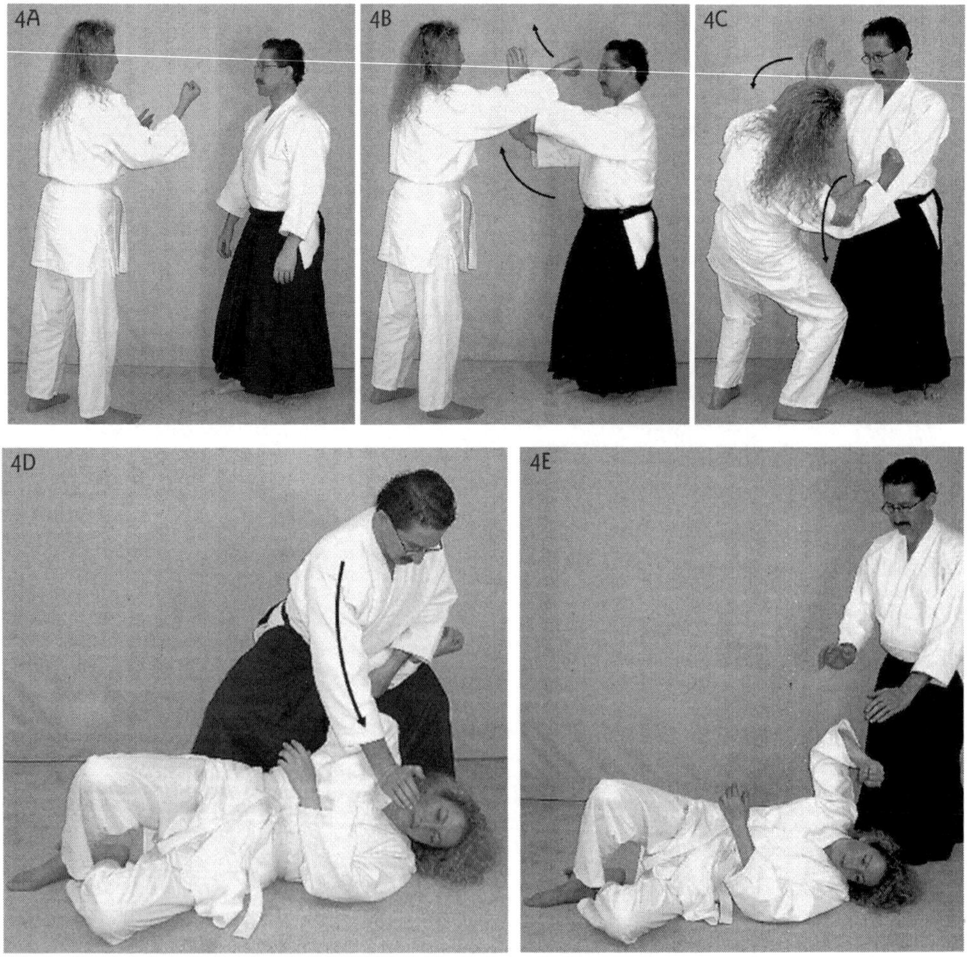

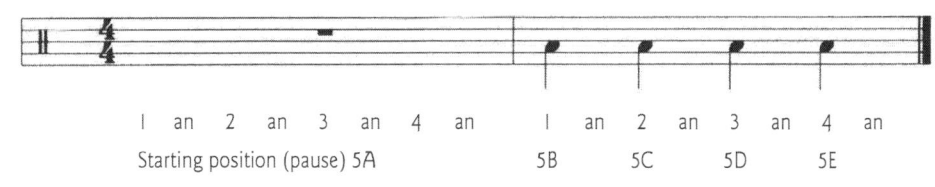

FIGURE 5: Neutralization of a two-handed lapel grab

5-A starting position: attacker (left) performs two-handed shoulder/lapel grab. Out-loud counting begins (time signature 4/4). **5-B one an:** defender (right) raises both arms (fingertips up). **5-C two an:** defender enters and hooks one of the attacker's arms with one hand at the same time that he redirects the attacker's chin up and to the side (detail). **5-D three an:** defender projects attacker down to her diagonal side. **5-E four an:** defender immobilizes the attacker by securing one arm and pressuring (or striking) just below the armpit area with a one-knuckle-fist (see detail). Be gentle, a slight pressure to this area generates pain. With practice, this routine should be performed fast (time signature 2/4).

| an 2 an 3 an 4 an | an 2 an 3 an 4 an |
| Starting position (pause) 6A | 6B 6C 6D 6E |

**FIGURE 6: Neutralization of a combined attack —
one-handed wrist grab and open-hand strike to the head/neck**

6-A starting position: attacker (left) performs one-handed wrist grab. Out-loud counting begins (time signature 4/4). **6-B-C one an:** attacker performs open-hand diagonal strike to the head/neck at the same time that the defender (right) raises the free hand to redirect the attack up and out (transition 6-B-C). **6-C two an:** Immediately, defender liberates his right hand and uses two of his fingers to deeply pressure slightly above the suprasternal notch. Be gentle, a slight accurate touch of this area generates pain. **6-D three an:** Defender projects attacker down by manipulating her arm and continuing pressuring above the suprasternal notch. **6-E four an:** defender immobilizes the attacker by securing her right arm with the hand, resting his right knee on her thorax, and maintaining the pressure on the suprasternal notch. With practice, this routine should be performed fast (time signature 2/4).

102

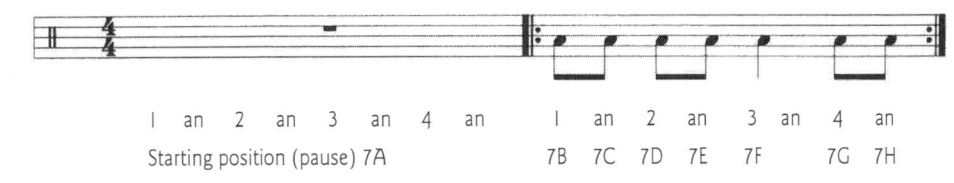

| an 2 an 3 an 4 an | 1 an 2 an 3 an 4 an |
| Starting position (pause) 7A | 7B 7C 7D 7E   7F   7G 7H |

WEAPONS

FIGURE 7: Draw and cut with a wooden sword (*bokken*)

7-A starting position (pause): sitting seiza, holding the sword with the left hand. Out-loud counting begins (time signature 4/4). **7-B one**: grab the sword with the right hand. **7-C an**: fast draw of the sword and horizontal cut (edge of sword out). **7-D two**: swing the sword next to your left shoulder area and prepare to cut again. **7-E an**: cut perpendicularly to the mat. **7-F three-an**: prepare to return the sword to the starting position (slower motion). **7-G four**: return the sword to the position in B (imagine you are inserting a sword back into its case). **7-H an**: return to the starting position. With practice, the two cuts should be performed very fast (time signature 2/4), while the intermediate motions remain gentle.

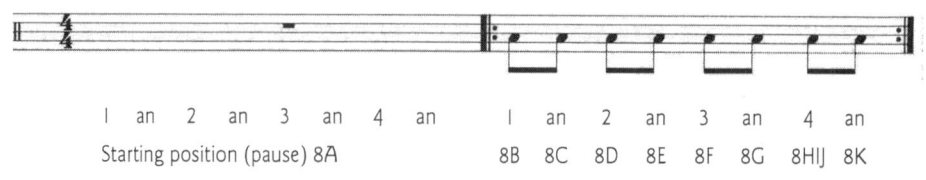

| an 2 an 3 an 4 an | | an 2 an 3 an 4 an |
| Starting position (pause) 8A | | 8B 8C 8D 8E 8F 8G 8HIJ 8K |

FIGURE 8: Staff routine

This whole routine should be performed in four seconds. **8-A starting position**: standing with the left foot forward and holding the short staff with the right hand. From a frontal view, the staff should not be visible to the opponent. To effectively hide it, place one end of the staff behind the lateral malleolus or uncle bone (inset) and the other end behind the armpit and shoulder area. Out-loud counting begins (time signature 4/4). **8-B one**: raise the staff and perform an over-head swing. **8-C an**: step forward with the right foot and execute a side-diagonal low-level strike. **8-D two**: another over-head swing. **8-E an**: step forward again with the right foot and perform a side-diagonal upper-level strike. **8-F three**: turn left 180° and swing the staff over your head. **8-G an**: step forward and strike vertically (upper level). **8-H four**: push one end of the staff with the left hand in the direction indicated in the figure; this will facilitate the rotation of the staff (centered in the right hand) like a propeller **(8-I)**. Continue swinging the staff **(8-J)**, at the same time turn left 180° in preparation to finish the routine. **8-K an**: return to starting position.

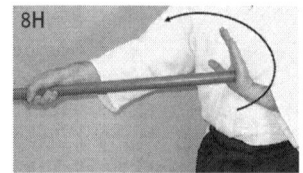

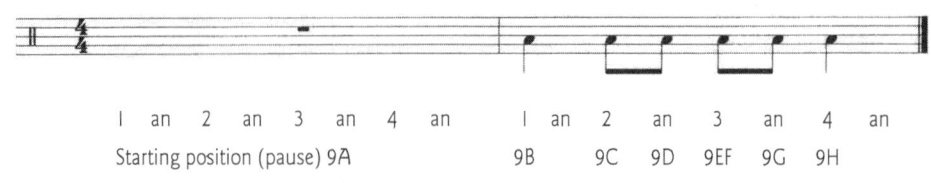

| an | 2 | an | 3 | an | 4 | an | | an | 2 | an | 3 | an | 4 | an |
Starting position (pause) 9A   9B   9C   9D   9EF   9G   9H

FIGURE 9: Neutralization of a thrust attack with a knife (*tanto*)

9-A starting position: standing, attacker (left) holds the knife with the right hand. Out-loud counting begins (time signature 4/4). **9-B one an**: the attacker thrusts the knife toward the defender's abdomen; defender redirects the attack slightly down and out at the same time that he secures the attacker's wrist (9-B detail). **9-C two an**: immediately, defender bends the attacker's wrist toward her shoulder (knife points upwards; see detail) which takes her down on her knees **(9-D)**. **9-E three**: defender steps forward and then turns right 180° placing himself to the side of and slightly behind the attacker **(9-F)**. **9-G an**: defender gains control of the knife with his left hand by redirecting the knife down in the direction of the attacker's shoulder (9-G detail). **9-H four an**: defender leads the attacker down and pins her by placing his left knee over the shoulder blade area (wrist control is maintained). Using the handle end of the knife the defender assures control of the attacker by pressuring behind and below the ear (inset). Be gentle, a slight pressure of this area generates pain.

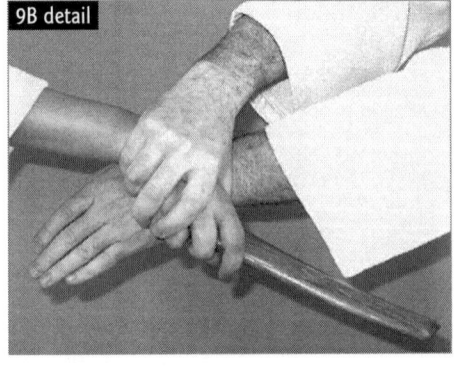

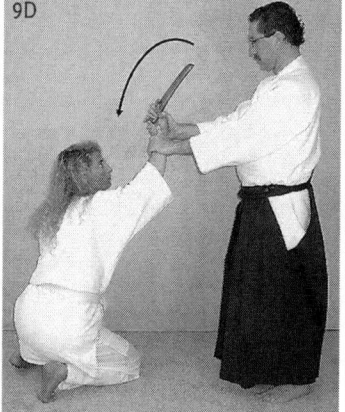
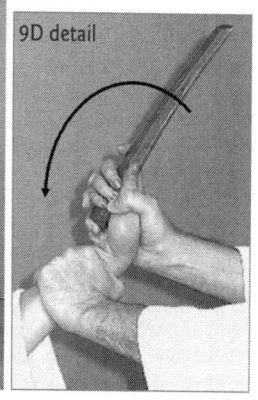
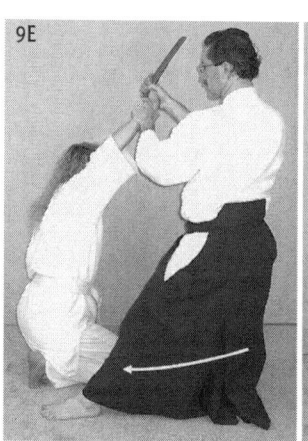

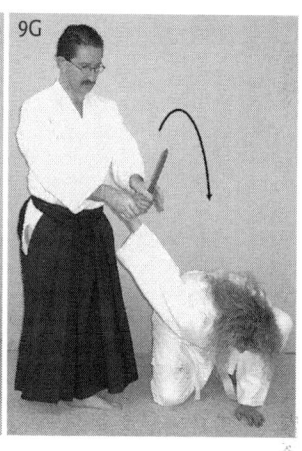
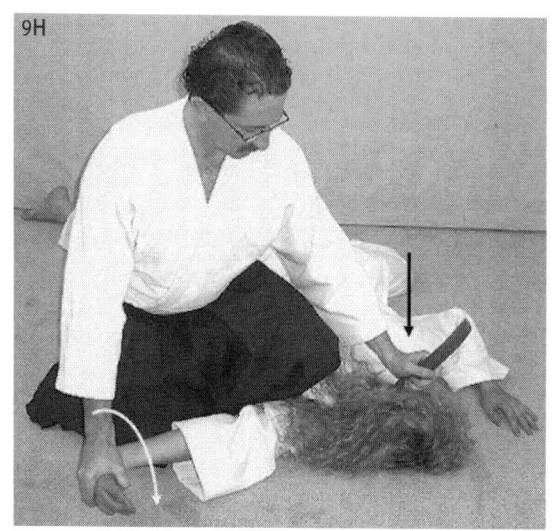
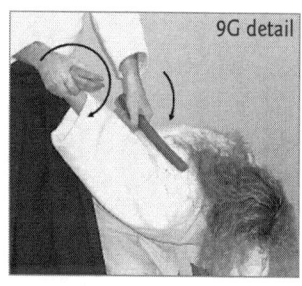
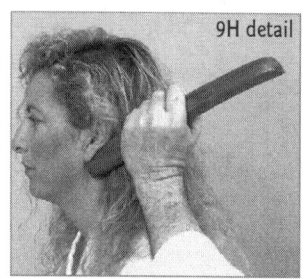

BREATHING EXERCISES

To discuss breathing in the context of rhythm, we must introduce another music notation element, the tie **(Figures 10-A-B)**. This symbol connects two or more notes together so that one sustains the note—therefore the sound—for a long period of time, e.g., like the continuous sound when an iron gong is struck **(Figure 10-C)**. Think of breathing as the sound of a gong which is rhythmically struck every sixteen seconds.

FIGURE 10A

| an 2 an 3 an 4 an | an 2 an 3 an 4 an | an 2 an 3 an 4 an | an 2 an 3 an 4 an

FIGURE 10B

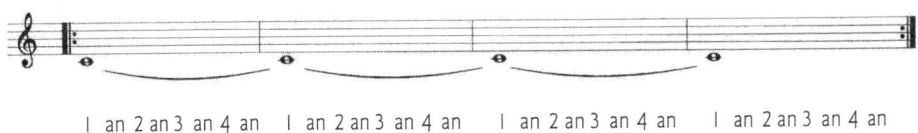

| an 2 an 3 an 4 an | an 2 an 3 an 4 an | an 2 an 3 an 4 an | an 2 an 3 an 4 an

FIGURE 10C

FIGURES 10 A-B-C

The tie lines symbolically connect notes together and indicates continuous sound. 10-A: Four quarter notes per measure are tied together (four measures). 10-B: Because a whole note is equal to four quarter notes (see Supplement), we can rewrite the passage in A using only whole notes. Aikido's breathing can be represented by music notation as the long-lasting sound from an iron gong (10-C), which is struck every sixteen seconds (see also Figure 11).

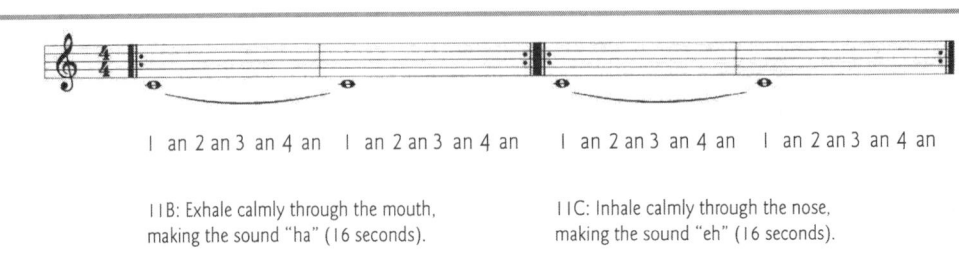

| an 2 an 3 an 4 an | an 2 an 3 an 4 an | an 2 an 3 an 4 an | an 2 an 3 an 4 an

11B: Exhale calmly through the mouth, making the sound "ha" (16 seconds).

11C: Inhale calmly through the nose, making the sound "eh" (16 seconds).

Practice breathing exercises in the following manner:

1. Set the metronome at 60 beats per minute.

2. Sit comfortably in an upright position, with the back straight as illustrated in **Figure 11-A**. Close your eyes.

3. Take in a deep breath of air (do this naturally with no effort at all!), open your mouth wide, placing your tongue behind your lower front teeth and begin to exhale calmly, making the sound "ha." When opening the mouth, try tipping the head slightly back, so that the jaw does not interfere with the airflow in the throat region (**Figure 11-B**). With practice and relaxation, you will be able to exhale for sixteen seconds, or more. This is analogous to the way a singer breaths.

4. Close your mouth, and gently begin inhaling through the tip of the nose. Try to listen to and feel the airflow deep inside the nasal cavity; the sound "eh" should be easily detectable (**Figure 11-C**). As with the exhalation, inhalation should last sixteen seconds, or more.

Rhythmic breathing is an essential aspect of aikido training. Practice sessions of 10 minutes before, between, or after intense bouts of physical activity. This will induce appropriate ventilation and efficient aerobic metabolism, which will improve your tolerance to endurance training. This method is based on relaxation. Do not hyperventilate!

MEDITATION

Meditation can be practiced in different ways. The method we recommend here is based on rhythm and works with almost anyone.

1. Set the metronome at 60 beats per minute. After a few sessions, you will probably want to slow it down to 40 or even 30 beats per minute.
2. Sit comfortably in the same upright position discussed in the breathing section of this article (above). Rest your hands palms up on your thighs and close to the knees. Close your eyes and breathe normally **(Figure 12-A)**.
3. Listen to the rhythm marked by the metronome and count in your mind "one an, two an, three an, four an," numerous times.
4. With each silent count, imagine feeling slight movements in your fingertips, like small contractions of the muscles which are perceptible but not necessarily visible (this will happen naturally). Starting with the left hand, match each count with the flexion of a specific finger, in the following order: "one an" will correspond to the index, "two an" to the middle finger, "three an" to the ring-finger, and "four an" to the little finger **(Figure 12-B)**. Ignore your thumb. Now, repeat the same routine with the right hand. Then, alternate left and right hands... Relax and free your mind of distracting thoughts, the key is to repeat this simple method over and over again.

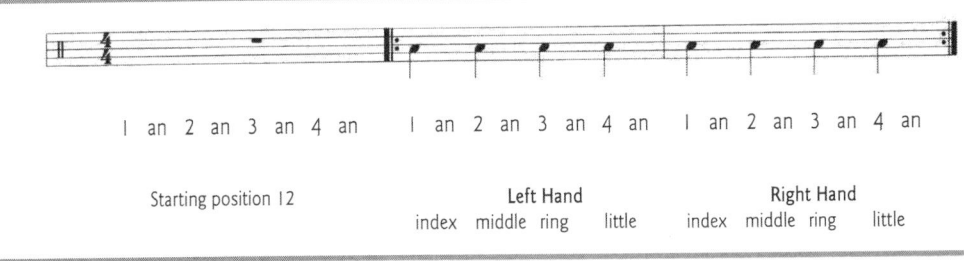

FIGURE 12:

Meditation (see text for details)

Meditation elicits what in scientific terms is known as the relaxation response, a state of mind-body interaction characterized by a reduced movement of the skeletal musculature, as well as decreased blood pressure and respiratory rate. Aikido practitioners meditate daily to calm their minds, concentrate their attention in complex mental/physical tasks, and minimize fatigue (by simply not thinking about it). Four elements are necessary to elicit the relaxation response: finding a quiet environment (this seems to be essential for beginners), consciously relaxing the body's muscles (e.g., physical relaxation while sitting), focusing for ten to twenty minutes on a "mental device" or constant stimulus repeated mentally (e.g., rhythmic counts that match the movements of your fingertips), and assuming an attitude of calmness, which includes disregarding distracting thoughts. With practice, only two of these elements become essential to elicit the meditative state: the mental device and a calm attitude.

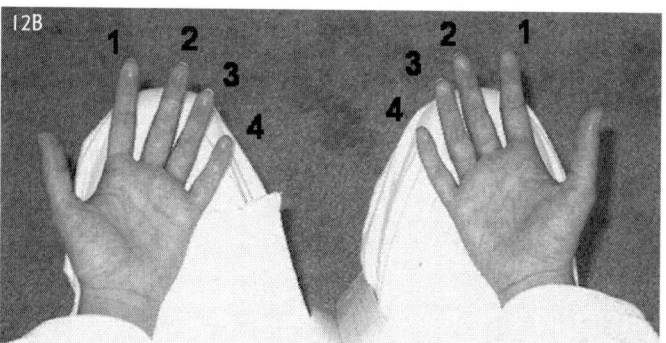

Concluding Remarks

Aikido implies a harmonious dialogue between the attacker and the defender. The defender must learn to detect the attacker's rhythm, match it, and blend with the intrinsic speed of the attack. Knowing when to pause and when to continue determines the outcome of this dialogue.

In this two-part article we have shown how music notation can help us "write" and understand the "rhythm" inherent to aikido. Keep in mind that aikido practitioners are just like musicians: at some point in their development they want to interpret aikido's rhythm in unique manners. Some learn to move fast, others emphasize motions in specific parts of a sequence (accentuating the expression of an "aikido note" or "pause"), and a few improvise by simplifying or prolonging the components of the "song". They all are, however, governed by the laws of physics that impose a natural pace to the movements of their common human anatomies.

Bibliography

Benson, H., Beary, J. & Carol, M. (1974). The relaxation response. *Psychiatry, 37*, 37–46.

Benson, H. (1975). *The relaxation response.* New York: Avon Books.

Curtis, C. (2001). *Ki-Aikido on Maui,* 3rd Ed. Maui, Hawaii: MAKS Publications.

Feldstein, S. & Black, D. (1990). *Alfred's beginning drumset method.* Van Nuys, California: Alfred Publishing Co.

Maruyama, K. (1984). *Aikido with ki.* Tokyo: Ki No Kenkyukai Headquarters.

Paz-y-Miño C.,G. & Espinosa, A. (2002). Dichotomous keys to fundamental attacks and defenses in aikido. *Journal of Asian Martial Arts, 11*(1), 8–27.

Paz-y-Miño C.,G. & Espinosa, A. (2002). Aikido: The art of the dynamic equiangular spiral. *Journal of Asian Martial Arts, 11*(4), 8–29.

Paz-y-Miño C.,G. & Espinosa, A. (2004). The rhythm of aikido, Part I. *Journal of Asian Martial Arts, 13*(2), 44–63.

Reed, W. (1992). *Ki: A road that anyone can walk,* 2nd Ed. Tokyo: Japan Publications.

Reed, W. (1999). *Ki: A practical guide for westerners,* 6th Ed. Tokyo: Japan Publications.

Shifflett, C. (1998). *Ki in aikido: A sampler of ki exercises.* Merrifield, Virginia: Round Earth Publishing.

Shifflett, C. (1999). *Aikido: Exercises for teaching and training.* Merrifield, Virginia: Round Earth Publishing.

Stewart, D. (1999). *The musician's guide to reading and writing music.* San Francisco, CA: Miller Freeman Books.

Tohei, K. (1962). *What is aikido?* Tokyo: Rikugei Publishing House.

Tohei, K. (1974). *This is aikido.* Tokyo: Japan Publications.

Tohei, K. (2001). *Ki in daily life.* Tokyo: Ki No Kenkyukai Headquarters.

Tohei, K. (2001). *The way to union with ki: Aikido with mind and body coordination.* Tochigi, Japan: Ki No Kenkyukai Headquarters.

Acknowledgments

We dedicate this article to Mark Rubbert, William Reed, Kashiwaya Koichi, and Andrew Tsubaki, who have inspired us to explore the fascinating complexity of Shin Shin Toitsu aikido (founder Koichi Tohei). Very special thanks to the St. Louis Ki Society and Kansas Ki Society members for continuous support and friendship. The material discussed in this article is not necessarily endorsed by Ki Society or any of its affiliates.

· 7 ·

Using Aikido Principles for Conflict Resolution In and Out of the Practice Hall
by Bryan Golden, B.A.

Harvey Konigsberg practicing aikido principles inside the dojo.
Photography by Sally Delmerico.

Introduction

This article is written to share personal experiences and perspective of aikido. The article is not intended as a technical discussion of aikido, but rather to show how lessons learned inside the training hall can be applied to conflict resolution in everyday life. Just as constant practice is required to develop into a competent martial artist, consistent repetition is needed to apply that art's principles for conflict resolution outside the training hall.

Although you may be a practitioner of a different martial art, the concepts and principles discussed here will be readily applicable to your style as well. All styles offer unlimited personal growth potential. To realize this potential, your primary motivation for practicing must be self-improvement rather than the acquisition of combative skill.

If one seeks personal development through training, martial arts practice should be a way of life. Martial arts training is ultimately learning to turn adversity to your advantage. Life inside and outside the training hall can and should compliment and reinforce each other.

Usually conflict is imposed on a person rather than being chosen, but in choosing to practice a martial art, the student intentionally places himself in a conflict filled situation where he learns his style's philosophy for conflict resolution. There is nothing within a specific style that makes it better or worse than another. Each style has its own particular approach. What does make a difference is the students' dedication and commitment to training and their willingness to apply their martial arts philosophy outside the training hall.

A truly accomplished martial artist radiates self-confidence that emanates from a realization that he doesn't need to prove anything or have to fight to win. A challenge doesn't obligate a martial artist to respond in kind. Although it's easy to imagine scenarios where martial arts techniques will produce a decisive victory, the epitome of self-development enables you to avoid such circumstances in the first place.

Conflict and the Human Condition

Conflict is a normal part of life. Each day presents challenges of varying difficulty. Every aspect of life has its own unique set of obstacles. There are family, friends, work, acquaintances, and strangers to deal with. No one else has exactly the same beliefs, opinions, and attitudes as you. So all interpersonal contact will have the potential for conflict.

When faced with conflict, it's easy to become emotional and lose sight of what is in your best interest. You will experience elevated levels of frustration and stress if you constantly try to force others to change. Any effort expended towards this end will typically be met with failure. Taking such a path will make each day feel like a conflict laden battle. You will feel more like a victim of fate than a master of your own destiny.

Outside the training hall, you have a great opportunity to put your martial arts training to work, and make your instinctive reaction to conflict the same as inside. Although conflict in the training hall is physical and conflict in society is typically not, the mental response in both situations should be the same. To fully experience all the benefits of martial arts training, the student needs to apply the principles both in and out of the training hall. Those principles can be applied equally to both physical and non-physical confrontations.

All too often, a student's attitude changes when he leaves the training hall. During practice, he is able to apply the philosophy of his particular martial art, but outside class, he becomes caught up in his usual mode of behavior and it seems as if all of his martial arts training goes out the window. He engages his opponent at the point of conflict in an attempt to overpower him. Not in the physical sense, but mentally.

Response to Conflict

Moreover, most of those with whom you contend outside of the training hall are people whom you will need to interact with long after the disagreement is forgotten. Can you win an argument by shouting louder and more wildly than the other person? Chances are that a screaming match will cause an argument to spin out of control and break off unresolved.

Even if you succeed in making an opponent do something because you are stronger or in a position of authority, you will elicit resentment and almost certainly create an adversary for future interactions. Most likely, after a confrontation is over, the other person will have nothing to do with you. You will soon be living as a hermit as you run out of people to interact with.

Suppose someone makes a grab at you. Most untrained people have an innate tendency, when engaged in conflict, to react with their mind and body at the point being attacked. When the mind is captured, the body locks up. All movement stops and their perceived range of options is reduced to breaking free. When this happens, your opponent has gained control.

In the training hall, the student trains to eschew anger when hit. All students experience being hit at some point. Sometimes, a blow is intentional, but often it's not. Ideally, the student doesn't get angry when hit. But this is not always the case. There are those students whose egos are easily bruised.

An ego can impede the student's progress. When he gets hit, his attitude changes. His reaction becomes heated and he loses track of his training. Although the behavior may remain within acceptable limits for the training hall, these types of students quickly earn a reputation as having low tolerance when techniques don't work perfectly.

A basic premise of aikido is redirecting an attacker's energy.

Ironically, the student who behaves in this manner is often more advanced with many years of training under their belt. He feels that with his higher level of training, he should always emerge from conflict unscathed. Training does not ensure that the student will never be hit. But it can help the student remain calm and maintain self-control in the face of adversity.

In the street, if an untrained person gets hit, he can become angry and irrational. If he manages to strike his opponent in return, without ending the confrontation, then the opponent will become more irate. The resulting punch, counter-punch exchange will not de-escalate a battle.

If an untrained person is stronger than his attacker, he may win the fight, perhaps even demolishing his opponent. Fortunately, there are few situations in life where the ruin of a foe is justified. Most conflict is not life and death, but even then, the repercussions of destroying another human being are always severe. Your ability handle an attack and limit damage is a combination of your fighting skill and mental attitude.

Skills that allow you to avoid physical or emotional injury, and turn an attack to your advantage, will serve for a lifetime. If you have a spectrum of responses available, ranging from barely perceptible to severe, you can match your response to the specific circumstances as required.

In any confrontation, avoidance, evasion, and escape without injury is the ideal strategy. With situations where there is no other option, you need the tactics and skills developed in the training hall. You can then apply appropriate techniques to the degree warranted by the nature of the attack.

Immobilizing an attacker without any blows.

Aikido Basics

The basic premise in aikido is the avoidance and redirection of an attacker's energy and intention. When applied correctly, aikido techniques demoralize an attacker. An attacker can find himself immobilized on the ground without experiencing any blows or force. Although aikido techniques appear to be simple, learning them requires a lot of repetition. Through constant practice, the student replaces bad ineffective habits with new potent techniques.

Aikido practice requires two partners who take turns being the attacker (*uke*) and defender (*nage*). There are no formal routines (*kata*). Aikido is non-competitive and there is neither victor nor vanquished. Both partners are learning from each other and striving to help one another.

As one attacks, the defender first moves off the line of attack and then redirects the attacker's energy and motion. The aggressor is at a disadvantage by initiating an attack. When attacking, one commits his energy and balance in one direction, taking his attention away from other dimensions. The aikido practitioner moves around the point of conflict and exploits the attacker's vulnerabilities. The harder one attacks, the more at risk he is.

An the attacker's movement can't necessarily be anticipated. Subsequently, the defender learns not to pre-plan a response. Instead, he trains to sense openings as they occur and move accordingly. In this way, the defender can survive in a constantly changing and unpredictable environment.

Each partner is responsible for the safety and well being of the other. The techniques being practiced are potentially devastating. The defender has an obligation to apply each technique in a manner that keeps the attacker safe. Over time, the aikido student develops an appreciation for just how effective redirecting an attack can be. This produces a sense of confidence that pervades one's being.

The spirit of cooperation and mutual learning that exists within the training hall doesn't necessarily occur outside it. Outside, an opponent doesn't have your well being in mind, yet always offers a lesson. Avoiding and reversing an attack requires that you remain calm, centered, and focused. If you feel a situation is hopeless, you will react accordingly. The aikido student learns that once an attack is initiated, he has many more options than the attacker. The student who realizes there are options and choices will never feel or act defeated.

The aikido student learns how to respond to all manner of attacks, from any direction. Advanced training involves learning tactics against multiple attackers. Defending against numerous attackers involves the same principles as defending against one. The critical ability is to neutralize one opponent at a time without becoming overwhelmed.

Tactical Advantage Conferred by Aikido Training

When a person's space is invaded by an opponent, their innate reaction is to become defensive and feel off balance. Your most productive strategy is not to engage or seek to vanquish an opponent bur rather move off the line of attack and redirect an attacker's energy. Especially when facing a tenacious, determined, and tricky adversary, your only option is to direct your movement to effect a positional advantage.

For example, what if someone tried to hit you and failed because you weren't there? He tried again and you seemed to disappear once more. The harder he tried to strike you, the more elusive you became. Since you are not being hit, you don't get upset and can continue to think clearly. Your opponent, on the other hand, is getting tired and frustrated. You retain a mental and tactical advantage while their thinking becomes clouded and endurance wanes. As this happens, you have the opportunity to throw or immobilize your antagonist.

When confronting conflict, you maintain your balance, position, and reaction. Although you can't force someone else to change, you can lead him. For example, when attacked with a punch, you move to the side and behind the attacker. To continue the aggression, an opponent must alter his tactics in response to your unexpected action. You have thus gained an advantage by causing the attacker to sacrifice his balance when he has to unexpectedly change direction. You are then in a position to end the attack by utilizing the attackers own momentum to bring him to the ground.

1) Redirecting the attacker's energy and motion.
2) Responding to conflict in an unpredictable way is the key to conflict resolution.
3) A foundation of aikido is that you only have control over your own movement.

An attacker serves as a formal challenge to your training in the practice hall, but outside, obstacles occur unexpectedly. There are situations where you will experience conflict despite the fact that there may have been no intention to engage you. Yet your reaction can be the same as if there were. When frustrated, it is normal to perceive the cause as a personal attack. To counter this, apply the principles of aikido and recognize the power you have over your response.

Imagine driving down an empty road. Ahead is a car stopped at an intersection. The car then pulls out right in front of you, forcing you to slam on your brakes. How do you react? If you get angry and start calling the other driver names, you have given him the power to control you. Although this response is common, it is unproductive and destructive. The other driver is probably in another world and not even aware of your presence. It's in your best interest to remain centered and not allow the incident to infect the rest of your day.

Encountering an obstacle is like walking down a path and tripping over a log you didn't see. Screaming at the log will have no positive effect. To avoid stumbling again, you must alter your course. For example, an accomplished sailor has no ability to change the wind or weather. Yet a sailor goes where he wants in virtually any condition. The sailor is skilled at adjusting the sails and steering the boat in response to prevailing conditions. As situations change, so does the sailor's actions. A sailor that refuses to adjust to circumstances, and alter his course when necessary, will not be sailing for very long.

4) Learn to move around conflict.
5) The harder the attack the more elusive you become.
6) Simple movement redirects attacker.

1) The very act of agression costs the attacker's balance.
2) Defense against multiple attackers.
3) Conflict becomes harmony.

Core Philosophies

There are a number of fundamental principles upon which aikido is built. As with many eastern philosophies, the essential beauty of these concepts is their simplicity and immortality. Although any one of these ideas could be the basis for an exhaustive dissertation, I want to provide you with a concise encapsulation that has daily relevance.

One of the foundation tenets of aikido is that while you have no control over someone else's actions, you do have total control over your own. You determine your reaction to conflict. No one can make you mad, sad, angry, irate, or anything else without your consent. By developing self-control, many problems and obstacles diminish in stature and become manageable, if not insignificant.

You determine your destiny and are responsible for where you are and what you do. It's easy and tempting to blame other people and circumstances for your situation, but no one else is responsible. The many options available to you become clear only when you accept responsibility for your situation.

Fight with your head, not your heart. If you allow an opponent to manipulate your emotions, you have lost the battle before it has begun. For example, anger will diminish your ability to clearly evaluate and select appropriate options. Once your opponent senses he has gotten under your skin, he will continue to push your buttons and your predicament will seem to degenerate.

Conflict can be diffused by doing the unexpected. You don't want your opponent to anticipate your actions. When someone yells—whisper. When someone frowns—smile. The expectation is that you will become upset when attacked. So don't become incensed by what others do. When you respond to anger with anger, it's akin to pouring gasoline on a fire.

4) A movement that redirects the attacker.
5) A more productive strategy is an approach that doesn't engage the conflict
6) When the mind is free the body responds.

Obstacles and challenges are an opportunity to practice your conflict resolution skills. There are no shortcuts; the more problems you master, the stronger you become. As your skill increases, you will be able to clear higher hurdles.

In the aikido tradition, a martial artist has a responsibility to never use his skills to dominate others or force situations. If he does, he will become a magnet for conflict and misery. The true martial artist strives to better all aspects of himself daily. Personal growth and development is a journey, not a destination. There is always room for improvement.

Treat everyone with respect. No one is above or below you. You never need to feel inferior nor should you ever make others feel that way. Don't hesitate to say you are sorry if you make a mistake. Ask people to assist you rather than barking out orders. You grow whenever you extend yourself to help others.

Be a humble, considerate, and receptive student for the lessons life has to teach. Become really skilled at applying fundamental strategies and daily frustrations will diminish. Your training hall has no entrance or exit for it is life itself.

Closing Remarks

Pursuing a martial art is a wonderful thing. The best martial artists are not necessarily the ones with the largest repertoire of techniques. Rather, a solid grounding in the basics and repetition to the point that the body's response becomes automatic, defines effectiveness. The same concept applies to everyday interpersonal conflict resolution.

The concepts presented in this article are intentionally fundamental. In my years as an aikido student and instructor, I have found that those who consistently incorporate the basics into their practice and their lives develop the most effective techniques. It's very easy to lose sight of simple solutions and erroneously search for complex resolutions to life's challenges. In aikido, the solutions to physical problems are to do less instead of more. The world is your training area. Practice daily. You are ever the student.

Acknowledgment
A special thanks to Mr. Harvey Konigsberg, 7th dan,
of Wood-stock Aikido, and to all who appeared
in the photographs in this article.

· 8 ·
Yoshimitu Yamada's Influence on Aikido in the West
by George Kennedy, M.A.

Yoshimitsu Yamada demonstrating Aikido at the World's Fair in New York City, 1964.

Yamada instructing at the Aikido Center of Atlanta, March 2005.

All photography courtesy of Yoshimitsu Yamada and George Kennedy, except where noted.

Introduction

In the spring of 1974, I attended my first aikido seminar. I was a young idealist with little more than one year's training under my white belt. The seminar was held at my home dojo in Atlanta, Georgia, under the direction of my teacher, Rodney Grantham. The guest instructors were Ueshiba Kisshomaru (son of aikido Founder Morehei Ueshiba) along with Yamada Yoshimitsu, and Mitsunari Kanai, both former disciples (*uchi deshi*) of the founder. There were approximately fifty people in attendance representing the entire southeastern region of the United States. Needless to say, we were all in awe of these Japanese masters who could effortlessly throw multiple attackers around while exuding an aura of calm serenity. We knew that we were especially fortunate to be affiliated with Yoshimitsu Yamada who had arranged for Ueshiba Kisshomaru's first visit to the continental U.S.

Yamada had arrived in the United States in 1964 to demonstrate this unknown art at the New York World's Fair and, gathering a handful of students, stayed to become Chief Instructor of New York Aikikai. A short time later he founded the United States Aikido Federation, which now encompasses over four hundred aikido schools in North and South America. Yamada still travels extensively, teaching in excess of thirty seminars per year in countries from the southern tip of South America to the northern reaches of the former Soviet Union.

In August of 2004, I joined with over one thousand other people from every continent of the world who gathered in upstate New York to celebrate Yamada's 40th year in the United States and his enormous contribution to the global spread of the art. This article is a short history of this one individual's impact on the spread of modern aikido from a relatively obscure, esoteric Japanese art to the world-wide phenomenon it has since become.

Aikido in Post-War Japan

In the years immediately following World War II, the practice of the martial arts was banned in Japan by the occupying forces under General Douglas MacArthur. Even after the ban was lifted, aikido was not well known even among most Japanese. Founded by Morihei Ueshiba, the aikido headquarters was one of the few buildings left standing in the Shinjuku area and was being used as shelter for neighbors left homeless by the war. Although the old wooden building has since been replaced by a more modern structure, the headquarters and Ueshiba's residence still occupy this space, one of the highest points in Tokyo.

Yamada demonstrating in Japan, circa 1959.

Gradually, as Japan began to rebuild, a new generation of students was attracted to the Ueshiba's teaching. The core group of these students, the live-in disciples or apprentices of the Founder, were to have a profound influence on the dissemination of aikido throughout the world. This group included Yoshimitsu Yamada, Mitsunari Kanai, Kazuo Chiba, and Seiichi Sugano. Foremost among those responsible for the growth of aikido worldwide is Master Yoshimitsu Yamada.

Yamada was born in Tokyo on February 17th, 1938, although he spent his early childhood during the war years outside of Japan. He lived in the town of Chinju, Korea, where his father was business manager of a mining company before returning to Japan. "I had a hard time when I came home [to Japan], but what could I do? It was war. I just looked at it positively: It was good for me." His father became a professor of business economics. Yamada describes his parents as "very unusual for Japanese at that time, being very liberal." He says his family never pressured him to go into business, aikido, or any other endeavor. "They respected individuality."

He was introduced to aikido at about the age of thirteen when he saw a demonstration by Ueshiba. Until then, he "knew nothing about it." Yamada's second cousin was Abe Tadashi, an early disciple of Morihei Ueshiba. "My father and he were cousins. However, my father's parents passed away when my father was seven years old. My father was adopted by Abe's family so I called him Uncle. Even though they were cousins, they were raised like brothers."

Yamada credits Abe Tadashi with being the first to introduce aikido to the west. "Abe's father respected Morihei Ueshiba and was supportive of him financially. Mr. Abe was very devoted to Morihei Ueshiba. I understand Abe was the first, even before Tohei [Koichi], to go overseas to introduce aikido, which was to France. At that time it was very difficult for Japanese people to go overseas. We were still under the American occupation and it was not easy to travel, but using his father's connections with certain VIP people, he was able to go. I think he had a very hard time because nobody knew what aikido was. In those days, like everyone else, he had to use judo people... Like it happened to me. In the U.S., I had to use judo and karate people in the beginning to do demonstrations. There was nobody else" (Bernath & Halprin, 1998).

Yamada had never had much interest in martial arts as a child; he was "just playing around, not serious," but when he graduated from high school in 1955, he felt that he "had better do something to straighten up my life. I was living the easy life and needed some discipline." In those days, not everyone could practice aikido, much less become a live-in student. "Just to practice, you had to have a good introduction [references]. In Japan at that time, aikido wasn't all that well known. Only a few people knew about it. They didn't advertise; there weren't any public demonstrations. I still remember the first public aikido demonstration because Morihei Ueshiba didn't give them permission to do that. I think [Kisshomaru Ueshiba, son of the founder] convinced Morihei Ueshiba that you have to show this to the public, but he didn't want to...in the old days, all the martial artists, they didn't want to show their technique to others...how to draw the sword, whatever...they didn't want to show just anyone. They would only teach certain students because they didn't want their enemies to see it. That's why in the old days, if you selected people to study, they had to have an introduction first. But that changed; just like our dojo was opened to the public. But not until then did we start to do public demonstrations...I think he [Morihei Ueshiba] had no choice. He had to make a living" (Bernath & Halprin, 1998).

Life as a Disciple of Morihei Ueshiba

Yamada relates that, because of his relation to Abe Tadashi, he had a "special connection" to Morihei Ueshiba and was immediately accepted. "It was a unique situation. My first day in aikido was my first day as *uchi deshi*. Other than me, they would come in like any other student and wait to get permission. At that time, although aikido was becoming more open to the public, there were only a few *uchi deshi*. When I joined, Arakawa [Sadateru] and Tamura [Nobuyoshi] were there, then myself, then Chiba [Kazuo], Kurita [Yutaka], Kanai [Mitsunari] and Sugano [Seiichi]" (Bernath & Halprin, 1998). There were many others in and out, but these are the ones I consider the real group. Sometimes others would come from branch dojo with an introduction to the Ueshiba family. Just like my dojo, sometimes people come, stay two, three months."

When asked if he had any stories about the other *uchi deshi*, Yamada said "Sure, a ton of them," but declined to share them for publication: "too personal." When asked if his cohort's personalities had changed over the years, he laughed and said, "Nah, still the same. They never change." Training as a live in student was quite rigorous, and the senior students engaged in a "weeding out" process that made it even more difficult. When asked how he was treated by his seniors when he started, Yamada replied emphatically, "bad!" Later he amends this statement, saying "They were nice. It was rough because it was so different from my lifestyle." [Judging from accounts by others who were *uchi deshi* at this time, Yamada's success in spreading aikido reflects not only his superior grasp of technique but also his considerable skill as a diplomat.]

"Already Tada [Abe Tadashi] and Yamaguchi [Seigo] had a regular class to teach, and I think Tamura [Nobuyoshi] too. At that time Tohei Koichi was the chief instructor. He went to Hawaii at about that time" (Bernath & Halprin, 1998). In a way, it was good because it was such a small community. Everyone knew everyone else. The dojo was an old wood building. It had a very good atmosphere. Morihei Ueshiba lived there. He had a house connected to the dojo." The daily routine of the *uchi deshi* was demanding. There were five classes per day. "We slept on the *tatami* [mats]. Morning class started at 6:30 so we had to be up earlier to open the gate for practice, cook, clean up inside the dojo and outside the Ueshiba family home. Of course we took care of the Ueshiba family too. The first class was taught by the late Kisshomaru Ueshiba, sometimes by the Founder when he was in Tokyo."

There were additional classes at 8:00 am, 3:00, 5:00, and 6:30 pm, the latter being the largest with "maybe 15 people" on the mat. "During the time in between regular classes there were many private lessons which people could buy with Morihei Ueshiba or Koichi Tohei. Every one of us had to be available for *ukemi* [break-falls] for those lessons" (Bernath & Halprin, 1998).

The white belt/black belt ranking system was already in place by this time. [There are five degrees of white belt and, theoretically, ten degrees of black

Author's note:

The Japanese term *uchi deshi* implies more than just being a live-in student. Although "apprentice" may be a rough English equivalent, the author has chosen "disciple" because of the deeply felt connection between these early students and the founder. No religious meaning is implied.

belt: in the original system, colored belts are not worn.] Yamada says, "I never took a test. You never ask for rank. You just wait for the master to say you are ready. Like the military, you don't decorate [promote] yourself… Unlike here [the U.S.A.] where sometimes people do!" Expressing shock that anyone would hint at gaining promotion Yamada says "people shouldn't say things like, 'just to remind you, I'm still 3rd dan.'"

Yamada enjoyed a close relationship with Morihei Ueshiba's son, Kisshomaru. While some have reported that Kisshomaru did not start training until fairly late in life, Yamada says this is not true. "He had to stop for a while because of World War II and later had to start a company to support his family, but he still came and trained at the dojo."

After approximately five years living in the dojo, Yamada got married, and moved out of the headquarters and into an apartment. He was still considered *uchi deshi* and was assigned teaching responsibilities at various universities and other branch clubs including teaching U.S. military personnel. Although he didn't travel a great deal with Morihei Ueshiba, he gained valuable teaching experience when he accompanied Kisshomaru on visits to other dojo throughout Japan.

During the war, the founder had moved to a small farm in Iwama prefecture where he built a training hall and shrine which was [and still is] maintained by the Saito family. When asked if he ever traveled to Iwama with Morihei Ueshiba, he replied, "Occasionally. I didn't like it. It's way out in the country. I'm more of a city guy. I wanted to stay in Tokyo." At one point, Yamada went through a period of doubt and actually stopped practicing for a short time. "I was young and had some questions. I thought maybe aikido was too sissified, you know? But I was wrong. It was a good education for me." Yamada was reluctant to discuss the specifics of how he became convinced of the art's effectiveness, saying with a wry smile, "I found out for myself that aikido is a powerful martial art."

Living with Morihei Ueshiba: "You Have to Steal the Technique"

Morihei Ueshiba was, of course, a very religious person. A devout follower of the Omoto-kyo faith, his religious beliefs certainly influenced his development of the strong moral and ethical foundation for which aikido is known. By most accounts, he never discussed technique, and most of his lectures were esoteric to the point of being almost incomprehensible. He began each day with ritual purification, chanting and prayer. According to Yamada however, "Although he was a very religious person, he never forced us to do the same. I don't think I would have stayed if he did."

Over the years, there have been many stories told about Ueshiba's supposed supernatural powers. When asked about Morihei Ueshiba's abilities to perform miraculous feats, Yamada states, "I'm not denying that he was a special person, but some stories just go too far. I don't like that." When pressed to give an example of a supposed miracle, Yamada was reluctant. "I don't want to make anyone mad."

However, he did relate that Morihei Ueshiba once found something which had been lost, saying that the Gods told him where to find it. "I thought it was cute." (Yamada keeps his own spiritual beliefs to himself and has always taken a very secular, technical approach to the art. He rarely discusses *ki* for example, allowing the power evident in his technique to speak for itself.)

Contrary to the popular myth that Morihei Ueshiba always exuded a saint-like demeanor of kindness and patience, he apparently also "sometimes showed his temper." According to Mitsunari Kanai, Morihei Ueshiba "had a voice like thunder!" When asked if Morihei Ueshiba was ever angry at him, Yamada said "sure, over small things. I didn't understand why he was mad. It happened, then it was over. That was what was good about him. He would just scream at me and that's it. It was over."

Regarding Morihei Ueshiba's technical skills, Yamada says, "He was in the later stage of his life when I met him and so his technique was very soft. Yet, for his age, he had a lot of movement which I liked. He used to say 'everyday my technique changes.' It is important not to take advantage of this and think that aikido has to be soft. That is not correct. If we have strong fundamentals and train very hard, *then* when we get older, our technique becomes mature, but not sloppy. This is so misunderstood. Sometimes people say, for example, Morihei Ueshiba never taught you hip throws so it should not be part of aikido, but they are just looking at the later part of Morihei Ueshiba's life. It's just an excuse. No matter what, still we are doing *budo*. It should be more positive, less brutal, but it is still budo." According to Yamada, Morihei Ueshiba never explained "the technical aspect" of aikido. "The way of teaching in the old days, the teacher didn't explain the technique. You had to steal it from the teacher. That's my philosophy too. I don't force a student to do exactly what I do. It's not possible. I just show the movement. You have to learn it, digest it. Unfortunately, students copy mostly the bad habits of the instructor anyway. It's funny. I wish they would copy the good parts."

Early Days in New York

Yamada came to the U.S. in 1964 partially for the purpose of demonstrating aikido at the Japanese pavilion of the New York World's Fair. "Originally, Tohei Koichi was going to be with me at the fair to do some aikido demonstrations, but he had an accident and couldn't come." Contrary to popular belief, Yamada was not sent by Morihei Ueshiba or the Headquarters. "That never happened" he said. "It was totally

Yamada at the New York Aikikai, circa 1973. *Photograph courtesy of Alicia Billman-Cordero.*

our choice. I always wanted to live in New York. I knew that New York was my kind of town. It was exactly the same as I thought it would be. I'm the kind of guy who adjusts very easily. I grew up with American culture, you know, music: Pop and Jazz, American movies… so it was nothing new to me. I don't think I'd have lasted this long here if I didn't love New York City." Leaving his wife and children in Japan for the first few years, Yamada lived in the New York Aikikai, again living a spartan lifestyle. Because he had come to the U.S. under a "cultural" visa, Yamada had a very difficult time with the immigration authorities. After bringing his family to the U.S., he was forced to return them to Japan for several years. Because of his visa restrictions, he was not even able to return to Japan for Morihei Ueshiba's funeral in 1969 for fear that he would not be allowed back into the U.S. Yamada expresses considerable regret concerning leaving his family. "I feel bad about my family. I don't have too many memories with the kids. We were separated and after they came back, I was busy and we weren't as well off as we are now. I couldn't just take them everywhere I went. That's my one big regret—the time I missed with my family" (Bernath & Halprin, 1998).

"In the early days, all of the students were ex-judo and ex-karate players. They were the only people who were interested." Many, if not most martial arts practitioners in the U.S. during the 1950's and early 60's, were former military personnel who had been exposed to the arts during post-war tours of duty in the orient. In aikido these pioneers included the aforementioned Rodney Grantham who had begun training in judo in 1950, achieving his black belt while stationed in Japan during the Korean War. Grantham founded the "Black Belt School of Judo" in Atlanta during the 1960's. He was first exposed to aikido when offered the opportunity to take falls for the legendary Koichi Tohei. He soon gave up judo altogether to study aikido under Yamada. In 1967 he founded the Aikido Center of Atlanta which is still in daily operation.

"We didn't advertise publicly. There were taijiquan people too. About that time, karate had started to boom. I had good relations with all of the American karate teachers, so every time they had a tournament, they always invited me to come and demonstrate at Madison Square Garden and other places. Almost every week they invited me. Of course they didn't pay me, but it was a good opportunity to spread aikido… That's why I don't like to do demonstrations anymore. I did so many, I'm sick of them. Just too much. But then we would go at any opportunity. I once demonstrated on the streets of the South Bronx, on the concrete. It was winter time so I wore black gloves. I remember this guy was saying like, "Oh! He's a killer! He's got the black gloves" (laughter)! At that time lots of people had crazy ideas about the martial arts. You know, they would copy Bruce Lee from the TV series [Green Hornet] he had." That show helped a lot to bring the martial arts popularity, more interest. I put a demonstration together with another guy, that movie star… he plays a Texas Ranger now…

Yes, that's right: Chuck Norris. Nice guy. We did a demonstration at the New York Hilton one time. He likes aikido" (Bernath, 1998).

There were only a "handful" of students practicing aikido in New York at that time including current USAF president Mike Abrams. Abrams, who now holds the rank of 7th dan, remembers, "We used to ask Yamada all kinds of intelligent questions like—What do you do if you're attacked by six guys on horseback with machine guns?—you know, intelligent stuff like that" (Abrams, 1994).

Growth of Aikido

From the moment he arrived in the USA, Yamada traveled a great deal teaching seminars and helping fledgling dojos get started. "Even then I traveled a lot. I went to Boston every Monday before Kanai [Mitsunari] came." (Kanai arrived in the USA several years after Yamada. He became Chief Instructor of the second oldest aikido school on the east coast, the New England Aikikai. Kanai passed away in 2004.) As dojos began to spring up along the east coast, Yamada began to travel more and more. "Not flying, like now. In those days Greyhound bus was my transportation." Yamada would travel by bus from New York to Atlanta to teach at Rodney Grantham's dojo. Yamada would then proceed on to Titusville, Florida, to teach at the school of another aikido pioneer, Dr. Tom Walker. An early student of New York Aikikai, Alice Billman Cordero (now 5th dan) remembers, "We would all pile into somebody's old car and drive to Connecticut in a snow storm. It was all very small in those days. Everyone knew everyone else. I was only a teenager and [Yamada] would escort me home on the subway to make sure I got home safe" (personal correspondance, 2003).

Over the years, Yamada's influence has left an indelible imprint on the art worldwide. His seminar schedule takes him to the far reaches of the globe, sometimes teaching two separate seminars in the same weekend. In 1996, the South American Aikido Federation (Federacion Latino Americana de Aikido) was formed with the approval of Yamada, bringing the combined membership of his organizations into the thousands. Throughout it all, he has remained focused on maintaining high standards of technical expertise while shepherding the growth of aikido throughout the world. Speaking about his role in aikido's growth, Yamada says: "I didn't know what it would be like. It was nice to have a small community, but I knew it wouldn't last forever. Now I am happy to see so many people involved. It's a good art. It's beneficial for the practitioners' life, so it's a good accomplishment, I think."

When asked about the quality of aikido now compared with the early days, he replies, "Because aikido is so individual, so personal, it depends on how each instructor sees it, so it is very difficult to keep a high standard… but I try. Aikido is different around the world because of the different mentality of each country. It is so difficult to try to keep everyone together. I try, but I don't know if I am doing a good job or not. Whenever you get so many people together you have problems, you have conflict. As a leader, I have to have a very flexible mind. Basically, I respect each individual no matter who they are. My philosophy is you must have trust, respect, and fairness, that's the most important thing for both the teacher and student."

TECHNICAL SECTION

Sixth-dan George Kennedy, helps spread the aikido style of Yamada in Atlanta, Georgia.

Kennedy blocks and evades a punch while simultaneously delivering a strike to the attacker's head. He quickly flows into a wrist and elbow lock, bringing the attacker to the floor
Photographs courtesy of Jeremy Wojcik.

Special thanks to Barry Kellerman, Aaron MacNeil, Ted Banta, Patrick Hardesty and Skip Chapman for assisting in the technical section.

George Kennedy side-steps out of the way from a strike, immediately unbalancing the attacker to throw him backwards to the ground. *Photographs courtesy of Jeremy Wojcik.*

Yamada demonstrating at the Aikido Center of Atlanta, March 2005.
Photographs courtesy of Jeremy Wojcik.

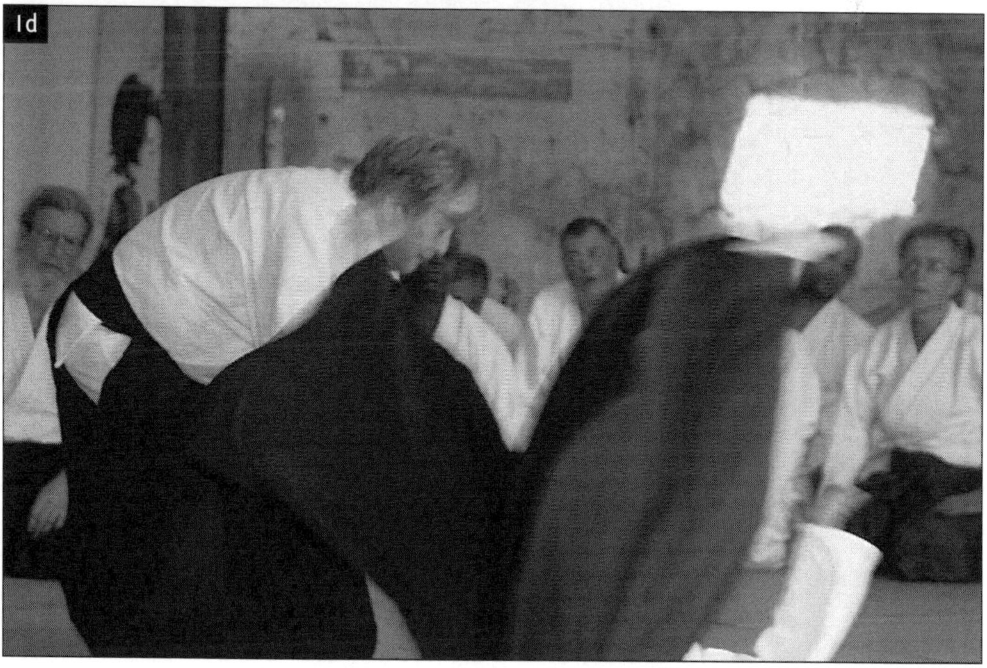

Yamada demonstrating at the Aikido Center of Atlanta, March 2005.
Photographs courtesy of Jeremy Wojcik.

References

Graham, M. (1994). *New York Aikikai's 30th anniversary: Past, present and future.* [video].
Bernath, P., and Halprin, D. (1998). Inside Aikido: Interview with Yamada Yoshimitsu. *Aikidoonline Magazine.* Available: www.aikidoonline.com.

· 9 ·

Optical Illusions in Aikido

by Guillermo Paz-y-Miño C., Ph.D. & Avelina Espinosa, Ph.D.

Photographs courtesy of A. Espinosa and G. Paz-y-Miño C.

Does the rim along the edge of this tatami mat appear to you as a straight line? It looks curved to me. Is it not true that if you extend this line out indefinitely, it will circle the Earth and come back to itself? Then it must be curved.

—Koichi Tohei (Reed, 1992: 296)

Introduction

Optical illusions are misleading images that deceive the visual perception of shape, size, color, or motion. Illusory visual stimuli make us believe we are seeing something that is not there or is not happening. The gentle and relaxed manner with which an aikido practitioner throws a partner creates the impression that no force has been involved in the technique. This is because the human eye tends to not see the entire sequence of the technique, but only its most conspicuous component (i.e., an opponent falling). Efficiency in causing imbalance, applying leverage, and using gravity (force) are the secrets of this "magic."

Aikido (*aiki* = harmony, *do* = path, the way of) is rich in optical illusions. They interfere with our perception of a throw, causing confusion in class and frustration in students and instructors. Here we discuss how illusory visual stimuli distort our interpretation of a variety of aikido routines, including rolling and falling, partnered neutralization techniques, projections-throws, and weapons. By dissecting the components of aikido routines, we can identify and understand the sources of the illusions. This can help us improve the methods for teaching aiki principles.

In this article, we divide aikido's optical illusions in two broad categories, static and dynamic. To comprehend the complexity of aikido's most deceiving and common illusions, the dynamic ones, we must first discuss the static illusions. We recommend that students and instructors follow this approach.

Static Illusions

Static illusions can be attributed to errors in perceiving contrast, size, orientation, or any combination of these variables. Below we provide three examples:

1) size-contrast
2) orientation-contrast, and
3) size-orientation-contrast illusions.

An example of size-contrast illusion is shown in Figure 1, where two identical calligraphies of the character *ki* (= life energy, spirit of harmony) are surrounded by four smaller (A) or larger (B) examples of the same character. For the observer, it appears that the calligraphy within the small symbols is larger than that within the large symbols. An even more impressive example of size-contrast illusion is depicted (C-D). When the human eye sees two mirror images of an aikido practitioner holding a wooden staff (*jo*), the attention is focused on the staff. If the practitioner keeps his arm bent (C), this creates the illusory effect of shortening the staff. In contrast, when his arm is extended (D), this has the effect of lengthening the staff. The illusion results from a misinterpretation of the staff's length (size) due to the position of the aikido practitioner in respect to the staff and the flexion or extension of his arm. An analogous example of this type of illusion is shown in Figures E–F.

Figure 1
Size-contrast illusions

The two calligraphies surrounded by four smaller (A) or larger (B) characters are identical.

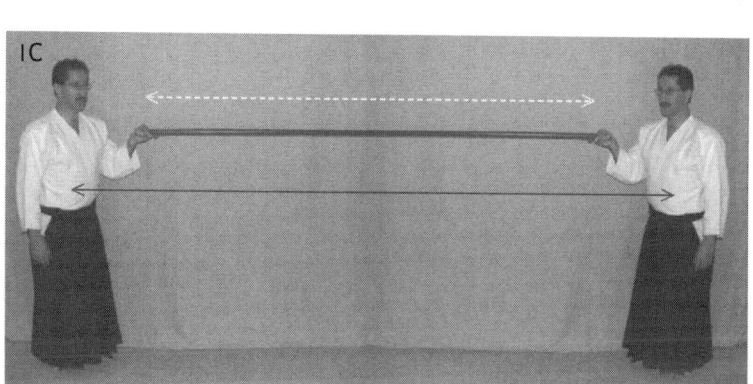
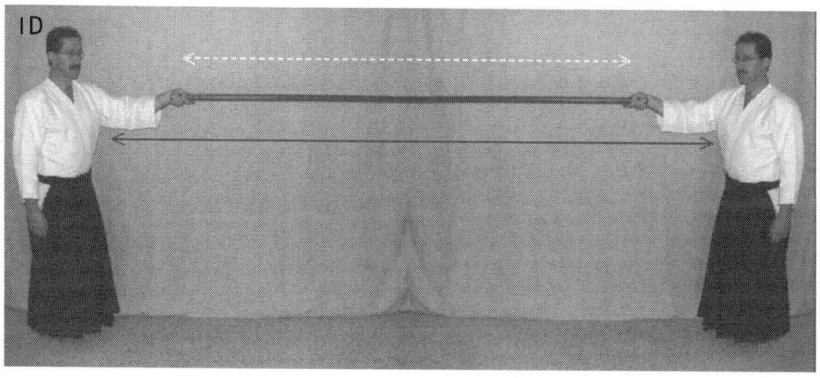

The length of the staff held by the aikido practitioner in the two mirror images (C-D) is the same (dashed line), but the position of the practitioner with respect to the staff differs (solid line) as a consequence of flexing or extending his arm.

The demonstration is simple yet powerful (E-F): when the practitioner holds the staff with his arms close to the body, the staff looks shorter than when he keeps his arms wide open. Although the length of the staff never changes (dashed line), the position of his arms does (solid line). In all these cases, the scale and distribution of the elements in the surrounding environment interfere with the perception of size.

An example of orientation-contrast illusion is illustrated in Figure 2. In this case, various wooden staffs (jo) are arranged equidistant and parallel to each other, while wooden knives cross them in opposite directions. This contrasting orientation of lines creates the illusion that the staffs merge near their ends.

Examples of size-orientation-contrast illusions are presented in Figure 3. The two suzu bells (A) (used for vigorous aikido chanting) are identical. However, the orientation of the lines in the background makes the bell on the left look larger than the one on the right. The three photographs of an aikido practitioner standing and holding a staff (B) are also identical, but the background creates the illusion that the one furthest away is the biggest. Finally, the arrangement of two wooden swords (bokkens) within two diverging staffs gives the impression that the upper sword is longer than the lower one (C).

Figure 2 Orientation-contrast illusion

The opposite orientation of the wooden knives (*tanto*) in respect to the staffs creates the illusion that the staffs merge near their ends.

Figure 3 Size-orientation-contrast illusions

The orientation and arrangement of the lines in the background give the impression that the suzu bells (A) and the photographs of the aikido practitioner (B) differ in size.

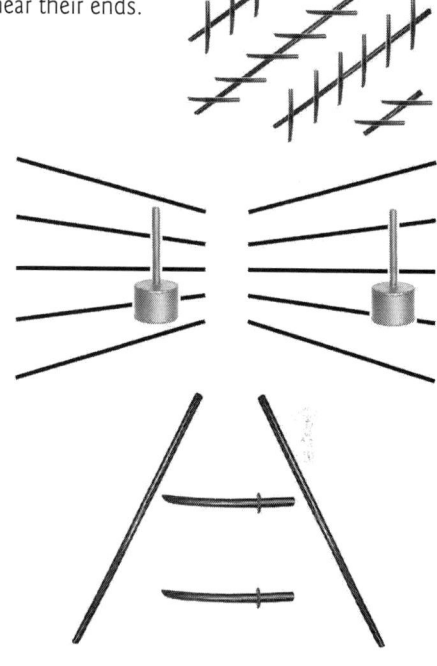

A similar illusory effect emerges when two wooden swords are arranged within two diverging staffs (C).

Dynamic Illusions

Dynamic optical illusions are also caused by errors in perceiving contrast, size or orientation, but these illusory visual stimuli emerge only when these variables interact in motion. Some illusions, for example, suggest movement of a stationary practitioner as a result of the motion of others around him. There are scenarios in which two or more practitioners move with similar velocities, however their speed can be perceived as different; moreover, if two practitioners move at the same speed, it may seem like the one performing the technique remains still while his partner is moving. Dynamic illusions arise from the interaction of the practitioners' kinetic patterns (unique to the human anatomy), with their relative speed of movement while executing a technique and the features of the environment (contrast, size, and orientation of objects; light, depth, and texture of the background; even sounds and/or noise can interfere with the perception of movement).

Aikido techniques include a complex combination of apparently independent movements in a three dimensional environment. The instructor usually performs all these "independent" components with accuracy and blends them into harmonious motions. Because the human eye captures the most conspicuous element of this blend, the student inadvertently disregards details. His visual perception of the instructor's performance is incomplete and illusory. Student and instructor are usually unaware of this phenomenon. Since the illusion is not conceptual but perceptual, knowing that the effect is illusory does not diminish the strength of the illusion. Shortly, student and instructor develop a negative feedback loop: the young practitioner continues to mimic only the most conspicuous element of the routine while the instructor struggles to communicate the important details within the entire technique. The illusion corrupts the correct understanding of those details because, in numerous cases, the student cannot even see them. At the end, student and instructor agree that only long-term training and arduous physical workout will take care of the problem.

We believe that this difficulty can be minimized, not by blindly fighting against the strength of the illusion (i.e., via long-term physical workout until the body, not the mind, finds the answer to the problem), but rather by consciously acknowledging its existence. Here are a few tips that can help you achieve this goal.

1. Assume that all aikido techniques include one or more optical illusions.
2. Acknowledge that when watching a technique the illusions emerge when the movements of the one-point (hara) "central point," or the body's center of equilibrium (located about two inches below the navel), interact with movements of the upper limbs (the "details," above). If the body moves up/down (by squatting), rotates (by turning), or shifts (by stepping), the arms will also move in these directions. In physical terms, this is true even if the practitioner never moves the joints of his arms. Why? Because the body cannot move without taking the limbs with it!
   In consequence, subtle motions of the arms, which are characteristic of aikido arts, will appear huge to the observer's eye given that they are enhanced by the motions of the one-point. The observer will tend to exaggerate and/or distort these or any other movement linked to the motions of the one-point.
3. Make sure you understand the movements of the one-point and the movements of the upper limbs separately before attempting to blend them.
4. Be critical about yourself and allow others to correct you. They should also be aware of the potential existence of illusions.
5. Be sensitive with yourself and others. Remember that, like viewing a magic trick repeated numerous times, knowing that a visual effect is illusory does not diminish the strength of the illusion. Below we provide examples of how dynamic illusions distort our interpretation of a variety of aikido arts. Each figure includes a detailed description of how to perform the routines. "Incorrect" execution of a technique or parts of a technique is indicated.

Figure 4

Forward roll from a formal sitting posture (seiza)

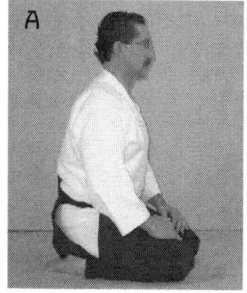

Starting position: formal sitting posture (A). Raise your body up and "throw" yourself into a forward roll (B). Continue rolling (C-D).

Slow down and prepare yourself to "knee walk" (E-F). The optical illusion makes the observer believe the practitioner quickly curls the body to execute the roll (incorrect B) and tries to stand up as soon as the back touches the mat (incorrect C).

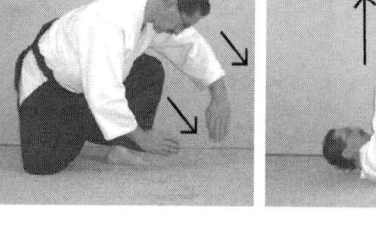

Incorrect-B   Incorrect-C

The early curling of the body compromises the entire technique preventing the practitioner from finishing the roll (incorrect E). The roll should be big, long, and forward, however, the student sees it as small, short, and compressed.

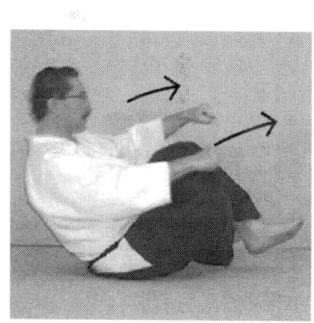

Incorrect-E

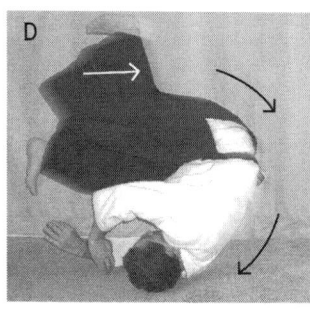
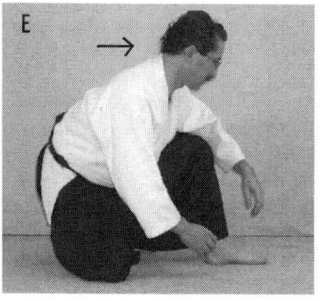

Figure 5
Three-palms-up lock

 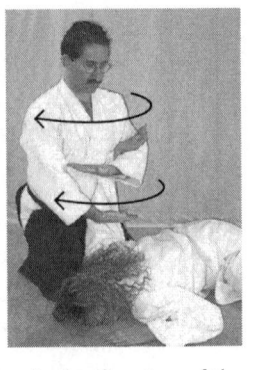

Incorrect-A

This lock relies on complex angular trajectories applied to the arm: one in the direction of each of the practitioner's hands (down and in), and another in the direction of the attacker's shoulder (see three arrows). These trajectories converge into a major center—the attacker's shoulder. The optical illusion misleads the interpretation of the technique, making the observer believe that the practitioner is turning his torso to his right (incorrect A), which actually frees the attacker or, even worse, injures her shoulder rather than simply restricting her movement.

Figure 6
Wrist lock

Incorrect-A

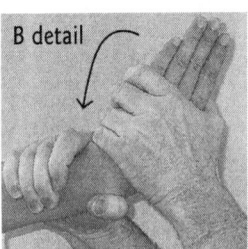 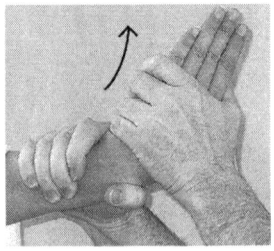

Incorrect-B

Keep the attacker's fingers pointing up and bend the attacker's wrist toward the one-point (A-B). The trajectory of the technique, which connects the wrist with the elbow, shoulder and one-point, forces the attacker to kneel. To the observer, it appears as if the practitioner is lifting the attacker's arm and projecting it over her head (incorrect A), which leads to a loss of control of the lock (incorrect B) and of the entire technique.

Figure 7
Lateral projection from
a formal sitting posture

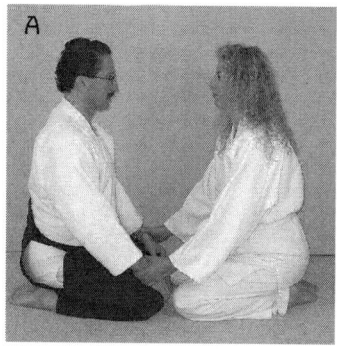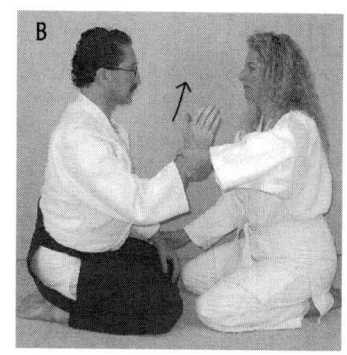

Attacker (right) performs a two-handed wrists grab (A). Defender (left) moves his right hand upwards, fingertips pointing to the sky (B). Defender's left hand mirrors the initial motion of the right hand and then he leads the attacker out and back down to her rear diagonal side (C). The defender's right knee rises up and he twists the attacker's wrist with his right hand at the same time that the left hand addresses the direction of her movement. Attacker turns completely over her hip and does a break fall (C).

Incorrect-B

The optical illusion in this technique is strong. It looks as if the defender pushes the attacker backwards (incorrect B) and attempts to walk over her (incorrect C). The successful execution of this throw relies on the rotation of the attacker's body, which is centered down and very close to the defender's right knee.

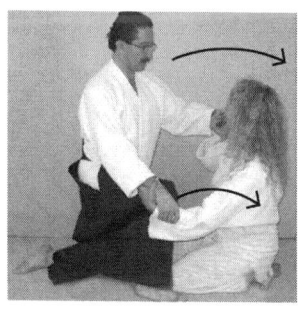

Incorrect-C

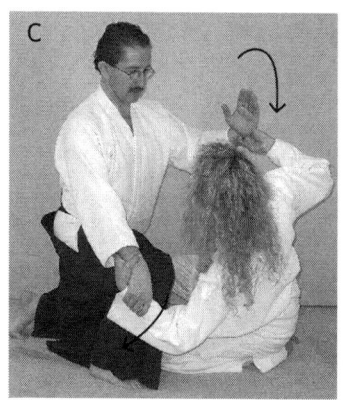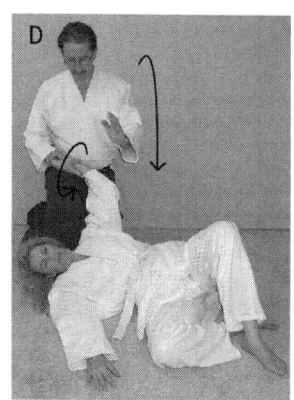

Figure 8

Harpoon throw

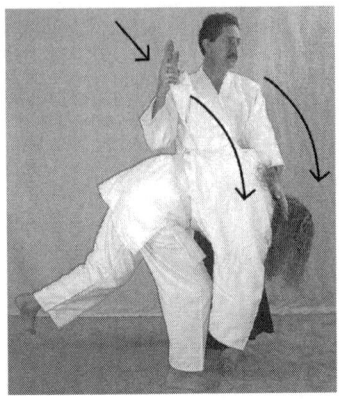

Incorrect-A

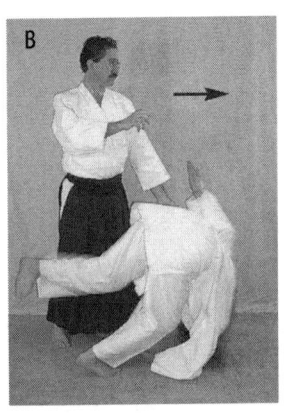

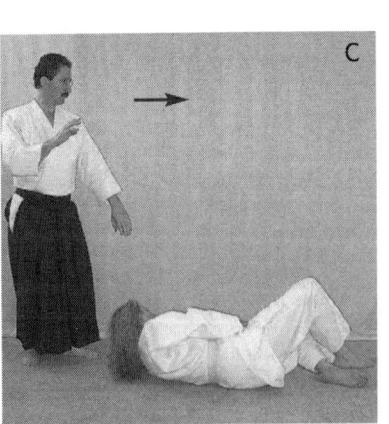

The practitioner (standing) leads the attacker into a stooped position (A) before projecting her into a forward roll (B) and a break fall (C).

The projection is gentle and parallel to the ground. However, the optical illusion makes it appear as a rough downward throw against the mat, mostly energized by the practitioner pushing the attacker with his arm (incorrect A).

The impressive power of this technique is generated by the movement of the practitioner's entire body (not his arm!) since he steps forward while leading the student in the same direction.

Figure 9

Wrist-bent-toward-shoulder throw

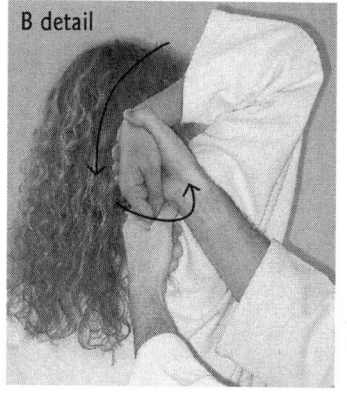

Incorrect-A

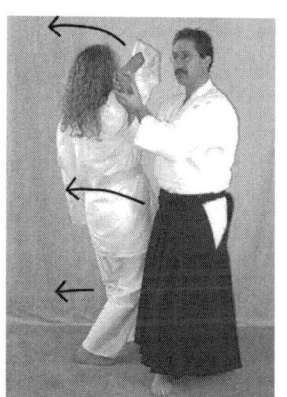

The practitioner (right) bends the attacker's wrist toward her shoulder (A-B), leading her to sit (C) or projecting her backward down onto the mat (D). To the observer, it appears as if the practitioner is walking forward (incorrect A), projecting the attacker's wrist over her head, and throwing her far away from him. The technique, however, takes place within the practitioner's individual space, with no significant walking, but with subtle squatting.

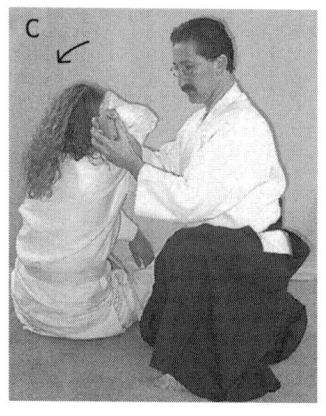

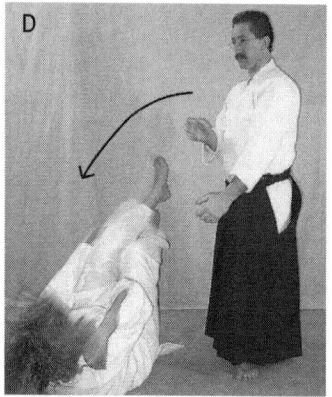

Figure 10

Neutralization of a thrust attack with a knife (tanto)

Incorrect-D Incorrect-E

Attacker (left) thrusts the knife toward the defender's abdomen (A-B). Defender redirects the attack slightly down and out at the same time that he secures the attacker's wrist (C detail). Defender bends the attacker's wrist toward her shoulder (D), which takes her down on her knees (E; knife points upwards, see detail F). Because the attacker kneels leaving her hand up, it appears to the observer as if the defender lifts the knife and projects it over the attacker's head (incorrect D-E). The lock is secure only if the attacker's wrist is firmly redirected down and toward her one-point.

Figure 11

Cut with knife (tanto), sword (bokken) and staff (jo)

The vertical cut with an open hand is identical to the cut with a knife, sword or staff (A-B-C). Since the weapon is an extension of the body, the adjustments to the length of it are important, but should not compromise the correct motion.

Because the aikido practitioner focuses his sight on the horizon while cutting with a weapon (D-E), it appears to the observer as if he is throwing the weapon forward trying to reach a distant target (incorrect D-E). In reality, the cut is close to the practitioner's body and directed to the ground even though his eye vector and intention converge on the horizon.

Incorrect-D

Incorrect-E

Concluding Remarks

To expedite the learning process, aikido's magic should be revealed to all students. In this way, students will understand critically and analytically the logic of aikido. They will also become efficient and independent in their development. Since errors in visual perception are universal to the eye, optical illusions might not be exclusive to aiki arts. Like aikido, other martial disciplines that rely on throws and projections can hide optical illusions in their forms. Throws and projections are based on equiangular (spiral) trajectories, with continuous wide rotations of the one-point. Combined with arm movements, these can create illusions. Striking arts, in contrast, emphasize on rotations of the one-point and linear blows, which communicate less confusing information to the eye (linear, of course, in relative terms). With this article, we hope that we have generated an awareness of some intrinsic difficulties in learning and teaching aikido principles, and we have suggested strategies to deal with them.

Bibliography

Carlson, T., Schrater, P. & He, S. (2006). Floating square illusion: perceptual uncoupling of static and dynamic objects in motion. *Journal of Vision* 6, 132–144.

Curtis, C. (2001). *Ki-Aikido on Maui*, 3rd Ed. Maui, Hawaii: MAKS Publications.

Gillam, B. (1980). Geometrical illusions, pp. 87-94. In *Scientific American The Mind's*

Eye. New York: W. H. Freeman and Company.

Goodale, M. & Humphrey, G. (1998). The objects of action and perception. *Cognition, 67*, 181–207.

Gregory, R. (1997). Knowledge in perception and illusion. *Philosophical Transactions of the Royal Society London B, 352*, 1121–1128.

Maruyama, K. (1984). *Aikido with ki*. Tokyo: Ki No Kenkyukai Headquarters. Paz-y-Miño C., G. & Espinosa, A. (2002). Dichotomous keys to fundamental attacks and defenses in aikido. *Journal of Asian Martial Arts, 11*(1), 8–27.

Paz-y-Miño C., G. & Espinosa, A. (2002). Aikido: the art of the dynamic equiangular spiral. *Journal of Asian Martial Arts, 11*(4), 8–29.

Paz-y-Miño C., G. & Espinosa, A. (2004). The rhythm of aikido: Part I. *Journal of Asian Martial Arts, 13*(2), 44–63.

Paz-y-Miño C., G. & Espinosa, A. (2004). Music principles applied to aikido techniques: Part II. *Journal of Asian Martial Arts, 13*(3), 64–81.

Plodowski, A. & Jackson, S. (2001). Getting to grips with the Ebbinghaus illusion. *Current Biology 11*(8), R304–R306.

Reed, W. (1992). *Ki: A road that anyone can walk*, 2nd Ed. Tokyo: Japan Publications.

Reed, W. (1999). *Ki: A practical guide for westerners*, 6th Ed. Tokyo: Japan Publications.

Schlag, J. & Schlag-Rey, M. (2002). Through the eye, slowly: Delays and localization errors in the visual system. *Nature Reviews Neuroscience 3*, 191–200.

Shifflett, C. (1998). *Ki in aikido: A sampler of ki exercises*. Merrifield, Virginia: Round Earth Publishing.

Shifflett, C. (1999). *Aikido: Exercises for teaching and training*. Merrifield Virginia: Round Earth Publishing.

Smeets, J., Brenner, E., De Grave, D. & Cuipers, R. (2002). Illusions in action: Consequences of inconsistent processing of spatial attributes. *Experimental Brain Research 147*, 135–144.

Tohei, K. (1962). *What is aikido*. Tokyo: Rikugei Publishing House.

Tohei, K. (1974). *This is aikido*. Tokyo: Japan Publications.

Tohei, K. (2001). *Ki in daily life*. Tokyo: Ki No Kenkyukai Headquarters.

Tohei, K. (2001). *The way to union with ki: Aikido with mind and body coordination*, 1st Ed. Tochigi: Ki No Kenkyukai Headquarters.

Acknowledgements

We dedicate this article to Mark Rubbert, William Reed, Koichi Kashiwaya, and Andrew Tsubaki who have inspired us to explore the fascinating complexity of Shin Shin Toitsu Aikido (founder Koichi Tohei). The material discussed in this article is not necessarily endorsed by Ki Society or any of its affiliates.

· 10 ·

The Loyal Opposition and the Practice of Aikido
by Jonathan Miller-Lane, Ph.D.

Photography by Dennis Curran.

Introduction

When a new student imagines enrolling in a martial arts class and learning an art of self-defense, it is unlikely that he or she is focusing on being the aggressor in training. For the most part, the interest is in learning how to respond to an attack. However, without the opportunity to practice with a strong aggressor it is difficult to learn how to become a strong defender with the ability to respond effectively. In the case of aikido, the process of learning to be an aggressor has an added layer of complexity due to the nature of the falls that an aggressor must take once the defender executes a technique.

Aikido is a relatively recent addition to the martial arts. The founder, Morihei Ueshiba (1883–1969) was from the city of Tanabe, Wakayama Prefecture in Japan and developed aikido after decades of intensive martial training in both open hand and weapons training techniques, particularly traditional Japanese sword training. He believed that aikido represented a martial system that was a true expression of *budo* (martial way) which he understood to mean "the loving protection of all things."

Ueshiba believed that aikido techniques were an effective means of self-defense, but most importantly they were a powerful means of refining the spirit and developing powerful compassion. Rather than respond to an attack with a killing strike or debilitating blow, aikido practitioners attempt to find an alternative response that enables the attack to be diffused without harming the aggressor. This is why aikido is often referred to as "The Way of Harmony" (Stevens, 1987).

While learning how to respond to an aggressor with compassion rather than an effective counter strike is a difficult task, the process of learning how to give a good attack and then react to the defensive technique is arguably even more difficult. An aikido aggressor must attack his partner with full commitment yet, at the same time, be sufficiently pliable to blend with the defensive technique itself in order to be able to train another day. Like all martial arts the process involves toughening up the arms, wrists, fingers, legs and back to withstand the physical strain. But, due to the many circular joint throws in aikido, a practitioner must learn how to take forward rolls, backward rolls, "high falls," and wrist throws at full speed. It is in this process of learning how to both strike and blend in the role of an aggressor that an aikido practitioner most resembles a member of the loyal opposition in a democracy.

The Loyal Opposition

The British historian Archibald Foord has traced the origin of the term "His Majesty's Loyal Opposition" to a speech given by Sir John Cam Hobhouse, a "radical statesman of moderate distinction," on the floor of the House of Commons of England in 1826. The phrase, "Loyal Opposition" soon came to denote a political party or group of parties that,

> operates wholly within the laws and conventions of the state, to which it is completely loyal. The Opposition is a responsible body, obliged not to take any action calculated to drive the country into chaos, and equally obliged to take office should its activities make government by those in power unfeasible or impossible.
> —Foord, 1964: 2

The loyalty is to the form of government: a democracy. The opposition is to the particular policies of the particular party in power, not to democracy as a form of government.

In the United States, among the more famous articulations of the concept of the loyal opposition occurred in a speech given by the Republican Party's nominee for president, Wendell Wilkie, on November 11, 1940 after losing the race for the Presidency to Franklin D. Roosevelt. Wilkie recognized and accepted Roosevelt's victory while arguing for the right and responsibility to continue to offer alternative perspectives.

Wilkie claimed that, "A vital element in the balanced operation of democracy is a strong, alert, and watchful opposition." He challenged the notion that during a time of war all opposition must cease and that there must be one dominant party to which all should swear blind allegiance; such a notion of blind allegiance was "a totalitarian idea... a slave idea... [and] must be rejected utterly" (Wilkie, 1940). Wilkie noted that a democratic government is one of laws and principles and that the war in Europe was being fought precisely to preserve the right to disagree and challenge the government in power:

> Any member of the minority party, though willing to die for his country, still retains the right to criticize the policies of the government. This right is embedded in the constitutional system... We, who stand ready to serve our country behind our Commander in Chief, nevertheless retain the right, and I will say the duty, to debate the course of our government.
> —Wilkie, 1940

For Wilkie, to be a loyal American in a time of war did not mean that one gave up one's First Amendment Rights, but rather that the need to exercise those rights became even more important. Loyalty to the democratic system was being demonstrated through open and heartfelt opposition. Disagreement and conflict were the lifeblood of democratic life. (It is important to note that the loyal opposition can refer to any and all political parties. During one's lifetime it is likely that one's own political party will be in power at one point and in the role of the loyal opposition at another. I am not advocating for a particular party in this paper, but rather for the embrace of a political principle that ensures the vibrancy of a democracy. The concept of the loyal opposition transcends political party affiliation.)

Being an Aikido Aggressor

As a practitioner of the unique, Japanese martial art of aikido as well as an educator and scholar of democratic education, learning how to be a member of the loyal opposition has often seemed surprisingly analogous to learning how to give a good attack and then receive the defensive response when practicing aikido. This process of learning how to take a fall, to blend with a defensive response, is called "*ukemi*" (oo-kehmee). Perhaps this unique martial art, traditionally taught in the authoritarian atmosphere of a martial arts dojo, may, in fact, offer opportunities to learn skills essential to democratic life.

In an aikido dojo, it is common practice for students to train in pairs with one student in the role of aggressor and the other, defender. After practicing a technique four times, students switch roles. As a result, during the course of a single class all students have been both aggressors and defenders numerous times. In the role of the aggressor, an aikido practitioner must give a "clean" attack to his or her partner in order for the defender to be able to practice a defensive technique. However, the aggressor must also be sufficiently pliable to absorb and blend with the technique that the defender (*nage*) chooses to employ (Saotome, 1993). By "clean" attack, I mean an attack that comes as close as possible to the perfect form of the strike called for by the aikido instructor. For the purposes of clarifying the analogy between *ukemi* and the loyal opposition, I will refer hereon to a clean attack as a loyal attack.

The rules of engagement in an aikido dojo generally involve experienced students training with beginners. Hence, an experienced student is expected to take into account the abilities of a beginner and modify the speed and intensity of the attack—this is also part of a loyal attack in a dojo. The senior student is still attempting to give the less experienced student a loyal attack, but at an appropriate speed and intensity. At more advanced levels of training, where both partners are skilled, a loyal attack will be a full speed attack. If I attack with a punch, the goal is to give the best punch possible regardless of whether I personally like or dislike the particular person with whom I am training. Ego and personality should have no place. A loyal attack is impersonal in the sense that the identity of the aggressor and defender does not matter. One must attack as instructed. The goal is not to destroy the defender, one's partner, but rather to try and offer, as best as possible, the perfect strike. Once the defender begins a response, the aggressor has the responsibility to cover her openings and protect herself. As Master Saotome (1993: 181) has stated, "The smartest way to accomplish this [self-protection] is to follow through with a committed attack and take [the fall] responsive to your partner's reaction, aware of all around you, ready to change and respond…." Stiff resistance to a defensive move is precisely what makes an aggressor vulnerable, as openings cannot be covered when muscles are stiff and tense. Flexibility and responsiveness are what aikido aggressors must learn—precisely the attributes necessary to be a defender. The aggressor is loyal to the etiquette of aikido training, the rules of the dojo, and the instructions of the teacher. By contrast, a disloyal attacker would be filled with the explicit intent to injure or maim one's partner for personal reasons and a person that demonstrated complete disregard for, and even a desire to overturn, the etiquette and rules of the dojo in which he or she was training. To paraphrase Foord, a disloyal attack would be calculated to drive dojo etiquette into chaos.

To be clear, I am not discussing the application of an aikido technique in an actual life and death situation outside the dojo in which the aggressor has no idea what *ukemi* is nor any desire to learn at that particular moment of attack. Rather, I am referring to the practice of *ukemi* within an aikido dojo, among aikido practitioners. The phrase "taking good *ukemi*" that is often used by aikido students suggests that learning how to absorb a defensive response without injury to oneself is a critical part of aikido practice. And, as anyone who wants to keep getting better knows, learning *ukemi* is essential to one's ability to return to the dojo to train another day. Can the skills learned in *ukemi* be usefully compared with the skills of constructive disagreement so essential to democratic life? Is the practice of *ukemi* analogous to the skills needed for a loyal opposition in a democracy? Perhaps.

Ukemi, the Loyal Opposition and Creative Tension

Once an aggressor has offered the strike and the defender begins to employ a particular self-defense technique, the aggressor must make a key adjustment. Suddenly, the aggressor must switch from providing a loyal attack to performing what might be called the loyal blend. This transition from aggressor to absorber is only possible if the aggressor remains pliable, that is, sufficiently flexible to respond physically to the self-defense technique that the defender has employed to diffuse the initial attack.

In the political setting, the transformation from loyal aggressor to loyal blender is exemplified in Wendell Wilkie's 1940 speech. During the election he had attacked President Roosevelt's policies. After the citizens of the United States had spoken, Wilkie had to blend with the result—his initial attack had been rebuffed. However, in his speech, Wilkie made the argument that he was not going to simply collapse and go away after his initial attack had failed. He was going to remain vigilant and look for openings or weaknesses in Roosevelt's policies. Wilkie's loyalty was to the system, i.e. Roosevelt as President not Roosevelt as the politician. Hence, Wilkie was reserving the right to challenge policies. During aikido practice, a good aggressor does the same thing that Wilkie advocated.

Imagine that an initial aikido attack is welcomed and neutralized by the defender. But, as the defender begins to execute a particular technique, he errs and moves into a position that in fact returns the aggressor to a strong, balanced position from where the attack can continue. In political terms, the policy that was initially selected failed to succeed and the opposition did not simply fall down at the first touch/presentation of policy, but rather maintained the focus and intent of the original line of attack. In the aikido encounter, imagine that the aggressor continues the attack until the defender rebalances himself and completes the throw properly. At the moment that the aggressor feels his balance taken, he must blend with the technique employed by the defender, take the throw safely, and return to attack again.

In the dojo, both aggressor and defender are playing by the rules of engagement of the dojo. One partner has agreed to attack in the manner requested by the teacher and the other has agreed not to intentionally seek the most injurious way to respond. In every aikido encounter, lethal options to an attack are noted but transcended. The goal is to respond with the least injurious, most harmonious and, thereby, effective option possible. In the political setting, both the party in power (defender) and the loyal opposition (aggressor) have agreed to play by the rules that have been democratically established. Neither seeks a military or violent overthrow—the equivalent of a strike with intent to kill. While in both the dojo and the political setting of a democracy the encounters can be intense and dynamic, there are rules that govern the engagement. The rules are intended to limit fatal injury to either the individuals or the system in which the individuals are operating and are specifically intended to allow for continued discussion and deliberation/training regardless of which political party is in which role. In 1940, the Republican Wendell Wilkie represented the loyal opposition. In 2007, the loyal opposition is likely to be led by Democrats. Whoever may be in power, the principle of the loyal opposition remains critical to democratic life.

Ukemi may be the most extraordinary and challenging aspect of aikido practice. In the rich, dynamic interchange between aggressor and defender lays the potential for aikido to make a positive contribution to democratic life in a multicultural society. In the field in which I work, educators constantly explore about how best to educate people for democratic life in a multicultural society. For such educators, there are two fundamental tensions that must remain vibrant if democracy is to remain a viable way of life. The first tension is built into the structure of the United States federal system—the checks and balances of our three branches of government. The United States federal system was created in such a manner that it assumes that the executive, legislative, and judicial branch will all compete for power. If the executive is dominant we have a tyranny. If the legislature becomes dominant, we are likely to have an hereditary aristocracy, and if the judiciary becomes dominant, we are likely to resemble a theocracy. Furthermore, in the US federal system, the states and the federal government argue over jurisdiction. The tension created by the three branches competing for power and the arguments over state and federal jurisdiction are essential for a vibrant democracy. Embedded in that pushing and pulling lies an essential and healthy tension of the United States federal system of government.

The second important tension that democratic educators stress is the unity-diversity tension created by the need for many voices to be heard within a single political framework. A fascist state has no unity-diversity tension as all citizens must envision their personal fulfillment as coterminous with their identity as subjects of the state; it is all about unity, diversity is forbidden. In a multicultural democracy, the need to constantly reexamine the political framework to ensure full inclusion for all citizens is a source of constant tension. Yet, it is the tension itself that sustains the rich interactions between individuals' political identity as citizens and their self-determined cultural identities of race, gender, ethnicity, sexuality, etc. Both the checks and balances and the unity-diversity tension illuminate the importance of the ability to negotiate and welcome tension as a source of creativity and possibility.

In 1963, The Reverend Dr. Martin Luther King Jr. wrote about the place of "creative tension" in a democracy from a jail cell in Birmingham, Alabama. He explained why he was using nonviolent resistance in the following manner:

> Nonviolent direct action seeks to create such a crisis and establish such creative tension that a community that has constantly refused to negotiate is forced to confront the issue. It seeks to dramatize the issue that it can no longer be ignored... This may sound rather shocking. But, I must confess I am not afraid of the word tension. I have earnestly worked and preached against violent tension, but there is a type of constructive nonviolent tension that is necessary for growth.
> —King, 1963: 79

The tension that Dr. King and thousands of Civil Rights heroes created challenged the physical barriers of Jim Crow by filling jail cells with human bodies. By accepting the punishment "lovingly and openly" the protesters filled the jailed cells beyond the point that the system could respond. The creative tension that these filled jailed cells created provided opportunities for political dialogue and change. The unified political framework was being stretched and pulled by diverse bodies demanding to be included more fully and equitably.

The transition from being a committed, loyal aggressor to a committed, loyal blender in aikido practice requires that a rich and "creative" tension be maintained. In particular, the aggressor must remain sufficiently resilient, attentive, connected, and pliable such that, during reversals practice (*kaishi-waza*), the aggressor can reverse the technique selected by the defender should the defender fail to execute the technique correctly. If the aggressor simply disengages from the attack there is no practice. Aikido training depends on the aggressor maintaining an attack and a connection as long as possible. Throughout the interaction, like the loyal opposition, the aggressor remains alert to regaining the position, "to take office" in Foord's definition, from where the selection of techniques or policies is made.

Learning how to be a good aggressor requires that one figure out how to attack honestly and loyally along a clear line, move from a low center of gravity, and maintain connection and tension with the defender and fall without injury. It is no wonder it takes years of training to become competent! Aikido practice provides the opportunity for a defender to welcome tension as the opportunity to connect and practice technique—to be creative. A single training class creates hundreds of miniature conflicts and many tension rich minutes of potential creativity. Such tension need not be feared whether in a dojo, a town meeting or workplace.

Summary

Like any analogy, there are places where the *ukemi* as loyal opposition comparison breaks down. For example, in introductory classes teachers may encourage experienced students to perform the proper *ukemi* even if the beginner has not actually executed the technique in a sufficiently effective manner. In such an instance, the senior student is helping the beginner by using her body, rather than her voice, to help a new person learn the defensive techniques. Here, the *ukemi* is in fact its own performance almost disconnected from, although in support of the defender (*nage*). Such *ukemi* performances can sometimes happen in tests where an aggressor may appear to be performing his own demonstration of athletic prowess outside of anything that the defender is doing. There are also times when a teacher might ask his or her students to "lock down" on a partner in order that the defender may practice from a stiff, rigid attack. Yet, even in these instances, the aggressor must learn how to attack with clear intent and sufficient pliability to be able to absorb the throw.

Learning how to respond as the defender, to a multi-person attack is excellent training for learning how to deal with any challenges that life may throw at you. Watching true masters (*shihan*) respond to such attacks in a manner whereby every aggressor is welcomed, connected with, and thrown safely, is to witness a level of awareness, calm, compassion, and focus that our political leaders of every stripe would do well to emulate. But, it is also extremely informative to watch skilled and dedicated aggressors perform their roles as well. Good aggressors do not fake an attack, but come in with clear, loyal intent to perform the perfect attack as a means to honor their partner and the practice of aikido. To provide a weak or distracted attack is to demonstrate disrespect to one's partner, one's teacher, one's dojo, and the practice itself, just as members of a political opposition disrespect the democratic system in which they live when their opposition is not strong and focused.

At the moment when the aggressor and defender physically touch in aikido, loyal aggressors do not collapse into a puddle, or fly off on their own predetermined flight path, but rather maintain the tension-rich connection, center to center, as long as possible. The image of a fire hose full of water is often used to describe the kind of strong pliability of a good aggressor. The aggressor is listening with his body to determine whether and how he will be thrown and the defender is listening to determine how best to establish a connection that provides the opportunity to respond creatively and compassionately. Master Mitsugi Saotome has said that the founder of aikido, Morihei Ueshiba is reported to have called *ukemi*, "a washing machine for the heart"—a practice through which ego, malice and anger can be cleaned into a loyal opposition.

Students and teachers alike could practice *ukemi* for decades without any awareness of its potential to inform democratic life. This would not make their *ukemi* any less beautiful. However, in this most fundamental aspect of aikido training may lie a rich store of potential for democratic education, should teachers and students seek to explore this possible analogy. Perhaps the study of *ukemi* offers a powerful means to extend the teachings of aikido beyond the walls of the dojo and into the tension rich world of democratic life in a multicultural society.

technical section

Sequence One

An important aspect of aikido is learning how to take a fall from a person much smaller than oneself. In this sequence the aggressor attacks with a right hand strike. The defender deflects the strike. The aggressor turns and strikes with the left, which is again deflected. However, this time the defender enters to the side, unbalances the aggressor and, before he can strike again, takes the center line throwing the aggressor to the ground. The aggressor must learn how to maintain the line of attack and yet, once unbalanced, absorb the throw.

Sequence Two

The aggressor begins with a punch. The defender turns and deflects. As the attacker strikes again, the defender hooks her arm and turns her inward so that the second strike is moot. As the aggressor attempts to find her balance and strike a third time, the defender steps to the side and brings the aggressor to the ground. Throughout this interaction, the aggressor has to keep attacking until final balance is taken in order for the "creative tension" to be maintained.

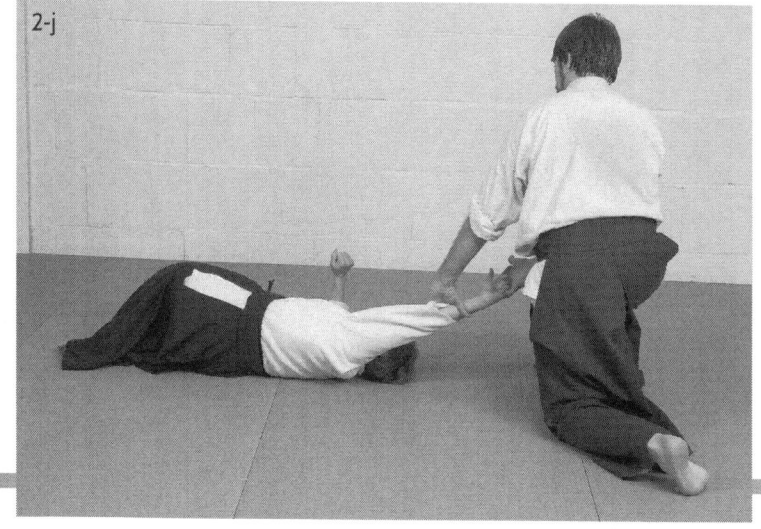

Sequence Three

The aggressor begins by grabbing the defender from behind with both arms and attempting to choke her with his left arm. The defender crosses over her chest with her right hand to grab the attacker's left hand as she turns to her right into the attacker thereby twisting his left wrist and weakening his right hand grip as well. Yet, as she attempts to apply the wrist technique to his left wrist, he overpowers her and strikes with his right. She steps back deflecting his punch and draws him in. With the aggressor off balance, the she then slides forward taking the center line and throwing him to the ground. For the aggressor, this interaction appears to stay in his favor until the sudden turn of events in the last move—it is the forward intent and commitment to strike that creates the possibility for the defender to respond creatively and effectively.

3-c

3-d

3-f

3-g

Sequence Four

This is an example of how quickly the aggressor must transition into the loyal blend. The aggressor begins with a punch and the defender slides to the side of the strike, catches the aggressor's elbow, slides it upward and enters. By doing so the aggressor is unbalanced and as he attempts to counter with the left fist, the defender keeps the aggressor unbalanced by sliding forward and throwing him into a forward roll.

Sequence Five

A left hand punch to the face is deflected downward by the defender's right hand drawing the aggressor forward and off balance. The defender continues the movement downward and turning the aggressor's neck forces him inward. As he rights himself and attacks again, the defender moves to the side and throws him into a wrist turn "high fall." Here the challenge for the aggressor is to maintain the connection and stay sufficiently supple whereby the final wrist throw is absorbed throughout the body thus avoiding permanent damage to his wrist. Both are staying within the rules of engagement. The aggressor commits to sustaining the attack and the defender finds an end result that enables the attack to the neutralized   but that also enables the aggressor to land safely.

Sequence Six

The aggressor grabs both wrists of the defender. The defender drops, rises up and extends forward to draw the aggressor off balance. The defender grabs the wrist, turns inward and steps back preparing to draw the aggressor to the mat. However, the aggressor recovers and strikes with his right hand. Again, the defender absorbs the strike and by drawing the aggressor downward unbalances him as she turns him forward by guiding him from the small of his back. Just when he turns to strike a second time, she enters and fills the center line throwing him to the ground.

Bibliography

Foord, A. (1964). *His majesty's opposition, 1714-1830*. Oxford: Clarendon Press.

King, M. (1963). *Why we can't wait*. New York: Mentor.

Saotome, M. (1993). *Aikido and the harmony of nature*. Boston: Shambhala Publications.

Stevens, J. (1987). *Abundant peace: The biography of Morihei Ueshiba, founder of aikido*. Boston: Shambhala Publications.

Wilkie, W. (1940, Nov. 11). Loyal opposition's constructive criticism. National Radio Address. http://www.usa-patriotism.com/tribute/speeches/willkie1.htm. Retrieved Sept. 15, 2005.

Acknowledgment

I wish to acknowledge the teaching and guidance of Kimberly Richardson of Two Cranes Aikido in Seattle, as well as photographer Dennis Curran, and the assistance of the following aikidoka of Blue Heron Aikido: Linda White, Holly Weir, and Nellie Pierce.

· 11 ·

Aikido as Myth
by Maurice Gauthier, M.Ed.

Illustration courtesy of Dante Lavidini. • www.dantelavidini

Once upon a time many moons ago when I was living in Tokyo, I ventured out one evening on a pub crawl with some aikido friends. At some point deep into the night, a karaoke sing-along we'd been having with a group of dockworkers somehow turned into a loud and disorderly argument. Before we knew it, we were all hauled off to the nearest police box to resolve matters.

Of course, we'd all had way too much to drink and the two stern police officers were anything but bemused. They somehow got us to calm down and began trying to clear up what had happened. This was when one of the dockworkers shouted, "Why are you asking them? You're supposed to be protecting us!"

In those days, Japanese police officers on duty outside these miniature police stations would be issued wooden staves (*jo*), like the ones we use in aikido. Most often they could be seen leaning on this short staff as they whiled away the long hours of their shifts in a peaceful (and gun-less) country with only the odd foreigner walking by whom they could stop and ask for an alien registration card as a way to practice their English.

On this particular night as well, one of the police officers was holding a jo. He raised it and gently placed the tip on this dockworker's shoulder. In one slow swoop, the dockworker collapsed helplessly to the ground. And it was in this pinning position that the officer, still standing and still casually holding his jo, calmly continued his interrogation.

I had never seen anything like this before. At that time, I already knew all the basic Saito staff and *bokken* (wooden sword) techniques as well as the long forms that Shirata Rinjiro (1912–1993) would demonstrate on his yearly trips down from Yamagata to the All-Japan Aikido Demonstration in the Nippon Budokan. I had even on several occasions witnessed Hikitsuchi Michio's (1923–2004) hauntingly beautiful *chinkon kishin* (lit. calming the spirit and returning to the divine) purification exercises, which he too (it is said) learned directly from the Founder, Morihei Ueshiba (1883–1969). Yet, I had always felt in a way hard to explain that weapon training in aikido was, to a large extent, mostly about little boys who didn't wish to grow up.

Whenever I picked up a weapon, either at the dojo or in the precincts of a local shrine, I invariably would feel a tad sheepish. As if I were not Musashi Miyamoto but Peter Pan, prancing around the befuddled Captain Hook, with that ludicrous alarm clock crocodile ticking ominously below. Fun, but not serious. Certainly nothing martial and certainly nothing that could lead to any sort of significant personal transformation.

This discomfort on my part was perhaps not even related to the Way of Harmony. After all, as a modern Japanese sport, aikido did resemble *kendo* (sword methods) and *kyudo* (archery), which were also practiced with weapon and *hakama* (traditional clothing), and which were also located somewhere between the past and the present, perched precariously between tradition and modernity. By ritualizing intention rather than outcome, these sports were elevated to the high aesthetic level of flower arrangement, tea ceremony and even the drama of Noh.

By fostering an external gesture through an internal cultivation of intuition, aikido was supposed to allow us to escape concept and enter directly into the immediacy of pure perception. So it went. In my experience, however, after having trained in Japan for almost two years, I was starting to feel that, if anything, I was just getting better at lying to myself. After all, if this were not so, why then was I being asked to explain myself inside this police box somewhere on the edge of a nightclub district?

The police officers slowly continued the interrogation. The odd sight of the brawny dockworker sprawled in a heap on the concrete floor had a great calming effect on the rest of us. Able to move but unable to stand up, he quietly answered when spoken to but otherwise lay there waiting. The wooden jo was wedged snugly across his shoulder. In a strange way he reminded me of myself.

The practice of aikido was not coming easily to me. Mashing my knees into the mat during the kneework and interminable seiza lectures, spraining my wrists and elbows in the locks and wrenching my back in the throws, I seemed to have (in those days) more energy than common sense. Which was fine for the time. But these painful reminders of my physical limitations were easy to bear in comparison to the growing sense that was slowly awakening in me. The late Founder's teachings had quickly and perhaps irrevocably become encrusted in a crude form of ancestor worship.

Even in those days it was crystal clear to me that aikido was, above all, an idea. It was something that Morihei Ueshiba had nurtured all his life. It had been transplanted in him as a toddler singing Shingon mantras in rural Tanabe. It had sprouted in his infantry days during the Russo-Japanese War (1904–1905). It had grown shoots during the harsh pioneering winters in Hokkaido. It had flowered during his later years in Iwama, where, for the longest time, he didn't even have a dojo in which to train.

Aikido was essentially about skillful means. Adapting to conditions. Coming up with the correct response. Being in the right place at the right time. What Morihei had discovered (as per the neat Japanese talent for inventing and not just copying) was a radically new and portable way to train. A kata one could toss into one's pocket and carry around at need. Not unlike its distant cousin, the Sony Walkman.

But just as Buddhism had long ago left India for China, and the dharma of Tibet fled to the West, aikido was dying a painful death in the land of its birth. With the Founder gone, all that remained was the cumbersome machination of a large bureaucratic organization. Also not unlike Sony, just another transglobal conglomerate.

Still, I honestly did enjoy the medieval pageantry and hushed religious dignity of the dojo. Removing and neatly placing our shoes in the main entrance. The obsequious flutter of bowing whenever the teachers were around. The conspiracy of codependence. The asymmetrical power relations of State Shinto.

I really dug starting and ending general practice with a solemn group bow toward the front of the dojo. At the large scroll hanging in the recessed alcove (*tokonoma*) and, just above, the photograph of Morihei Ueshiba. Often though, I would catch myself wondering whether the Founder weren't roaring with laughter at us for having so misrepresented his teaching.

Finally the police officers put away their notepads and decided we were all free to go. Unruffled and unharmed, the dockworker was allowed to stand up. For a short while, we stood there together in the hollow police box under a dim ascetic beam of light.

Outside I could see the dazzling neon art frenetically flashing above groups of office workers, university students, and busloads of tourists from the countryside who were merrily carousing along the street. Far far away from the comfortable certainties of the monochrome world of Kurosawa Akira, I watched people in expensive clothes vomiting all over themselves.

After an ostentatious profusion of apologies, we walked out of the police box and along the crowded street. At the sign of the first bar, our friends the dockworkers invited us in for yet another karaoke sing-along. I, however, did not follow. Instead, I bolted down a side lane and ran back all the way back home. The last thing I remember is setting my alarm clock as I dropped off. Catching a few hours sleep before the morning aikido class.

· 12 ·
Aikido Defenses Against Real-World Attacks
by Roy Y. Suenaka and Chad Taylor, M.S.

Painting by Feodor Tamarsky • Email: feodor.tamarsky@gmail.com • www.artsglobe.com

Foundation of Traditional Aikido

Traditional aikido has only a few "orthodox" attacks for which one practices defense. Of these, there are just three strikes: *yokomen uchi*, *shomen uchi*, and *mune tsuki*. These terms describe a knife-hand strike to the side of the head, a vertical knife-hand strike, and a thrusting punch to the midsection, respectively. The delivery of these strikes during practice can at times seem laughable, as they are usually performed in an entirely unrealistic manner for the benefit of one's partner. Coupling this with the unlikelihood of encountering such attacks in the real world, one is left questioning why such attacks are considered orthodox in aikido at all.

To answer this question, one has to understand aikido's major influences. Most aikido practitioners will correctly cite Daito-ryu Aiki-Jiujutsu as the predecessor of aikido, but neglect to mention the profound influence of sword and spear-fighting arts, which founder Morihei Ueshiba mostly learned prior to his training in Daito-ryu. It is within these arts that the origin of traditional aikido strikes can be found, corresponding directly with the sword techniques of similar mechanics.

In addition to this historical tradition, these attacks persist because they represent a wider variety of attacks. *Mune tsuki* is practiced in place of any thrusting-type punch. *Shomen uchi* is used for any vertical overhead strike. *Yokomen uchi* represents any lateral, circular attack. In these loose definitions, one can indeed see where some real-world attacks are located, but is this an optimal way to train? Do these attacks, and the ways they are performed, truly embody the attacks people are likely to encounter in the real world? In most cases, no.

Aikido in the Modern World

The representation argument above is no more than an excuse to follow tradition, and this loyalty to the founding techniques should be applauded. However, one has to wonder what attacks Ueshiba would have stressed if the culture in which aikido was developed had been influenced by today's standards. Boxing, MMA, wrestling, and the like were simply not an integral part of the early and mid-1900s Japanese culture, and were not likely to influence the developing art, or an attack on the street. So the question should be, if Ueshiba were alive to witness the kinds of attacks that are prevalent now, would he optimize aikido training to defend against them?

Although Ueshiba wanted aikido to embody love, peace, and harmony, he did not intend for that goal to be at the expense of self-defense. Aikido, as Ueshiba taught it, should be maximally effective on the street, and with respect to this goal, he likely would have incorporated defenses against attacks not directly represented by the three orthodox strikes currently used in aikido. In essence, he would want his aikido to address every aspect of self-defense, and not just the traditional ones.

Many practitioners, wanting to accentuate principles they themselves deemed most important from Ueshiba's teachings, filtered out other aspects. In many cases, what was filtered was this self-defense mind-set. They speak of Ueshiba's later years, claiming he had evolved into a softer, more spiritual practitioner. While he unquestionably did become more spiritually motivated, "soft" is a vastly misleading term. The "soft" aspect, that is frequently referenced refers to blending and avoidance of force-against-force techniques that are ineffective against larger assailants. For those serving as *uke* (the attacker), Ueshiba's techniques were anything but soft, at times bordering on excruciating.

There are those who claim adding elements to aikido is bastardizing the art. But adopting this view is a fallacy that in itself is contrary to the principles of aikido. Ueshiba once said,

> Even though our path is completely different from the warrior arts of the past, it is not necessary to abandon totally the old ways. Absorb venerable traditions into this Art by clothing them with fresh garments, and build on the classic styles to create better forms.
> —Stevens, J., 1992: 49

"[C]lothing them with fresh garments..." That bears repeating. Ueshiba saw the need to adapt to the changing times, to the changing culture, while still holding true to the principles on which the techniques were based.

This sentiment was echoed to Roy Y. Suenaka at a private dinner, and later to others, when Ueshiba told him, "I am but a student of aikido. Take what I teach and improve upon it." That is a daunting task for a master to bestow on his students. It is a responsibility, not just to one, but to all practitioners. As Ueshiba understood while developing aikido, the task he bequeathed to his students was to allow aikido to evolve and grow while maintaining its principles. If this is indeed Ueshiba's will, then maintaining a static, inflexible aikido is in fact crippling it.

In that spirit, practicing one's techniques against real-world attacks in the practice hall, rather than assuming the necessary adaptation will occur in the street, is paramount in optimizing one's training. "You respond as you've trained," is often heard in the practice hall, describing the close relationship between learned instincts and repetitive training. Certainly, adaptability is vital in addressing the infinite variation of subtleties in a street encounter, but the more closely represented those variations are and the more well-rounded one's training, the better prepared a practitioner will be when faced with a real-world attack. Necessity may breed creativity, but experience breeds skill.

Influencing an Attack

Before exploring the types of attacks one is likely to encounter, it is important to understand what can be done to influence an attack before it even begins. With respect to this, traditional aikido works best with committed attacks that possess sufficient momentum to be controlled and redirected. Therefore, assuming one cannot avoid the assault altogether, the goal is to entice the attacker to commit.

Of all the elements inherent in a proper technique, only one directly affects an attack prior to its launch: *ma-ai*. Proper ma-ai can best be described as the distance between oneself and the attacker such that the attacker is required to move in order to make contact. Simply put, one should stay out of range. This is often measured in the practice hall by having the attacker and defender extend their arms toward one another and just barely touch fingertips.

This required movement to close the gap forces employment of the attacker's hips, which in turn generates momentum and thus increases the commitment of the attack. This gives an aikido player time and energy with which to work. This also makes the attacker readable. An aware defender can observe the attacker's hip movement and weight shifts to deduce the initial attack and respond to it. As attacks in the street happen too quickly to consciously think through them, this deduction and response should occur on a subconscious, instinctual level through repetitious and closely representative training.

The other factor to consider is one's stance. An obviously trained, ready-for-action stance will elicit caution from an attacker, which in turn makes the attacker less committed. While it is ill-advised to keep oneself open and indefensible, if one maintains proper distance, one's stance can be subtle and inviting of a committed attack. Generally this means being ready and balanced, but with hands lowered and slightly in front. The effect is to appear unthreatening while tempting an attacker to use a committed attack into one's disguised readiness. If one has maintained proper distance, then there will be ample time to bring one's hands up in defense or application of technique.

Rarely does an attack occur for the pure joy of the encounter. There is a motive behind it, whether anger, desperation, or financial gain. The attacker is not looking for a long, drawn-out fight, but rather wants to end it quickly. The means to this end is usually understood to be more powerful, committed attacks. Therefore, if presented with the opportunity to use such an attack and end the encounter quickly, the attacker will generally take it. It is this rationale that makes the stance above useful in luring an attacker to commit for the benefit of one's technique.

Atemi: The Use of Strikes

Atemi refers to striking techniques, usually performed to distract an attacker, create or close openings, or dissuade a continuous assault. Atemi should be an integral part of aikido techniques, although many practitioners have reduced or eliminated their usage, claiming Ueshiba removed strikes from aikido to emphasize its spiritual side. This is a misguided claim based largely on demonstrations performed by Ueshiba later in his life.

While it is true that Ueshiba lessened his usage of strikes in his later years, that is not to say he devalued striking, nor wished for its usage to cease. Rather, Ueshiba wished the prevailing strength of aikido, i.e., harmonizing, to be focused upon during his demonstrations. This was especially true for videos publicized to non-aikido practitioners who could misinterpret striking as part of a violent art.

However, Suenaka vividly recalls frequent conversations during that same time in which Ueshiba stressed the use of strikes when applying aikido in self-defense. So while Ueshiba used physical techniques as embodiments of the spiritual principles he wished to relay in his demonstrations, his advocacy of strikes in effective street aikido had never diminished.

In aikido, strikes are used to distract an attacker and create openings for one's techniques. Without such, many aikido techniques would fall prey to resistance or counters. This is especially true when an attacker maintains a strong stance and provides insufficient momentum to reliably control the attack. By employing strikes, the aikido practitioner weakens the attacker's resolve, directs the attention away from the defense, and reduces the possibility of subsequent counters. Those who do not use strikes are severely limiting their techniques against real attacks.

It should be noted that atemi allow for a broad range of intention in their usage. The primary goal is simply to distract. Therefore, a simple hand motion to the face is sometimes adequate in situations where the attacker should not be harmed. In other times, you may need to apply more severe, debilitating atemi. Although aikido striking is rarely power oriented, its aptitude for disabling an attacker lies in the delivery to vulnerable areas, such as eyes, knees, groin and throat.

Attack Scenarios

It should also be understood that just as one will not always be able to control distance, neither will an attacker always provide ample momentum. Unfortunately, most aikido schools operate under this false assumption. Almost all attacks in the practice hall are committed and launched from proper distance. Ideally, all attacks would conform to this paradigm, but that is not realistic. Therefore, it is important to understand and address scenarios failing to meet these assumptions.

In confined areas, the luxury of proper distance may be unachievable. These situations require decisiveness. If one believes an attack is eminent, then one should not wait for such an attack. Rather, the first physical move should be from the defender upon acknowledging the inevitable attack. This is still a defensive philosophy, although offensive physically, since the attack has been initiated by intent. To wait in close proximity for an attack is to invite defeat.

By initiating the first physical move, there is no momentum with which to work, and the attacker is generally well balanced. Therefore, the energy behind the technique is entirely generated by the defender, and utilizing strikes is important to stop a potential counter. There is a similar effect when confronting an uncommitted attack, except the attacker has already engaged an offensive mentality, so striking and timing are even more important.

Furthermore, in the street one is rarely guaranteed a strictly one-on-one fight, so training must address multiple attack scenarios. Aikido does practice *randori*, or free-style

defense against multiple attackers, but usually in succession, so the defender only need be concerned with one attacker at a time. This is effective in creating responsive techniques, but does not adequately address awareness of simultaneous attacks which can potentially overrun even the most skilled one-on-one practitioner. This fault is not attributable to the practice hall itself, which for safety reasons, should keep throws away from walls or non-matted areas. However, instructors should encourage more realistic movements, even if safety does not always allow full application of techniques.

When faced with multiple attackers, the first rule on the street is to stay out of the center, such that the defender can face all adversaries and not expose one's back to unseen assaults. The second rule is to keep moving; a static target is an easy victim to a coordinated attack. Finally, one needs to take the attackers out quickly, which generally means moving aggressively, straight into a technique (*irimi*), and avoiding longer indirect entering techniques (*tenkan*) with multiple blends and redirections.

The ability to evade attackers and subsequently disable them quickly is a strength of aikido not found in most arts. Although strikes should be intimately integrated into one's defense, a pure striking strategy would be insufficient in such scenarios, as it effectively requires overpowering all foes or uses a level of precision hard to maintain in such dynamic circumstances. Likewise, a purely throwing mentality may not allow a defender sufficient time or openings to apply one's techniques. For truly efficient defense against multiple attackers, one needs to supplement throwing techniques with strikes and vice versa.

Attacks

It are to one's benefit to practice defenses from a wide array of feasible attacks, both traditional and modern. This is an area in which many aikido schools need improvement. Perhaps they focus too much on the defense that they neglect to learn how to properly attack. Whatever the reason, this shortcoming should be addressed if practitioners are to prepare themselves for the street. This includes learning to deliver the orthodox strikes as well as strikes most commonly encountered in the street.

What are most commonly seen in aikido schools are strikes that are effectively presented for the defender to use, but not realistically delivered. Frequently, the midsection punch (*mune tsuki*) finds its full extension well before its target and is subsequently run into the defender. The downward knife-hand attack (*shomen uchi*) is delivered with its loading stage moving close to the defender without following through with the strike itself. The strike to the side of the head (*yokomen uchi*) is blatantly telegraphed and follows a wide arc. Essentially, the attacker focuses not on the attack, but rather on the opponent's defense. Contrary to popular belief, this is not being a good attacker (*uke*), as the attacker's job is to prepare the defender by offering a realistic attack.

Although there are as many stylistic philosophies behind proper striking techniques as there are methods of defense, two simple facts reign in almost all styles: striking power comes from the hips, and the apex of the strike should penetrate several inches into the target. If one analyzes the methods employed by many schools, one finds they conform to neither requirement. Since aikido is primarily a throwing art, some argue this weakness is expected and acceptable, but how do students learn defense against real strikes if they're never attacked with such in the practice hall? Therefore, it is recommended that practitioners acquire a well-rounded understanding of attack mechanics to further their defensive skills and those of their practice partners. Likewise, practitioners should understand the limitations of the three orthodox strikes, what they represent, and how variations therein affect their techniques.

The midsection punch (*mune tsuki*) purposes to cover all thrusting-type strikes. However, no singular strike can adequately cover such a wide range of attacks and their inherent complexities. One who is trained only against a midlevel punch may discover too late his unpreparedness to circumvent a higher-level strike, such as one to the face or an overhand strike that may impose both a lateral and downward element. Jabs are frequently encountered, especially at short range, and their quickness and lack of commitment will foil many techniques aimed at the wrist or arm.

The strike to the side of the head (*yokomen uchi*) represents any circular or lateral strike, and does a fair job simulating one of the most common attacks: the haymaker. This telegraphed, overcommitted, looping-style punch is anything but proper form, but it's used by more untrained attackers than just about any other attack. It's reasonably easy to defense against, because it's highly telegraphed, but its inherent power makes it formidable if contact is made with the intended target or a block. Not as easily translated from *yokomen uchi* is a hook punch, a very common strike for anyone exposed to basic boxing techniques.

The vertical knife-hand strike (*shomen uchi*) has limited usefulness, especially given its typical execution. Running toward someone with one's hand raising in the air in belated preparation is no kind of an attack at all. Likewise, even a proper preparatory move, that allows for forceful delivery, does not prepare one for an attacker loading up from the side or behind. These variations will greatly complicate or completely circumvent typical entering (*irimi*), defenses against the vertical knife-hand strike (*shomen uchi*). Furthermore, most downward strikes tend to be rare, weapon-oriented attacks that present further complications that should be addressed more directly.

Of even greater concern to aikido practitioners are strikes that are completely dissimilar to the orthodox three. Uppercuts, jabs, hooks, overhands, and flurried strikes are increasingly common, but generally unaddressed in most schools. The same principles are applied to these attacks—blending, redirection, and slipping—but significant modification of techniques is required to adequately control them. While a textual description of defenses against these attacks would prove uninformative, a pictorial representation of the more common attacks and a select defense is included for a more practical explanation.

Kicks are not as common, but still a concern that is often overlooked. Defenses against kicks fall into two categories: application of techniques directly to the attacking leg, similar to ones applied to an arm, or deflecting the kick and moving in for a throw. While most kicks are reasonably easy to avoid, it should be noted that some kicks, in particular a quick roundhouse kick to the defender's leg, is very difficult to avoid completely. In fact, trying to move away from the kick will usually shift the defender's weight onto the attacked leg, which forces full acceptance of the blow. Aikido has no defense against such kicks. Therefore, it is necessary to borrow techniques from other arts, such as karate or Muay Thai, and learn to accept the blow with the minimal amount of dispersive damage. In doing so, one can in effect nullify the attack or leave the attacker off balance in the process.

Aikido is very adept at defenses against grabs, but there are a few that fall to the wayside. For one, men rarely get attacked with just a grab, unless the intent is simply to intimidate; normally grabs are succeeded by strikes, unless the defender moves quickly enough to remove the potential. Conversely, women will be grabbed much more frequently that struck. Finally, one of the most common grabbing attacks is a football tackle, where the attacker rushes in to jam or take the defender to the ground. Movement is the greatest tool against such an attack, as shown in the pictorial section.

• • •

Technical Section

A Roy Suenaka faces an attacker (Chad Taylor), but assumes an open, non-threatening posture, which encourages commitment with an attack (A-1). At close range with reduced reaction time, Suenaka raises his guard (A-2).

B The attacker threatens Suenaka and tries to move closer (B-1). Suenaka responds by maintaining distance, disallowing the attacker's advance (B-2).

C The attacker again moves closer (C-1), but this time, Suenaka decides an attack is imminent. Suenaka responds by preemptively jamming the attacker's closest arm and strikes with the palm of his hand, disallowing the attack (C-2). Following through with the strike, Suenaka pushes the attacker's chin (C-3) and torques slightly to throw the attacker off-balance (C-4) and to the ground (C-5).

D The attacker throws an overhand right punch (D-1). Suenaka traps the arm (D-2), and applies downward pressure to the radial nerve, just above the elbow (D-3), while allowing the attacker's momentum to continue through and down (D-4 through 7).

D-1

D-2

D-3

D-4

D-5

D-6

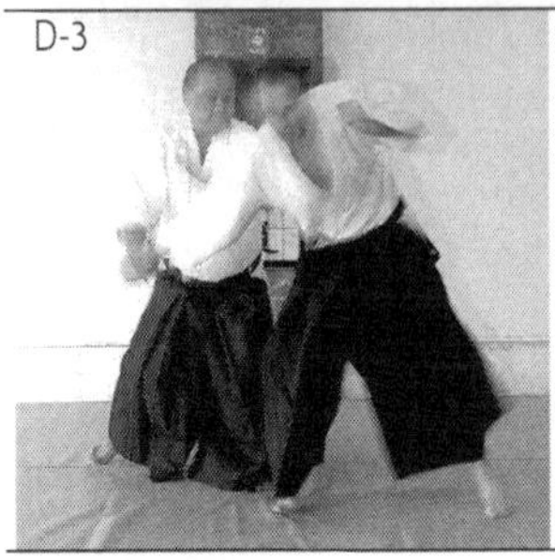

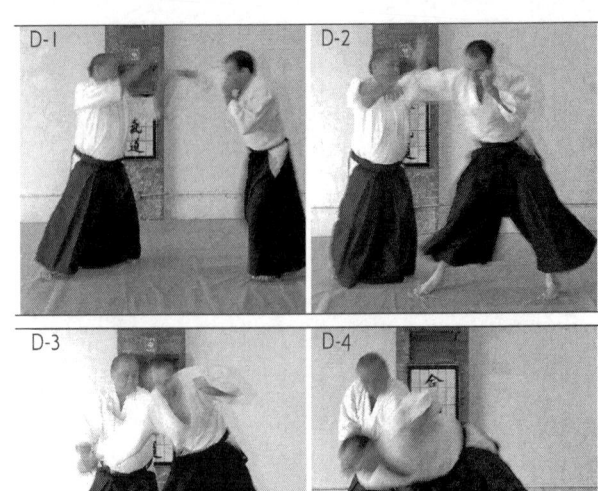

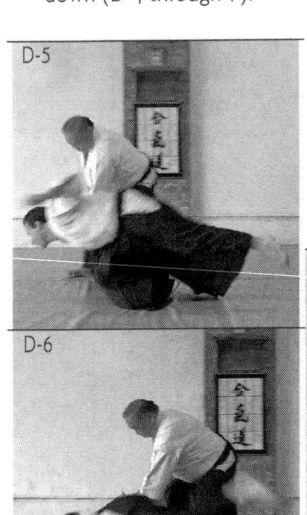

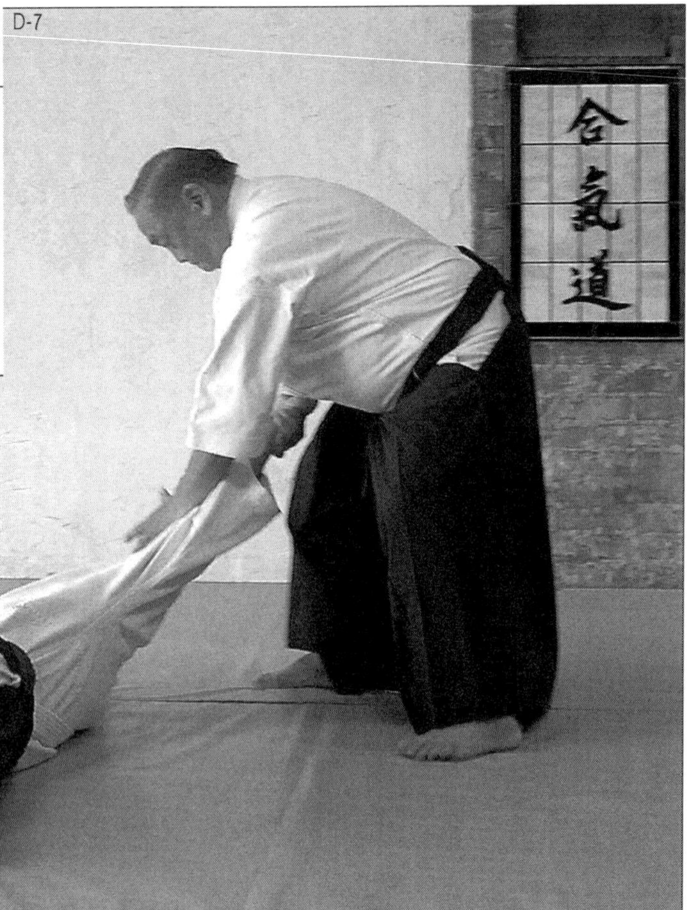

D-7

E Suenaka evades a right-cross and strikes the attacker's ribs (E-1). Shifting back slightly, Suenaka traps the extended arm (E-2) and applies downward pressure (E-3), driving the attacker to the ground (E-4).

F The attacker moves in for an uppercut (F-1), but Suenaka blends to the outside (F-2) and traps the arm (F-3). Suenaka continues the upward torque, using his elbow to apply painful pressure to the attacker's shoulder (F-4).

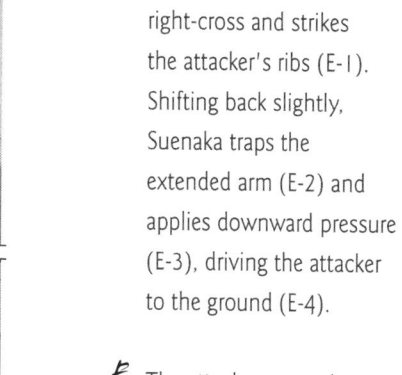

G Again, the attacker attempts an uppercut (G-1), but Suenaka jams the arm down and into the attacker's body (G-2). Suenaka then drives his arm alongside the attacker's jaw (G-3), throwing his head back (G-4) and down (G-5), and directs the attacker to the floor (G-6).

H The attacker rushes Suenaka in a common "football tackle" (H-1), but Suenaka jams the closest arm (H-2) and throws it across the attacker's back while applying downward pressure on the head (H-3). The attacker for forced to tuck and roll to save himself (H-4-5).

I Again, the attacker attempts a football tackle (I-1), but Suenaka jams the closest arm and strikes with his knee (I-2). Suenaka continues the jam by moving the arm behind the attacker's back (I-3), applying pressure to the shoulder (I-4) and locking the arm securing it to the ground (I-5).

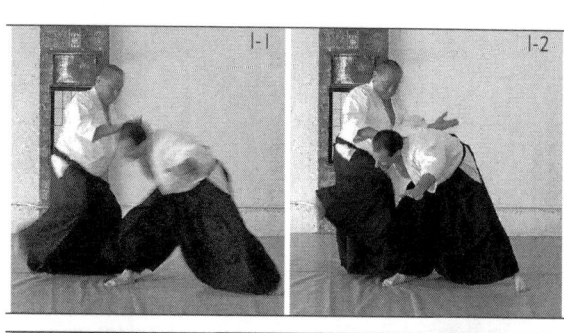

J The attacker performs a quick, non-committed roundhouse kick to Suenaka's thigh, who has no choice but to lift his leg and defuse the force along his entire thigh and shin (J-1). As Suenaka steps down, he begins to enter (J-2) and jam the threatening closer hand (J-3). Delivering a palm-heel strike to the attacker's chin (J-4), Suenaka continues through and torques the attacker's head (J-5), redirecting him to the ground (J-6).

K Suenaka is threatened and knows an attack is imminent (K-1). He immediately turns the attacker's body by jamming the closest arm and pushing the opposite shoulder (K-2). Moving behind (K-3), Suenaka positions himself for a choke (K-4) and locks it down by applying pressure along the attacker's carotid artery (K-5).

L The attacker attempts a hook punch, only to be met with a quick, entering jam (L-1). Suenaka torques the attacker's arm, so that it locks the shoulder (L-2). Suenaka then pushes the attacker's head back (L-3), and torques it down to the floor (L-4), while maintaining the lock (L-5).

M-1

M-2

M-3

M-4

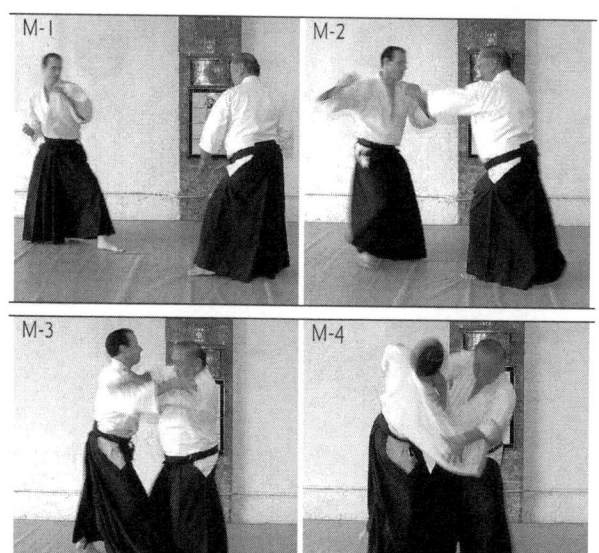

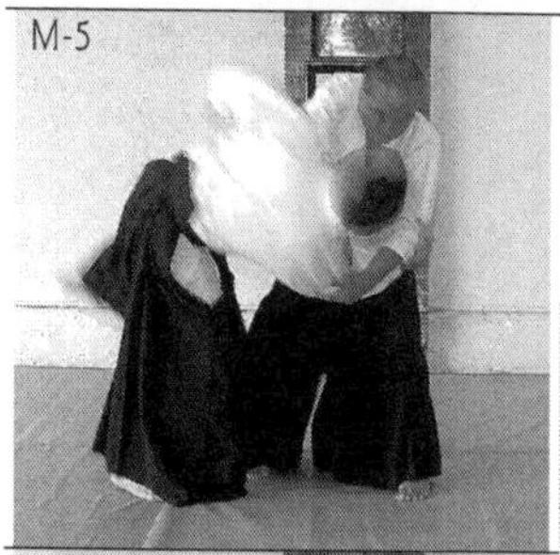

M-5

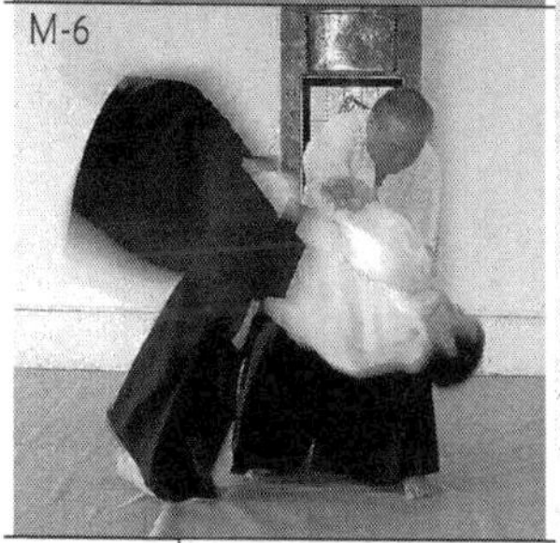

M-6

M The agressor loads up in preparation for an attack, but the distance is too great for an easy jam (M-1). As the attacker launches the haymaker punch, Suenaka begins his blend (M-2) and closes the gap (M-3). Suenaka applies downward and outward pressure on both the arm and shoulder (M-4), throwing the attacker off-balance (M-5) and launching him forward (M-6) to the ground (M-7).

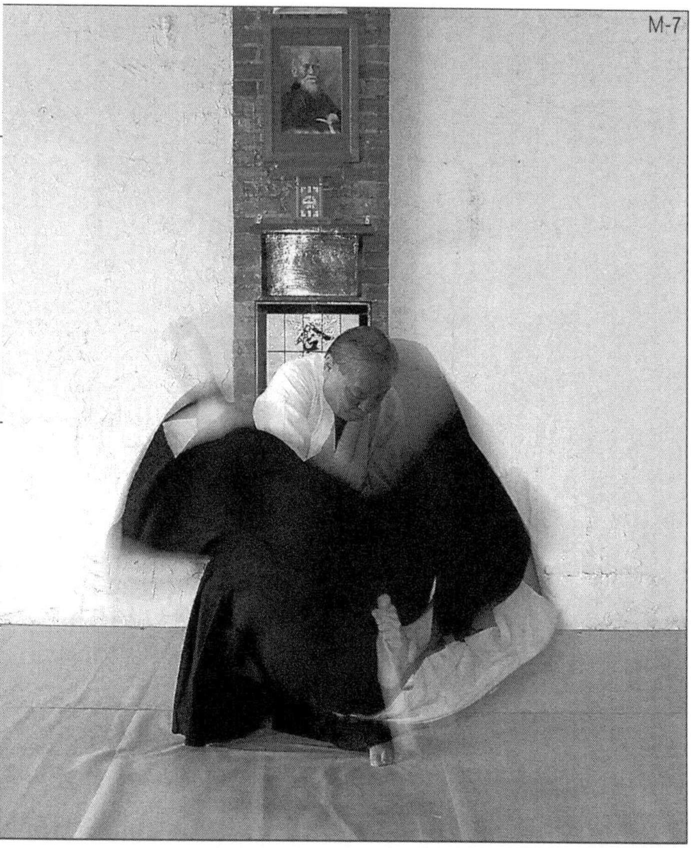

M-7

N Four attackers surround Suenaka (N-1), who responds with a quick throw to the closest aggressor (N-2-7), who lands between Suenaka and two of the other attackers, slowing them down and keeping them from attacking simultaneously (N-8). Suenaka responds to the next attack with another quick throw, knowing long, draw-out techniques would give the other attackers time to close the distance (N-9-13). Suenaka stays to the outside of the danger-zone, keeping all attackers in his field of vision (N-14). As Suenaka quickly throws the third attacker (N-15-18), he is immediately attacked by the fourth (N-19-20). Suenaka does not delay as he addresses this final attack (N-21-26). Suenaka maintains his position on the outside of the danger-zone, watching all attackers (N-27-28).

**takemusu
aiki
武産合気**

"To spontaneously execute the perfect aikido technique in any given situation."

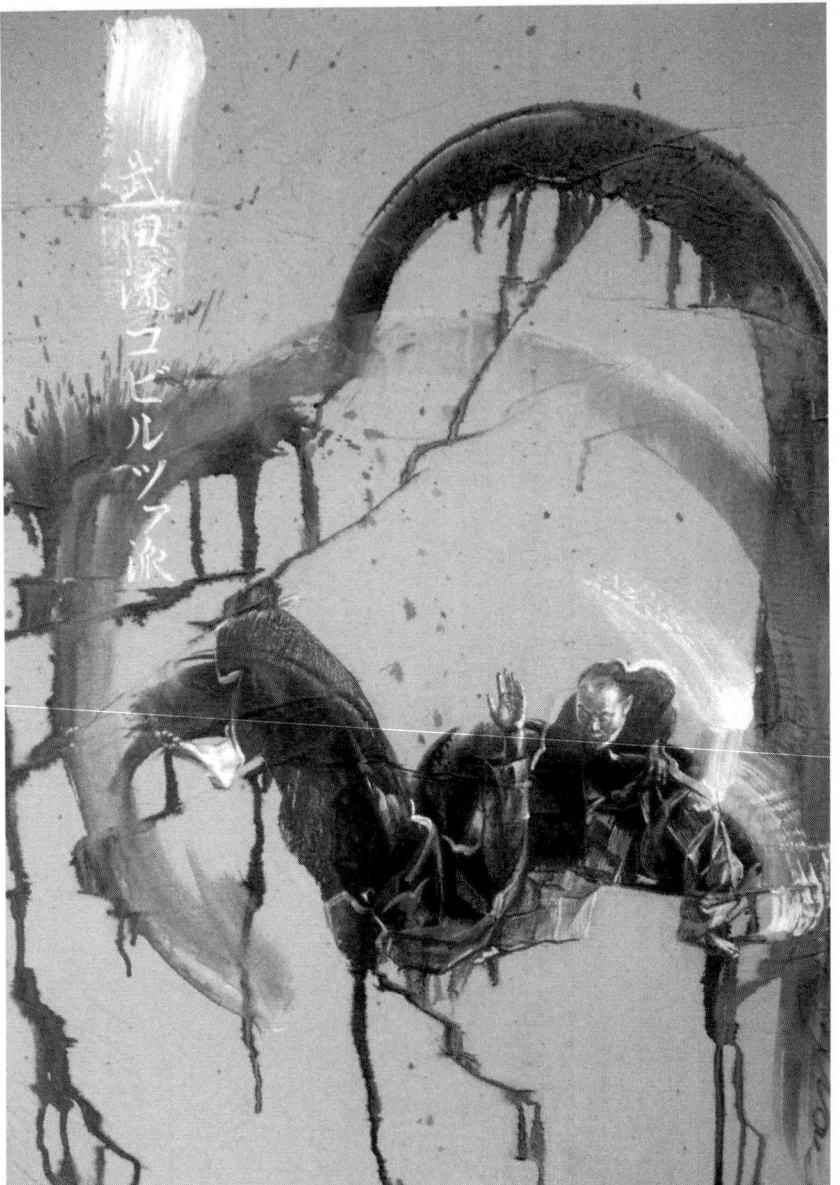

Conclusion

Takemusu Aiki is a term meaning "to spontaneously execute the perfect aikido technique in any given situation." A similar interpretation is "infinite creativity," which describes the adaptability of aikido. Acknowledging that no two attacks are exactly the same, this concept emphasizes the importance of making microadjustments in one's techniques to compensate for variation. Teach an aikido practitioner one technique, and a thousand should unfold. It is this adaptability in combination with blending that embodies the strength of aikido. Moreover, without the ability to adjust one's technique to any given situation, one would surely fail, regardless of the art studied.

Likewise, aikido itself should be adaptable and evolve with respect to Ueshiba's teachings. To refuse to address common attacks, simply because they were not in the original repertoire, limits one's defensive capabilities. Aikido is a wonderfully adaptive art, but to maximize one's response efficacy, a broader understanding of attacks and their respective defenses should be achieved. In doing so, one transcends traditional limits applied to modern encounters and allows aikido to achieve maximum effectiveness.

Glossary

aikido	合気道	the Way of unifying with life energy
atemi	当て身	blows to the body
Daito-ryu	大東流	Great Eastern School
irimi	入り身	entering straight into a technique
jujutsu	柔術	gentle or yielding; art/technique
ma-ai	間合い	space between two opponents
mune tsuki	胸突き	middle level punch
nage	投げ	person who exicutes a technique
randori	乱取り	free-style practice or sparring
shomen uchi	正面打ち	vertical knife-hand strike
tenkan	転換	"divert"; a 180 degree pivot to one's rear
tsuki	突き	thrust
uke	受け	person who "receives" a technique
yokomen uchi	横面打ち	side-of-the-head strike thrust

Bibliography

Stevens, J. (1992). *The art of peace.* Boston: Shambhala Publications.

Suenaka, R. & Watson, C. (1997). *Complete aikido: Aikido kyohan; The definitive guide to the way of harmony.* Boston: Tuttle Publishing.

Acknowledgment

The authors would like to thank Trey Davidson, Chris Mennona and Jennifer Saunders for their assistance with the multiple attack scenario. Photography by Ausar R. Vandross.

· 13 ·

Aikido and Body-Awareness Training for Peacemaking and Combat
by Paul Linden, Ph.D.

Photographs courtesy of P. Linden; graphically adjusted by Via Media Publishing.

It would seem that the personal requirements for combat and for peacemaking would be vastly different. However, on the level of body-awareness training, they are essentially the same.

The key lies in the nature of the body's distress responses. When people are stressed, challenged, or threatened, they typically contract or collapse their breathing, posture, movement, and attention. This is experienced as feelings of fear, anger, strain, body numbness, or dissociation. In situations of conflict, these powerful physical response patterns undermine the ability to think rationally, interact empathically, and act peacefully. In situations of combat, these responses interfere with perception, movement, and coordination.

The focus of aikido is on understanding and using effectively the philosophy and strategy of *aiki*, which translates roughly as "harmony." I have been practicing aikido for forty years, and my process for understanding aikido has been to break broad, complex processes down into simpler modular units of body-awareness practice. These practices are implicit in aikido training, but I found that making them explicit allowed me to work with them more easily on the mat and apply them more easily off the mat in my daily life. It also enabled me to teach them to beginners in aikido far more easily and rapidly.

Beyond that, making the practices explicit allowed me to teach them as a simpler, more rapid stand-alone training, which I call *Being In Movement*® mindbody education, and which nonmartial artists can practice and then apply in their daily lives.

The term "aiki," as it is used in aikido, has outer and inner meanings. When talking about the movement structure of a typical aikido defense technique, aiki means not going against the flow/movement (direction, speed, timing) of the attack, but instead sidestepping the power of the attack, joining into its flow (called "blending"), then smoothly adding to the flow so as to unbalance the attacker (called "leading"), and in the end controlling the attacker's capability to move/attack (with a throw or pin).

In terms of inner functioning, *aiki* refers to a state of relaxation, stability, unrestricted breathing, full awareness of the environment, and respectful, compassionate, and protective receiving of the attacker. The inner meaning is what I am referring to as body-awareness training. Examining some body-awareness exercises is the easiest way to explain what this means.

Stand in a deep T-stance and resist when your partner pushes on your chest. It should be a safe and gradual push, not a sudden impact. Relax your belly and your breathing, lean forward a bit into the push, and resist it. Most likely, you will be hard to move.

Now make one small change. Raise your eyebrows while you resist your partner. Almost certainly you will now be easily pushed back. Why?

When would a person ordinarily raise her eyebrows? When she's startled or afraid. And what other body actions would she perform when her eyebrows went up? Most likely she would pull back. It's the fear/startle response.

So when you raised your eyebrows, that evoked the rest of the reflex package. When your body goes into the fear/startle response pattern, your posture gets weak. **In order to fight well, you have to attend to all the components of the fear/startle (fight-or-flight) response.**

Let's try the exercise again, but this time the focus will be on the voice. Have your partner push on you again and as he does, count aloud from one to ten with a loud, clear voice. Notice what you feel and how you respond to the push. Then, as your partner continues to push on you, shift to counting aloud in a mumbled, indistinct manner, as though your mouth were filled with marbles. What happens to your posture and your ability to resist?

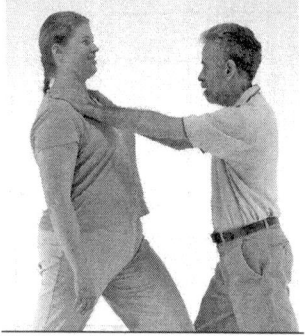

Almost always people experience that when they mumble, they are unable to resist strongly. The body is a web of muscles. When one part of that web goes slack and limp, the whole does. **In order to fight well, you have to be clear and focused.**

Let's try the exercise a third time. As your partner pushes on you, feel anger and resentment that this jerk should be touching you in this insulting manner. What happens to your posture? Again, most people will find that they become weak and unable to resist effectively. By contrast, as your partner pushes on you again, think and feel that he is a long-lost friend whom you are so glad to see again. Most people will feel that this produces strength and stability. Your body is stronger and more stable when you feel friendly, kind, and respectful. **In order to fight well, you have to feel kindness toward your opponent.**

Let's try another experiment. Have your partner stand in front of you and poke your chest with one hand. (It is more interesting to try the exercise with a punch.) Block the poke with a simple inward block and, as you block, say aloud, "Don't touch." Now do the same maneuver, but as you block, say, "Thank you." Most people experience that when they say "Don't touch," they become tense and awkward—just the opposite of what is needed to block the poke. And saying "Thank you" makes their movement smoother, easier, faster, and more effective. In other words, the mere words which express gratitude are sufficient to induce in the body a state of relaxed power. **In order to fight well, you have to feel gratitude toward your opponent.**

What is underlying these different body-awareness and movement experiments? It is what I call *projecting an intention*. Another body-awareness exercise can make this clearer.

Put a pencil on the floor, and then stand about ten feet (about three meters) away. Stand up comfortably. Look at the pencil. This is a magic pencil. With this pencil, anything you write will come true. Wouldn't you love to go over and get that pencil? Build up within yourself a feeling that it is a wonderful pencil and you would really like to have it. Actually *intend* to go over and get the pencil.

It is important to be clear about what wanting the pencil means. "Want-ing" is not the same as "going." Don't actually walk over and get the pencil. However, don't freeze up and physically prevent your body from moving in order to focus on wanting to move. "Wanting" does not mean merely *thinking* about getting the pencil. "Thinking about" is a disconnected intellectual picture, but *feeling* is an action you do with your "heart" and your body. Relax, be natural, and create an authentic feeling in your mindbody of desire and intention to walk over and get the pencil.

What happens when you stand and focus on wanting the pencil? Take some time to let the feeling build. Once you establish the feeling, you will probably feel yourself "involuntarily" tipping toward the pencil. For most people, this movement will be a small drift toward the pencil, perhaps a quarter of an inch (about half a centimeter) or so, though some people will actually move quite a bit. Most people will feel as though the pencil were a magnet gently drawing them toward it.

What you're working with is the interface between "mind" and "body." If you pay attention to the feeling of reaching out into space, in a particular direction, with a particular intensity, you'll notice that process underlies all voluntary movement. And by sensitizing yourself to that process, you can improve your own movements and better perceive and disrupt your opponent's movements. **Learning effective movement control requires working from the intentional level.**

The distress response involves constriction or collapse, two different ways of becoming smaller. Replacing fear with kindness is one element in the process of body-awareness training. In the next exercise, we'll go into the process of expansion. Expansiveness is the physical, psychological, and spiritual opposite of distress. The expansiveness will be accomplished through a systematic process of intentional projection.

Stand up with your feet about shoulder width apart and your hands down by your side. With the soles of your feet, reach down into the earth. You could reach toward the center of the earth, or you could find a closer point to focus on, as close as you need for it to be a clear sensing process for you.

Don't just visualize or think about reaching down, but actually sense in your body and through your feet a reaching toward the middle of the earth. Stay with that sensation/action for a moment.

Then let go of reaching down. Now, with the top of your head and shoulders reach upward to feel the sky. This should be a very gentle action, an intention or micromovement without any strain. Try reaching forward with the whole front surface of your body. And then reach back behind you with the whole back surface of your body. Reach out to the right with the right side of your body. And then reach out to the left with the left side of your body.

Now, do all the directions together. Reach down and up, left and right, and forward and back. How does that feel?

Most people experience this as spacious and energizing. You don't have to give in to the distress response and shrink. You can take up space.

Some people find it easier to use a more concrete focus. Instead of simply reaching outward, you could imagine reaching toward slices of pizza or something of the sort.

You can practice the *Six Directions Reaching* exercise as you walk around during your daily activities. That will help you practice being more present and more alive. You can also use the *Six Directions Reaching* to help you maintain your inner spaciousness when you feel threatened. That will help you respond with more clarity and strength. **In order to fight well, you have to be spacious.**

I'm sure you can see the point. Being kind, grateful, relaxed, stable, focused, and spacious will allow a person to be adaptable and effective in resolving conflicts or in fighting. On the level of body awareness, the foundations for the ability to fight well and for the ability to resolve conflicts peacefully are just the same. To resolve a conflict peacefully, you must be able to resist the body's natural distress response, and the best way to do that is by consciously constructing a body state of spaciousness.

I think that the core values and practical training methods of the martial arts will be crucial in creating a new, harmonious way of living on the planet, but aikido and the other martial arts are too profound and too labor intensive to be widely practiced. Practicing body awareness and intentionality separate from aikido makes the training simpler, more accessible, and more quickly applicable to daily life.

For many people—both martial artists and people outside the martial arts—it is a new and surprising idea that practicing combat skills is a way of training yourself to create peace. However, through martial arts and body-awareness training, we can replace fight-or-flight aggression with a mind/body state of calm alertness and compassionate power, which is the foundation for both combat and conflict resolution.

· 14 ·

Aikido and Body-Awareness Training for Peacemaking and Combat
by Josh Paul, M.A.

Photograph courtesy of Dreamstime.com

Introduction

Martial arts are paths of physical, intellectual, spiritual, and social growth. Among children, adolescents, and college students, martial arts training is associated with reductions in inappropriate social behaviors, violence, and aggression (Daniels and Thorton, 1992; Lamarre and Nosancuk, 1999; Woodward, 2009; Zivin et al., 2001), as well as increased prosocial behaviors, improved classroom conduct, and improved sleep quality, mood, and mental health (Caldwell, Harrison, Adams, and Triplett, 2009; Lakes and Hoyt, 2004; Wang, 2008; Woodward, 2009). Although the research is limited, there is evidence that martial arts also improve confidence, self-esteem, and quality of life among children with intellectual and physical disabilities (Conant, Morgan, Muzykewicz, Clark, and Thiele, 2008; Gleser et al., 1992; Wall, 2005; Woodward, 2009; Wright, White, and Gaebler-Spira, 2004).

Autism spectrum disorders (ASD) are the second-most-common developmental disability in the United States, affecting more children than childhood cancers, juvenile diabetes, and pediatric AIDS combined, and the prevalence of ASD is increasing 10–17% annually (Autism Speaks, 2011a). As the prevalence of ASD increases, martial arts instructors will be increasingly faced with the question of whether to enroll children with ASD in their dojo and how to best teach this population. Aikido, and martial arts in general, have the potential to fill many of the psychosocial needs of this special population by providing a recreational activity that fosters intellectual, physical, and social growth, as well as much-needed "normal" childhood experiences.

Since 2007 I have taught short-term aikido courses to children with medium- and high-functioning ASD and other developmental disabilities enrolled in New York City public schools. Through a process of trial and error, I developed a cumulative curriculum of selected aikido exercises that emphasize focus, body awareness, and awareness of others. This article provides a background on ASD, and, based my experiences, discusses general considerations and curriculum for teaching children with ASD. Although the curriculum presented is specifically aikido based, the exercises could be adapted to any martial arts environment.

Autism Spectrum Disorders: Facts and Figures

In the broadest sense, ASD are a group of developmental disorders characterized by difficulties in communication and social interaction (Brasic, 2011). Autism is considered a "spectrum" disorder because of the extraordinary variability in the type and severity of symptoms and behaviors (Table 1).

According to a 2009 study from the Centers for Disease Control and Prevention (CDC), which reviewed medical records for eight-year-olds in eleven U.S. cities, 1 out of every 110 children, or nearly 1% of all children, in the United States is on the autistic spectrum (CDC, 2009). The study also found that the prevalence of ASD increased 57% between 2002 and 2006. This increase was partly attributed to changes and improvements in screening systems, diagnostic methods, and broadened definitions, but part of the increase represented real growth in the number of children with ASD.

A more recent study reported an even higher prevalence (Kim et al., 2011). This study screened all children ages seven to twelve years old (approximately 55,000) in a single community in South Korea rather than reviewing medical records. Using this methodology, the investigators found a prevalence of 2.64%, equivalent to approximately 1 in 38 children. The findings suggest that the prevalence in the United States might be higher than currently thought if calculated using a similar method.

ASD occur in both genders, and all racial, ethnic, and socioeconomic groups, but are four to five times more common in boys than girls (CDC, 2009; CDC, 2011). An estimated 1 in 70 boys and 1 in 310 girls are affected (CDC, 2009). ASD are also frequently associated with intellectual disability: 41% of children with ASD have an

IQ of 70 or less (a normal IQ is considered between 90 and 109) (CDC, 2011).

Autism Spectrum Disorders: Categories, Diagnosis, and Treatment

There are three broad categories of ASD: autistic disorder (classic autism), Asperger syndrome, and pervasive developmental disorder (CDC, 2011). Autistic disorder is characterized by profound difficulties with language, communication, and social interactions. Children and adults with autistic disorder often exhibit unusual behaviors and interests, and it is frequently accompanied by intellectual disabilities and other conditions, such as seizures, Down syndrome, and mental health issues.

Like autistic disorder, Asperger syndrome is characterized by difficulties with social interaction and communication, but not the speech problems or intellectual disabilities typical of autistic disorder (CDC, 2011). Children and adults with Asperger syndrome are usually socially awkward with tendencies to engage in one-sided conversations and exhibit unusual nonverbal communication. They may appear to lack empathy or connection with others, and may have obsessive, narrow interests, among other qualities (Table 2) (Mayo Clinic, 2010; CDC, 2011).

The third category—pervasive development disorders (PDD)—is a nonspecific description of children and adults with some, but not all, of the characteristics of autistic disorder or Asperger syndrome. The symptoms, severity, and intellectual disabilities among those with PDD are variable, but most have social difficulties and unexpected responses to noises, lights, and other sensory information (NINDS, 2011).

ASD are diagnosed by observation and evaluation. There are no blood tests or imaging studies. The disorders are detectable very early—symptoms appear within the first one to two years of life—and a trained physician can reliably diagnose ASD by age two (CDC, 2011). Treatment of ASD consists of multiple types of behavioral therapies designed to improve communication and social skills and intellectual abilities (Autism Speaks, 2011b). Different diets (e.g., gluten-free diets) have been associated with reductions in symptom severity, at least temporarily, as has regular exercise. Medications can be used to treat specific symptoms or associated conditions (e.g., depression and anxiety) (Autism Speaks, 2011b). Interventions started early in life produce the best results.

ASD and Aikido

Like all children, those with ASD and other developmental disabilities experience emotional and psychiatric problems. Depression, anxiety, low self-esteem, and feelings of isolation and unmet needs for intimacy are common (Lundström et al., 2011; Mukaddes, Herüner, and Tanidir, 2010; Müller, Schuler, and Yates, 2008; Sebastian, Blakemore, and Charman, 2009; Twyman et al., 2010; Vickerstaff, Heriot, Wong, Lopes, and Dossetor, 2007). Children with ASD and other disabilities are more likely to be bullied, victimized, and ostracized than other children (Twyman et al., 2010), which can precipitate or exacerbate already existing self-esteem and emotional issues. What is sometimes misunderstood is that although children with ASD may not demonstrate or express a need for social belonging or connection, they do in fact have such needs, and many children with ASD aspire to be productive members of a community and develop social skills and friendships (Müller, Schuler, and Yates, 2008).

Compounding such social challenges are physical challenges: children with ASD and other disabilities are two to three times more likely to be obese than the general population, and more likely to suffer from illnesses and emotions secondary to obesity such as high blood pressure, high cholesterol, depression, fatigue, and low self-esteem (Rimmer, Yamaki, Lowry, Wang, and Vogel, 2010). Also, unlike their counterparts without special needs, children with ASD spend an extraordinary amount of time in therapy.

Within this psychosocial context, there is a clear and pressing need for recreational activities like martial arts that promote community and social interaction, as well as hold the potential to improve physical and psychological health. Aikido, as a physical practice, develops balance, coordination, body awareness, focus, and sensitivity to others. As a path of personal development, it encourages nonverbal and verbal connection and communication, collective learning, community involvement, and self-awareness. And, like all martial arts, aikido has the potential to improve self-esteem and overall mental health.

Considerations for Teachers

Children with ASD are diverse, with unique and sometimes unexpected behaviors warranting some special considerations. The most consistent characteristic of children with ASD is that they do not (cannot) always follow or respond to verbal instructions. At times, it may look and feel as if a student is ignoring you or deliberately looking past you, but this is emblematic of ASD. Other times the same student may seem completely present (like everybody, children with ASD have good and bad days). Special efforts such as physical touch, repeating a student's name, standing next to the student, and other strategies may be needed to elicit responses and focus.

As might be expected, children with ASD have difficulty understanding and engaging in partner practice, which is the core of aikido practice. Although part of a typical aikido class includes group stretching and exercises, most of the practice is done with a partner, with each person alternating between uke and nage (attacker and defender, respectively). There is very little individual kata practice in aikido. Among children with a disorder specifically characterized by difficulties in communication and relating to others, establishing partner practice is difficult, and may require more diligence than with other students. The instructor cannot simply say, "Get a partner" and expect something to happen. However, the physical, verbal, and nonverbal communication that occurs during practice is part of the uniqueness of the experience.

Teaching and maintaining partner practice ultimately requires more individualized attention, and classes may require a higher teacher-to-student ratio than other classes. Teenaged teaching assistants are an option, as are parents, guardians, and siblings. Additional supervisors do not have to be practitioners of the art being taught, as long as they understand how to maintain class structure. Likewise, when enrolling new students, keep the parents/guardians/ therapists—whoever brings the student to class—in the dojo until you feel comfortable and confident.

Talking with parents, guardians, siblings, therapists, and teachers (if possible) is important too, as children with ASD and other disabilities may have unique health risks that could endanger their safety in a martial arts class. For example, up to 30% of people with Down syndrome have a structural deformity at the base of the skull known as atlantoaxial instability, which increases the risk of neck and spinal cord injuries (Alvarez, 2010). Other behaviors to be aware of include unexpected reactions to lights, noises, colors, and shapes, issues with physical contact, and behavioral issues/aggression. Ask questions about individual needs, risks, and behaviors more than once and on an ongoing basis. Children and adults with ASD are not static; symptoms and symptom severity change over time. If you have any doubts, concerns, or questions, do your own research and find your own answers. Table 3 lists some reliable resources.

Photograph courtesy of Dreamstime.com

What to Teach?

What to teach children with ASD? The short answer: aikido (or another martial art), but in small, sequential steps, using exercises that cater to the needs of the students. Over the course of multiple short-term programs (five to twelve weeks), I tried many standard aikido exercises—*aiki taiso* (ki exercise), *tai sabaki toshu* (basic body movements against various attacks), strikes (shomenuchi, munetsuki, yokomenuchi), kokyudosa, shikko walking, ukemi, etc. I eventually found a core group that students were able to successfully perform after a few classes. These were accepted as recognizable martial techniques (students responded better to movements they had seen in movies or computer games), and they were fun.

Aiki taiso exercises, also called ki exercises, are a series of exercises developed by Koichi Tohei (1920–2011) designed to improve body awareness, posture, breath control, focus, balance, and coordination. They also serve as the building blocks of techniques. There are more than a dozen ki exercises, but, at least at the beginning of a program, I focus on six of them (Figures 1–6):

1) unbendable arm (*orenaite*)
2) rowing (*funakogi*)
3) blocking (*shomenuchi ikkyo*)
4) pivoting (*zengo*)
5) turning (*tenkan*)
6) rolling backward and forward (*koho tento*)

* Note: For complete descriptions of all the ki exercises, see Shifflett, 2000.

Figure 1:

Unbendable Arm (*orenaite*). Maintaining a relaxed but unbendable arm is important for blocking and deflecting, rolling, and controlling an attacker. To test orenaite, have a student stand in a front stance and press down on the elbow and up on the wrist simultaneously. Students wiggle their fingers to demonstrate relaxation.

Figure 2: Rowing Exercise (*funakogi undo*).

This is a four-step exercise. From a front stance: hips rock forward and arms extend (**2a**); hips rock backward and arms retract (**2b**). The arms should make a small figure eight, as if rowing a boat. Rowing exercise performed with a partner (**2c**). Hands should just touch when students row forward. To perform dynamically, have students face each other and perform the exercise with one student stepping forward and the other backward.

Figure 3:
Blocking–Deflecting Exercise (*shomenuchi ikkyo undo*).
This is a four-step exercise. From a front stance: hips rock forward; unbendable arms rise from shoulders (**3a**), unbendable arms drop, and hips rock back to a neutral front stance. Blocking–deflecting exercise performed with a partner (**3b**). Partners work in unison. Fingertips should just touch when arms are in the raised position. To perform dynamically, have students face each other and perform the exercise with one student stepping forward and the other backward.

Figure 4: Pivoting Exercise (*zengo undo*).

This exercise is the blocking–deflecting exercise, but performed in two directions. There is a 180° pivot between each blocking movement. When performed with a partner, the fingertips should just touch. In this picture, zengo undo is practiced with multiple people in a circle. This requires students to maintain spacing in two directions.

Figure 5: Turning Exercise (*tenkan undo*).

This is a two-step turning exercise. From a front stance, the student turns 180° on the front foot (**5a–c**). The movement is repeated, continuing in the same direction, to return to the start position.

Figure 6a-c: Rolling Exercise (*koho tento undo*)

From a position kneeling on one knee, students roll back and return to the seat position. The same can be performed from kneeling and standing positions. When performed from standing, students kneel, roll back, kneel, and return to a front stance. Make sure hands are kept in front, and not used to stop the roll.

Figure 7a: Forward Roll (*koho tento*).
Figure 7b: Backward Roll (*koho tento*).

Figure 8:

Knee Walking (*shikko*). This exercise emphasizes movement from the hips, is fun, and usually easily learned by children. Have students start by sitting in seiza, lifting one foot and placing it squarely on the floor (**8a**), and pushing the knee all the way down while simultaneously rotating on the opposite knee (**8b**). Rather than reach out with the foot and leg, the rotation pushes the leg out from the hip.

Figure 9:

Escaping from wrist grabs.

Figure 10:

Breathing Exercise (*kokyudosa*). There are many variations to this exercise. In the one shown, partners sit on their leg (*seiza*), their knees barely touching, with the attacker holding the other's wrists (**10a**). The defender separates her arms and extends up, toward the attacker's head, lifting her center. She then turns slightly to throw the attacker (**10b**).

Ki exercises are particularly useful when teaching children with ASD. In addition to the primary intent of developing body awareness, coordination, etc., ki exercises can be performed solo and with a partner, and statically and dynamically (that is, standing still and with motion). They provide a vehicle for safely introducing partner practice while improving balance and coordination, and by checking balance during the practice (ki testing) the exercises provide feedback about a student's body awareness and coordination. Unlike tai sabaki toshu exercises, there is no uke or nage when performing partnered ki exercises —each person does the same thing—making the partner aspect more comprehensible. Other well-received individual practices are *ukemi* (backward and forwards roll) and *shikko* (knee) walking (Figures 7 and 8).

I continue partner practice and introduce uke/nage roles with escaping from grips (wrist and maybe lapel holds) and kokyudosa (Figures 9 and 10). In this latter exercise, partners sit on their legs (*seiza*) with knees barely touching. Uke holds nage's wrists, and nage tries to unbalance uke by stretching uke beyond her balance point (this should not be a wrestling match). The practice teaches each participant about his or her balance and coordination. Kokyudosa can then be performed standing as the students' first throwing technique (kokyunage), and as skills are acquired and improved, more can be introduced.

This curriculum is not a therapeutic intervention; however, there is ongoing research into using an aikido curriculum as a therapeutic option (Kramer, 2011). Although I have had repeated success with this format, there is no guarantee that this approach will work with all students, in all environments, and for all instructors. It can and should be adapted to individual circumstances and students.

Instructor Expectations and Conclusions

Children with ASD are all different and change over time. They should not be expected to conform to any specified set of expectations or requirements. As instructors, it is important that our expectations be flexible and our teaching style responsive and observant. Some extra patience will be required when teaching this unique population, and given the diversity among children with ASD, some trial and error should be expected. As the prevalence of ASD increases, recreational activities like aikido and other martial arts that foster physical, social, and emotional health will be increasingly important.

Table 1: Common Autistic Behaviors

- Not responding to name by 12 months
- Not pointing at objects to show interest by 14 months
- Not playing "pretend" games by 18 months
- Avoiding eye contact and wanting to be alone
- Having trouble understanding other people's feelings or talking about their own feelings
- Delayed speech and language skills
- Repeating words or phrases over and over (echolalia)
- Giving unrelated answers to questions
- Getting upset by minor changes
- Obsessive interests
- Flapping hands, rocking bodies, spinning in circles
- Unusual reactions to sounds, smells, tastes, or how things look or feel

SOURCE: Centers for Disease Control and Prevention. Facts about Autism Spectrum Disorders. Retrieved May 25, 2011, from http://www.cdc.gov/ncbddd/autism/facts.html.

Table 2: Common Behaviors among Children and Adults with Asperger Syndrome

- Trouble understanding other people's feelings and talking about their own
- Difficulty understanding body language
- Avoiding eye contact
- Wanting to be alone; or wanting to interact, but not knowing how
- Narrow, sometimes obsessive, interests
- Talking only about themselves and their interests
- Speaking in unusual ways or with an odd tone of voice.
- Difficulty making friends.
- Appearing nervous in large social groups.
- Clumsy or awkward
- Rituals that they refuse to change, such as a very rigid bedtime routine
- Developing odd or repetitive movements
- Unusual sensory reactions.

SOURCE: Centers for Disease Control and Prevention. Asperger Syndrome Fact Sheet. Retrieved May 25, 2011, from ww.cdc.gov/ncbddd/actearly/pdf/parents_pdfs/Asperger_Syndrome.pdf.

Table 3: Additional resources for learning about ASD	
Autism Collaboration	www.autism.org
Autism Research Institute	www.autism.com
Autism Science Foundation	www.autismsciencefoundation.org
Autism Society of America	www.autism-society.org
Autism Speaks	www.autismspeaks.org
Centers for Disease Control and Prevention	cdc.gov/ncbddd/autism/index.html
Medscape	www.medscape.com/resource/autism
National Autism Association	www.nationalautismassociation.org
National Inst. of Neurological Disorders & Stroke	www.ninds.nih.gov
U.S. Autism and Asperger Association	www.usautism.org
WebMD	www.webmd.com/brain/autism/default.htm

References

Alvarez, A. (2010). Atlantoaxial instability in Down syndrome. Retrieved May 18, 2011, from http://emedicine.medscape.com/article/1180354-overview.

Autism Speaks (2011a). What is autism? Retrieved May 18, 2011, from http://www.autismspeaks.org/whatisit/index.php.

Autism Speaks (2011b). Treating autism. Retrieved May 18, 2011, from http://www.autismspeaks.org/treatment/index.php.

Brasic, J. (2011). Autism. Retrieved May 17, 2011, from http://emedicine.medscape.com/article/912781-overview.

Caldwell, K., Harrison, M., Adams, M., & Triplett, N. (2009). Effect of Pilates and taijiquan training on self-efficacy, sleep quality, mood, and physical performance of college students. *Journal of Bodywork and Movement Therapy, 13*, 155–163.

Centers for Disease Control and Prevention (2009). Prevalence of autism spectrum disorders—Autism and Developmental Disabilities Network, United States, 2006. *Morbidity and Mortality Weekly Report Surveillance Summary, 58*, SS–10.

Centers for Disease Control and Prevention (2011a). Autism Fact Sheet. Retrieved May 17, 2011, from http://www.cdc.gov/NCBDDD/ actearly/facts.html.

Centers for Disease Control and Prevention (2011b). Facts about Autism Spectrum Disorders. Retrieved May 25, 2011, from http://www. cdc.gov/ncbddd/autism/facts.html.

Centers for Disease Control and Prevention (2011c). Asperger Syndrome Fact Sheet. Retrieved May 25, 2011, from www.cdc.gov/ncbddd/actearly/ pdf/parents_pdfs/Asperger_Syndrome.pdf.

Conant, K., Morgan, A., Muzykewicz, D., Clark, D., & Thiele, E. (2008). A karate program for improving self-concept and quality of life in childhood epilepsy: results of a pilot study. *Epilepsy Behavior, 12*(1), 61–65.

Daniels, K., & Thornton, E. (1992). Length of training, hostility and the martial arts: A comparison with other sporting groups. *British Journal of Sports Medicine, 26*(3), 118–120.

Gleser, J., Margulies, J., Nyaka, M., Porat, B., Mendelberg, B., & Wertman, E. (1992). Physical and psychosocial benefits of modified judo practice for blind, mentally retard children: a pilot study. *Perceptual and Motor Skills, 74* (3 part 1), 915–925.

Kim, Y., Leventhal, B., Koh, Y., Fombonne, E., Laska, E., Lim, E., … Song, D. (2011). Prevalence of autism spectrum disorders in a total population sample. *American Journal of Psychiatry*. Epub version published May 9, 2011, doi: 10.1176/appi.ajp.2011.10101532.

Kramer, E. (2011). Life is growth: An adapted martial arts program. Unpublished graduate thesis, Harvard Graduate School of Education, Cambridge. Retrieved via personal e-mail May 18, 2011.

Lamarre, B., & Nosanchuk, T. (1999). Judo—the gentle way: a replication of studies on martial arts and aggression. *Perceptual and Motor Skills, 88* (3 part 1), 992–996.

Lakes, K., & Hoyt, W. (2004). Promoting self-regulation through school-based martial arts training. *Applied Developmental Psychology, 25,* 283–302.

Lundström, S., Chang, Z., Kerekes, N., Gumpert C., Råstam, M., Gillberg, C., Lichtenstein, P., & Anckarsäter, H. (2011). Autistic-like traits and their association with mental health problems in two nationwide twin cohorts of children and adults. *Psychological Medicine, 22,* 1–11.

Mayo Clinic.com. (2011). Asperger's Syndrome. Retrieved May 17, 2011, from http://www.mayoclinic.com/health/aspergers-syndrome/DS00551.

Müller, E., Schuler, A., & Yates, G. (2008). Social challenges and supports from the perspective of individuals with Asperger syndrome and other autism spectrum disorder. *Autism, 12*(12), 173–190.

Mukaddes, N., Hergüner, S., & Tanidir, C. (2010). Psychiatric disorders in individuals with high-functioning autism and Asperger's disorder: similarities and differences. *World Journal of Biological Psychiatry, 11*(8), 964–971.

National Institute of Neurological Disorders and Stroke. NINDS pervasive developmental disorders information page. Retrieved May 9, 2011, from http://www.ninds.nih.gov/disorders/pdd/pdd.htm.

Rimmer, J., Yamaki, K., Lowry, B., Wang, E., & Vogel, L. (2010). Obesity and obesity-related secondary conditions in adolescents with intellectual/developmental disabilities. *Journal of Intellectual Disability Research, 54,* 787–794.

Sebastian, C., Blakemore, S., & Charman, T. (2009) Reactions to ostracism in adolescents with autism spectrum conditions. *Journal of Autism and Developmental Disorders, 39,* 1122–1130.

Shifflett, C. (2000). *Aikido: Exercises for teaching and training.* Sewickley, PA: Round Earth Publishing.

Twyman, K., Saylor C., Saia, D., Maias, M., Taylor, L., & Spratt, E. (2010). Bullying and ostracism experiences in children with special health care needs. *Journal of Developmental and Behavioral Pediatrics, 31*(1), 1–8.

Vickerstaff, S., Heriot, S., Wong, M., Lopes, A., & Dossetor, D. (2007). Intellectual ability, self-perceived social competence, and depressive symptomatology in children with high-functioning autistic spectrum disorders. *Journal of Autism and Developmental Disorders, 37*(9), 1647–1664.

Wall, R. (2005). Tai Chi and mindfulness-based stress reduction in a Boston Public Middle School. *Journal of Pediatric Health Care, 1*(4), 230–237.

Woodward, T. (2009). A review of the effects of martial arts practice on health. *Wisconsin Medical Journal, 108*(1), 40–43.

Wright, P., White, K., & Gaebler-Spira, D. (2004). Exploring the relevance of the personal and social responsibility model in adapted physical activity: A collective case study. *Journal of Teaching in Physical Education, 23*(1), 71–87.

Zivin, G., Hassan, N., DePaula G., Monti, D., Harlan, C., Hossain, K., & Patterson, K. (2001). An effective approach to violence prevention: Traditional martial arts in middle school. *Adolescence, 36* (fall), 443–459.

index

Abe, Tadashi, 126–127
Aikido Center of Atlanta, 130
Aikikai Hombu (headquarters), 49, 50, 62, 125
Aikido World Federation, 62
Arakawa, Sadateru, 127
atemi (striking technique), 10, 176–177
Billman Cordero, Alice, 131
Bu Jin Design, 62
bokken (see wooden-sword)
bowing, 28, 50, 172
Boulder Aikikai, 62
breath throw (kokyunage), 207
center (hara), 54, 142
Chiba, Kazuo, 125, 127
choke, 9, 164
Daito-ryu, 174
dichotomous keys (defined), 1–2, 6
elbow lock, 132
entry technique (irimi), 6, 11–12, 178, 180
fifth teaching (gokyo), 11, 14
first teaching (ikkyo), 4, 11, 14, 18, 202
four direction throw (shihonage), 4, 11, 15, 18
Goju-ryu, 47, 58
Grantham, Rodney, 124, 130–131
hakama, 50, 171
halbred (naginata), 47
Hikitsuchi, Michio, 171
hip throw (koshinage), 16
iaido, 47
Iizasa, Yasusada, 47
Ikeda, Hiroshi, 62
International Ki Society, 3
kagura-kotodama staff, 48
Katori Shinto-ryu, 47, 54, 57
Ki-Aikido, 3
knife-hand strike (shomen uchi), 10, 174, 179–180, 202
ki exercises, 202, 207
kicks, 2–3, 8, 10, 36, 45, 88, 180
Kurita, Yutaka, 127
life energy (ki; qi), 138
meditation, 69–70, 94, 97,
Kanai, Mitsunari, 129

Miyagi, Yasuichi, 47
New England Aikikai, 131
New York Aikikai, 124, 130–131
Nippon Budokan, 171
Omoto-Kyo, 51–53, 128
Otake, Risuke, 47
Russo-Japanese War, 172
Saito, Morihiro, 50
sankyo (third teaching), 11, 14
Saotome, Mitsugi, 62, 155, 159
second teaching (nikkyo), 4–5, 11, 14
Shin Shin Toitsu Aikido, 3
Shintoism, 50–53, 172
Rinjiro, Shirata, 171
South American Aikido Federation, 131
spear, 51, 174
staff (jo), 27, 44, 47–55, 75–88, 104–105, 138–140, 149, 170–171
Suenaka, Roy Y., 175, 177
Sugano, Seiichi, 125, 127
taijiquan, 47, 130
takemusu ("inexhausible fount"), 52, 190
Tamura, Nobuyoshi, 127
tanto knife, 43–44, 106, 148–149
Sugawara, Tetsutaka, 47–48
Tohei, Koichi, 69, 126–127, 129–130, 137, 202
turning (tenkan), 6, 11–112, 178, 202
Ueshiba, Kisshomaru, 124, 126–128
Ueshiba, Morihei, 47–57, 125–130, 152–153, 159, 171–172, 174–177, 191
United States Aikido Federation, 124
Walker, Tom, 131
wooden sword (bokken), 27, 43, 54, 103, 140, 149, 171
World War II, 125, 128
wrist lock, 144
wrist turn (kotegaeshi), 167
Xing, Yanling, 47
Yamada, Yoshimitu, 124
Yamaguchi, Seigo, 127
yonkyo (fourth teaching), 11, 15

Printed in Dunstable, United Kingdom